'When I was writing *Unapologetic* more than a decade ago, I knew the job would soon need doing again. And again. Because the bridge between faith and contemporary experience constantly needs to be rebuilt as times change. So here it is, then: the bridge for the present moment, across which seekers for more meaning in their lives can travel in the knowledge that they won't be bullied, browbeaten or talked down to. This book. This one. In your hand. Right now.'

Francis Spufford, author of *Golden Hill* and *Unapologetic*

'Elizabeth Oldfield has a gift for writing about the things that matter most in a way that's honest, warm-hearted, and down-to-earth in the very best sense of the term. This remarkable book points not to some unreachable ideal of life but to a deeper, more soulful and meaningful experience of the lives we're actually living.'

Oliver Burkeman, author of *Four Thousand Weeks*

'I will be buying this book for everyone I know who is interested in what makes for a good life. In dark times, this book is an invitation to have another look at a way of seeing the world; a way that has brought light and hope to many.'

Gwen Adshead, psychiatrist, psychotherapist, and author of *The Devil You Know*

'Reading *Fully Alive* was like sitting down for coffee with a well-read and passionate friend. Elizabeth is courageous, insightful, generous and gentle. Her book is a rare find: it never rejects complexity in its search for clarity and never allows authority to crowd out compassion and curiosity – I felt very nourished by the work – there is wisdom here.'

Jenn Ashworth, author of *Ghosted*

'In turbulent times, what is there for us to hold onto? In *Fully Alive,* Elizabeth Oldfield suggests gratitude, humility, connection, community. Her writing is honest, touching, often funny and always thought-provoking. I loved it.'

Charlie Gilmour, journalist and author of *Featherhood*

'Plainspoken, fearless, disarmingly tender. Oldfield is a leader by example, and her book is a glowing argument for faith – one that speaks urgently to our fractured world.'

Rhik Sammader, journalist, broadcaster and actor

'This is the book I didn't know I needed, Elizabeth Oldfield the Sherpa who might persuade me not to give up climbing the mountain. I know few people as committed to living deeply as Elizabeth but in spite of that she's neither pompous nor pious (phew). This is deep stuff, personal yet learned, funny and vulnerable. If you loved Francis Spufford's *Unapologetic*, you will love this.'

Sally Phillips, actor and comedian

'In this beautiful book, Elizabeth Oldfield gives voice and vigour to a paradox of our time – that even as Christianity is officially on the wane, it is a bearer of wisdom, intelligence and rituals of lavish value to our world in all its pain and its promise. It is for modern humans who, like her, have gone "off script" in finding religion more relevant, not less so, in this young century.'

Krista Tippett, author of *Becoming Wise*

'A rich and soul-searching exploration of what it means to believe in a shifting age. This is a rare thing – an open, human and vulnerable profession of faith. I learned a lot.'

Katherine May, author of *Wintering* and *Enchantment*

FULLY ALIVE

Tending to the Soul
in Turbulent Times

ELIZABETH OLDFIELD

First published in Great Britain in 2024 by Hodder & Stoughton
An Hachette UK Company

4

This book tells parts of my story, which necessarily intersects with other people's. Everything in it is true to the best of my recollection, but memory is faulty and only ever from one person's perspective.

A CIP catalogue record for this title is available from the British Library

Hardback ISBN 978 1 399 81076 0
ebook ISBN 978 1 399 81078 4

Typeset in Sabon MT by Palimpsest Book Production Ltd, Falkirk, Stirlingshire

Printed and bound in Great Britain by Clays Ltd, Elcograf S.p.A.

Hodder & Stoughton policy is to use papers that are natural, renewable and recyclable products and made from wood grown in sustainable forests. The logging and manufacturing processes are expected to conform to the environmental regulations of the country of origin.

Hodder & Stoughton Ltd
Carmelite House
50 Victoria Embankment
London EC4Y 0DZ

www.hodderfaith.com

The authorised representative in the EEA is Hachette Ireland, 8 Castlecourt Centre, Dublin 15, D15 XTP3, Ireland (email: info@hbgi.ie)

'I find the soul a valuable concept, a statement of the dignity of a human life, and of the unutterable gravity of human action and experience . . . I find my own soul interesting company'
Marilynne Robinson

'The glory of God is a human being fully alive'
St Irenaeus, second century ad

For Edith and Auden

May your roots grow down deep into Love

CONTENTS

INTRODUCTION

A few years ago, I was driving along a dual carriageway with my husband and kids. It was hot and the air was stale, my passenger-seat footwell strewn with tepid water bottles and keep-cups and empty Pom Bear packets. We'd long outgrown our tiny bashed-up city car, but couldn't stretch to a bigger one and so packing involved a complex Jenga game of maximising space while avoiding a child being crushed by a suitcase. My daughter was in the back singing along to 'When I Grow Up', a song from the musical *Matilda*. In her reedy, unselfconscious voice she belted out Tim Minchin's deceptively simple lyrics, which predict a future in which the children singing will be grown up enough to know how to answer hard questions, strong enough to carry heavy things and brave enough to fight the monsters underneath the bed.

The chorus, beloved by kids everywhere, is all about eating sweets and staying up late to watch endless TV, but it was these verses and their childlike melody that landed that day like a punch in the heart. The irreconcilably bittersweet nature of adulthood was suddenly too much. I am purportedly a 'grown-up', but don't know the answers. I feel bone-weary from carrying around heavy things. I hate that the monsters exist, and that they often win, and that some of them live in me.

I broke down and started sobbing, my heaves so abrupt that my husband pulled the car over in concern. I didn't want my daughter to have to grow up into this world. I wanted her to find, as the song promises, that being a 'grown-up' really is about doing what you want in a cartoon world of freedom, not this discombobulating cocktail of beauty and heartbreak, despair and delight, the longing for justice and our own utter and bewildering failure to enact it. I don't think this conviction that the world should be different, that *we* should be different is unique to those who procreate. Honestly, I think the grief is also for myself, for the child I used to be, the innocence I have lost. I would like to put the apple back on the tree, please, because the knowledge of good and evil is just too damn painful.

I don't think I am the only one who feels this. We joke about 'adulting', the drudgery of paying bills and sorting out a pension, but it can't be just me who hears the seriousness thrum underneath. What kind of person am I becoming, with all this living? What kind of person do I *want* to be becoming? What part am I playing in the tragi-comedy we all find ourselves in?

Growing up must, surely, be about more than ticking (or failing to tick) achievements off an arbitrary list. It must be about something deeper, yet the stories that used to orient and guide us, handed down through generations of our ancestors, seem to have got lost in transit.

Today's plural, secular, Western societies have gifted us many things, but reliable sources of communal meaning isn't one of them. So many people I speak to crave places to belong and ways to settle their soul. Technology has freed us from drudgery and offers endless ways to increase our comfort and convenience. Product after product promises to boost our status and performance. Optimise and maximise. Up and to the right. In lots of ways, we've never had it better. But still there is a malaise, a sense of impending threat, which many of us feel in our least defended moments and don't know how to speak about. The news scrolls unendingly with stories of war, disease, deepening division, the rise of authoritarian governments and the unimaginable but rapidly approaching prospect of climate collapse. Accelerating advances in AI may turn the world upside down in ways no one can predict. Against this ominous global mood music, we have unlimited choices in framing our identity, but this freedom can sometimes induce vertigo rather than exhilaration. Many of us feel isolated and anxious, or too distracted and overworked to feel much at all.

In the 1930s a man called Thomas Merton was part of a group of 'irreverent and hard-drinking . . . proto-beatniks' who were similarly dismayed at the state of the world. University-educated as they were, the prospects that mainstream society offered looked less and less appealing: 'The world is crazy, war threatens, one has lost a sense of identity . . . People are dropping out . . . The rest of us are just lost.' The cry of Merton and his friends then echoes now: 'I am not [only] physically tired, just filled with a deep, vague, undefined sense of spiritual distress.'[1]

I don't want to live in spiritual distress. I want to be fully alive.

As I head for my forties, I wonder where all the grown-ups have gone. They don't seem to be leading us. I am longing for there to be more people I can trust, who reliably act with integrity. I want to be trustworthy myself. I crave morally serious people, which is not the same as just being no fun, or being good at pointing fingers at others. My instinct is that morally serious people don't have to perform their virtue. They've learned and suffered and let stuff go. They are resilient, kind and open. They know how to laugh, even on dark days. I want to be like them.

My ambition now is to be a 'non-anxious presence', to make people feel more peaceful when I'm around.[2] I'm currently too scattered for that. I want to be brave and generous and free, and on those I also have a way to go. Sometimes, when I catch myself moaning about some triviality, trudging through a day made grey by my inattention, a voice wells up inside and shouts, 'There must be more!' Yes, I can be sort of intense.

This longing to be fully alive, to know how to steady myself, has made one thing clear. My aim is not, now, a big glitzy hedonist life, nor staying within the tram tracks of a tidy conformist life. I want depth. I feel the need for roots, for spiritual core strength. As I look at the future, I want whatever is the equivalent of Pilates for my soul.

Every generation thinks the world is ending, but maybe we are right. Maybe the apocalypse is coming and we can't stop it. Once I've processed the emotions that thought provokes I want to be the kind of person that is needed at the end of the world. If we're headed into (even more) turbulent times I want to be someone who is of use, not overwhelmed and panicking but steady and hopeful, able to contribute to weaving a canopy of trust under which other people can shelter. Instability can make us (me) close ranks and cease to care for those beyond our immediate family and friends. I want to resist that impulse. I aspire to become the kind of person who would have hidden runaway slaves or people escaping the Nazis. Not least because I want to live in a society in which someone might hide me, my friends, my kids. I know I am not that kind of person yet. I am probably not going to grow that kind of character accidentally. If it turns out it is not the end of the world, well, we always need those people. If nothing else the attempt to become one feels more interesting and meaningful than just polishing my CV and going to actual Pilates.

This book is about my search for a deep life, for a place to steady my self amidst the waves. Partly it's vanity. I want to be luminous. Yes, because I buy too many serums, but mainly because of my soul. I want a luminous soul. (I assume people with a luminous soul think less about serums but I'll deal with that when I get there). I'm done with cool. That isn't quite true. I *want* to be done with cool. I'm old enough now, surely. It is true that I'm increasingly drawn to wisdom.

There are a million places to look for this, now the world is at our fingertips. Online influencers know wisdom is good for their brand. And there is much that is genuinely helpful among the recycled quotes, pop psychology and life hacks. Few of us have had a set of directions passed down, so the default among many of my friends is a choose-your-own-adventure approach to the treasures of Buddhism, yoga, Sufi Muslim thought via Rumi, astrology and more. For others more allergic to anything that sounds too woo, Stoicism, therapy, mindfulness and, more recently now the research looks solid, psychedelics, are routes to growth.

This is why part of me is surprised at the richest seam of wisdom I have found. I am British, marinated in the irony, scepticism and critique of our dominant liberal culture. I have two degrees. I'm a feminist. I have worked at the BBC and in Westminster. I have a subscription to the *New Yorker* (I liked the bag) and know who is on the Booker shortlist, though my actual reading skews increasingly heavily towards golden age detective stories.

In summary: I am supposed to be one of the growing

majority of people who have long relegated Christianity to the scrap heap. For my friends who are also desperately seeking ways to settle their souls, it's the last place they'd look. I should have been one of them, dropping the mild cultural Christianity still around in my childhood without regret like most of my generation, retaining only a socially acceptable taste for choral music or Gothic architecture, the festive habit of tipsy Midnight Mass.

That isn't what happened. My story went off script.

*

The cold presses up through my hoodie and jeans. I can feel the roughness of the concrete surface under my fingers, designed to not get slippery but be easily sluiced of animal droppings. As I become aware of my surroundings again, I can see ranks of shiny red flip-down chairs and a tin roof overhead.

I've been lying here for an hour, or maybe five minutes. The woman who has been quietly praying for me nearby gives an 'Everything ok?' look and, when I nod, smiles a beatific smile and wanders away to hover near another teenager. I stay on the floor, enjoying the cold, enjoying the roughness, listening to the guitar music from the front of the barn and the murmur of voices around me. I want to stay here, in the glow of life-altering love, and begin to process what has just happened.

When I was a teenager I had an ecstatic experience. I'd come to a Christian festival, invited by a friend, mainly for the boys. My parents weren't especially interested in God. My mum comes from a working class, atheist family and my dad retained a quiet cultural Christianity but actual engagement with the subject never happened at home. This was different. A field full of eager young evangelicals gathered every evening to sing and pray in tongues and ask to be 'baptised in the Holy Spirit', whatever that meant. They were fine – I'd gone along to my friend Kirsty's youth group a bit, and didn't mind them, but I was mainly there for a week of low adult supervision and because Kirsty fancied an impossibly glamorous American boy called Jake, whose blond curls bounced as he skateboarded. She'd promised a week of sunshine and freedom and no need to come to any of the sessions. Every morning we applied thick layers of Rimmel make-up in the dim light of the tent and hoped we looked like the girls in *Buffy*. Clearly though, something was sinking in by osmosis, because on the last night I went to sit, not by the skatepark as I had every other night, but in the main arena, a temporarily converted livestock sales building. I listened to a large man in a Hawaiian shirt give a talk about the relentless pursuit of God's love. I could feel something aching in my chest, some kind of longing, some kind of lack. Around me people were singing and praying in unrecognisable languages, and the joy that had seemed cringey and earnest was now deeply attractive. So I prayed: 'God, if you are there, show me.'

I don't know how to describe the next period of time. There are limits to language, and these moments of 'unselfing', in the great Iris Murdoch's phrase, necessarily escape from the net of our words. I remember the prayer, and the aftermath, but in between is a shining gap, a shift so profound I can't speak of it. Decades later, I could explain it in terms of neurology, or crowd dynamics, the power of suggestibility and the credulity of teenagers. I have done these things, seeking to explain it away, to tidy it into the boxes my education allows. But I'm not being fully honest when I do.

When I look back over my life, this moment is the hinge.

My question had been answered with an overwhelming felt presence, an encounter with a 'you' defined by love and acceptance and peace. The change felt like it happened at a cellular level. When I eventually stood up, still in clothes that smelt of damp tent, still with spots around my hairline and a belly I constantly sucked in, I was different. I was loved. I was seen. I was, somewhat to my horror, a Christian.

And apparently it showed. I vividly remember walking in the door after the festival with my rucksack, grubby and tired, and my mum saying, 'What on earth has happened to you?' She could see a change in my face, immediately. The transformation was so stark it prompted her to sign up to an Alpha course and become a Christian herself a few months later.

I had brought home with me a different kind of teenage volatility. There was a woman in the church I started attending who joked about having worn a box of tissues on a string round her neck for the first year after she'd converted, and I understood. I cried all the time, the feelings hot and strong and mixed – relief at encountering this love, yes, and joy, but also grief, like a child who holds their sobs back until they hit the safe enclosure of a parent's arms. All my feelings suddenly had somewhere to go, somewhere I wouldn't be too much. Christianity was the most intense thing I had ever experienced in my sheltered village childhood. It opened the door to the adventure I'd longed for since I first started racing through novels. My life had acquired another dimension, bursting out of the boundaries of maths classes, torturous cross-country runs and long rides on stale coaches. It now seemed to stretch beyond the boundaries of my own existence even, back before my birth and forward into eternity. I felt drunk on it.

*

It is nine years later, and I have just decided I am no longer a Christian. I am pushing my bike along the verge of a roundabout outside Manchester in the dark. It is raining, hard. I can hear the rustle and squeak of my waterproof trousers as I walk, feel the damp seeping into the seams of my canvas Vans. Water is running down my neck, and clouding my glasses, but by following the metal barriers I can see enough in the sulphurous glow of streetlights to get me and my poor punctured bike back to the house I'm lodging in. It all feels appropriately bleak, a fitting setting for the end of a love affair. As I trudge, I am saying goodbye to my faith. It feels like letting my own house fall in on itself, the inevitable result of a series of small erosions of the foundations, rather than continuing to desperately patch and prop. As I pass the sign saying 'Welcome to Salford' I realise it's gone. My home is down. And my feet are sodden. I hate this city.

Manchester will forever be associated in my memory with wet asphalt: shining black and streamer-streaked with the white and red of car lights. Striking, in a graphic eighties blouse kind of way, but not welcoming.

I hadn't expected to be there. I'd graduated straight into a job at the BBC in London, surprising myself and pissing off the entire volunteer staff of the university student radio into which I'd never set foot. My job was dogsbody in the Radio Drama department, a strange backwater of the corporation staffed entirely by theatre types and sardonic studio managers who could make a knife and a melon sound like the eye gouging in *King Lear*. Our offices were in the bowels of Bush House, the resplendent neoclassical marble hallways otherwise occupied by the BBC World Service. Standing in the canteen I could hear eight different languages, microwave my soup while smelling six different home-cooked cuisines.

This was the building from which a BBC reporter had walked out onto Waterloo Bridge and been stabbed by a poison-tipped umbrella during the Cold War, like something from a Le Carré novel. Due to a now-closed loophole, I could legitimately claim theatre tickets on expenses in the name of research, so went several times a week. I found a church packed with other shiny young people and sang with my hands in the air every Sunday. I loved London, and London loved me.

Life was exciting, but the job couldn't hold my attention for long, mainly because I was terrible at it. I wanted to make programmes, not just plan and budget for them, but the leap from production assistant to researcher felt like jumping between moving trains. Most of my applications, typed on windows hastily minimised when my boss passed, went unanswered – not least because I had little actual knowledge or experience to offer. One job, though, required something I thought I had – knowledge of the Bible. The Religion and Ethics department in Manchester had been commissioned to create a six-part, big budget, bells and whistles television dramatisation of the book of books, and they needed help.

I'd been a Christian for seven or eight years by this point, and had spent many hours of quiet times reading the nice fridge-magnet bits of the Bible over and over. I felt this qualified me perfectly. I was offered the job, threw a fabulous leaving party, packed my hippie pillow cases, fairy lights and IKEA lamp and moved into the spare bedroom of a friend of a friend in Salford.

The BBC headquarters in Manchester is now the shiny glass splendour of Media City, but then it was a long, low, brutalist building beside a busy A road, an Ugly Sister to Bush House's Cinderella. Where in London I'd walked under cherry blossom along the architectural grandeur of the Aldwych, here I dodged lorries in the rain. It rained all the time. It is entirely possible that my over-dramatic imagination, in a fit of pathetic fallacy, has added more rain to my memories than ever actually fell. I know I did pack waterproof cycling trousers in my pannier every single day.

The family I was living with were kind but distracted, dealing with young children and a house renovation I hadn't expected. I crept up to my attic room over dust sheets and open toolboxes to eat my pesto pasta perched on the edge of a single bed. I knew no one except a brother of a university friend who took me for one drink. My new colleagues were kind and fun, high energy and experienced television producers. I kept it quiet that I didn't really watch TV.

I could probably have coped with the loneliness, and the rain, but the work itself was a problem. I was tasked with researching a section of the Hebrew Bible that I'd barely opened before – Judges, Joshua, Kings and Chronicles. It was like dropping directly into an ancient Near Eastern version of *Game of Thrones*. Warring tribes, massacres, child sacrifice, rape, adultery – it was clear these stories would make excellent telly but neither God nor his people came out looking especially appealing. I made research calls to world-leading scholars about how to read these books, how to present them on screen, and attempted to ignore the nagging sensation in my soul.

I tried to find a church, but struggled to connect. The fissures that had started in the Old Testament cracked outward, riddling the whole book, the whole edifice, with questions. I found myself muttering cynically under my breath through services, so stopped going. Every day at work chipped away at my certainties, and there wasn't anyone on the team

I could talk to. They all knew this stuff, having done theology degrees, and most weren't Christians. I was ashamed to be so late to it, embarrassed at the way I'd failed to apply my intelligence to my faith. I looked back on, looked down on, my perky London self as painfully naive and blind to complexity.

My identity had been so intertwined with my Christianity that the tunnelling underneath felt like existential threat. I wanted it to be true, willed myself to believe, but the intellectual gaps gaped wider. Until the day by the roundabout, when living in two worlds became too much, and I made myself look it in the face. My faith had gone. The presence I had encountered in the cowshed had somehow bled out of the world, washed away by the rain, and I was alone.

The story of how I found my way back is less dramatic than these two moments. It was much slower. They say the first time you fall in love can never be repeated, that heartbreak forever changes us. My teenage conversion did feel like first love to me, and the collapse of my faith like some kind of death. In asking 'If you're there, show me' I had allowed myself to hope, and that hope required excruciating vulnerability. Vulnerability betrayed becomes a hard crust of reserve and self-protection.

The following months in Manchester were spent drinking a lot and throwing myself into friendship with my colleagues. I began running obsessively, whittling my body to a leanness unknown before or since. I wrote bleak poetry and performed it at open mics in dark bars. Despite it all, I couldn't seem to shake the damn thing off. Writer Julian Barnes begins his memoir with 'I don't believe in God, but I miss him.'[3] I missed God, and I missed church, the community, the rhythm, the place where I could sing and dance and cry, where I could sit in silence with others. I missed the sense of being part of something bigger, of my life having purpose. I missed confession and absolution. I missed the regular call to be better, to be kinder, more truthful, more generous, more free. I wanted more to be asked of me than just doing a good job at work and trying to look hot.

Meanwhile, I was reading and listening to atheists who shared my concern about the Bible, but who were not offering any kind of positive alternative to what I'd walked away from. Instead, they seemed to glory in meaninglessness. In some ways it was the aesthetic that put me off, the vibe that only the truly intelligent can cope with the austere emptiness of life. I felt I was supposed to admire the nobility of staring into the abyss and not flinching, but I didn't. I flinched, and flinching felt more human.

The moral freedom I had supposed would arrive once I'd shed the shackles of religion was also a disappointment. Anonymous sex seemed much less appealing in reality than in my fantasies, and anyway, no one was offering.

Drugs sounded more inviting, specifically mushrooms, which struck me as vaguely organic, less likely to have brutal criminal activity and child labour in the supply line. I'd always thought paganism would be a good plan-B religion and mushrooms sounded a suitably tree-hugging source of transcendence. I think what stopped me was the fear I'd end up worshipping. Even clubbing felt vaguely risky in this respect; the ecstatic hands-in-the-air high of a drop into dirty bass was too close to the feelings I was trying to wean myself off. It was, fundamentally, the feelings that I missed. The intensity of worship and the relief of prayer. My faith had been a source of comfort and awe and inspiration. Everything else felt flat. It wasn't, I now know, the city's fault. I have come to the conclusion that I am a strange kind of hedonist, that I am less (though not totally un-) intrigued by drugs and orgies but am hungry for meaning, for experiences of encounter.

My deepest fear is not being fully alive. Even as I write this I know 'fully aliveness' is at odds with most people's impressions of Christianity. Especially in the UK, we associate faith with weak tea and polite restraint. It's a sort of boring background noise to the nation, like Radio 4 turned down low. In the US the associations are angrier and more judgemental. Neither are at all attractive, but neither have been my experience. For me it was a portal, a shimmering layer over ordinary life. For years I had been able to get high on my own existential supply, and now it was gone. And I missed it.

I also became aware, as months passed, that the statement 'I don't believe in God' wasn't quite true. Despite myself, the sentence that floated up when my mind was quiet was 'I don't believe in you.' The presence was not completely gone, but lurking. Poet Francis Thompson wrote of God as a relentless 'hound of heaven':

> 'I fled Him, down the arches of the years; I fled Him, down
> the labyrinthine ways
> Of my own mind.'[4]

I fled God too. I argued with this thing I didn't believe in while riding my bike in the rain. I wanted a clean break, to reinvent myself as liberated and impressive, for a man like Josh Lyman from *The West Wing* to call me a smart cookie and ask for my number. I wanted to be wry and mysterious, to drink martinis alone at a bar reading Sartre, in no need of an imaginary friend. It felt time to grow out of this childlike longing like I'd shed the tooth fairy, but I didn't know how. I was left with a deep ambiguity.

Many years later I discovered a poem by Jeanne Murray Walker, which takes me right back to that time:

> Oh, we have only so many words to think with.
> Say God's not fire, say anything, say God's
> a phone, maybe. You know you didn't order a phone,
> but there it is. It rings. You don't know who it could be.
>
> You don't want to talk, so you pull out
> the plug. It rings. You smash it with a hammer
> till it bleeds springs and coils and clobbery
> metal bits. It rings again. You pick it up
>
> and a voice you love whispers hello.[5]

It was smart Christians who showed me a way out of my tortured, existential paralysis. I was invited on a theology study weekend by a friend from my old church in London, who said someone had dropped out and I could come for free. A weekend in a hotel she said, hot meals, a bar, she said, no need to come to any of the sessions, I know you're not into that at the moment. I should have heard the echoes.

That weekend I met highly intelligent, kind people, who'd been where I was. People who weren't surprised by the intellectual collapse, by the questions about science and suffering and all the sharp edges and inconsistencies, but had found a way through. They seemed to be able to hold together the questions with the rootedness, the peace, the fundamental belovedness I remembered.

It took a long, long time before I felt close to comfortable in church again. I still often feel like an alien there, but I no longer mind. I discovered that there are a lot of us, disgruntled but devoted, allergic to glib certainties but compelled by a love we can't fully explain. I found there was a constellation of poets and mystics and morally courageous saints I could listen to and learn from. So here I am, fifteen years later. I have a husband and kids and live in a monastic-inspired intentional community, sharing rhythms of prayer and hospitality, pooling our resources with others (I'll tell you the whole story of this later in the book). Our enormous table is crowded with friends who also want to think about what a good life really is, what it might take to be a grown-up at the end of the world as we know it. They are Marxist and post-liberal, polyamorous and celibate, Jewish, Muslim, pagan, Buddhist, Stoic, atheist, confused. Many want to talk about religion after taking psychedelics, finding they have made their materialist worldview unsustainable. I love it here, with our art student and anarchist neighbours. As I approach middle age I am in what philosopher Paul Ricoeur called my 'second naïveté', discovering this tradition to be richer and deeper and more capacious than the first time round,[6] more interesting for me and for others. All the messages our culture gives us about Christianity lead me to expect primary colour stories for children, oily Easter Egg chocolate, not this Old Master narrative world, this complex red wine. Yes, I deconstructed my home, but I'm now very happy living in the renovation. I'm a contentedly failed atheist, who retains a soft spot for those who would still call themselves that.

This, then, is the wisdom I want more people to know about. I've lived all the arguments against my tradition, am very familiar with the ways its people and institutions disappoint.

I've looked elsewhere for the stability my soul craves, tried to talk myself out of it. But I've given that up now. I'm increasingly convinced there are deep and applicable insights, rituals and practices here helpful even for those who would never go to church. The long, withdrawing roar of secularisation has left the vast resources within increasingly inaccessible. This worries me. We are living in a time of endings and are going to need all the help we can get. While newer disciplines bring much insight and comfort, religions have a many-centuries head start in mapping the mysterious terrain of human depth. These stories were written in, and have been told through, more turbulent times than ours. They have provided forms of collective resistance, existential steadying and meaning-making material for billions. And there is power in them yet.

That is why, that day on the side of the dual carriageway, heart pierced by the song from *Matilda*, I did something you (statistically) probably don't do. I went to the place I go with this feeling, and with most of my intense emotions. I prayed. I don't remember exactly what or how. It may have been a few breaths of a Christian meditation practice, or the Jesus prayer ('Lord Jesus Christ, Have Mercy on Me'), that ancient Eastern Orthodox mantra, which I have prayed so often it now rises unbidden on any panicky inhale. I know I reached for the old, old story, the habits that have grounded me so many times before. They remind me that I don't have to be the ultimate grown-up, that my life, my daughter's life, doesn't just rest with me. They imply, improbably, that it is possible to see the world as it really is, and still not be afraid. Whatever it was, I reoriented my emotions, my soul settled, and we were able to drive on and go about the mundane business of the day – getting petrol, cleaning up travel sickness, bickering over dinner.

Thomas Merton, who recognised the spiritual distress of his generation in the 1930s, eventually became a cloistered Trappist monk. I haven't gone that far yet, but I know the draw of it. I think if I wasn't married with kids, I would be exploring being a nun, though now I think about it I can see the obedience and silence bit being a problem. Also, the poverty and chastity. Instead, I've taken the way more travelled, but committed to seek a deeper life in my everyday. I am trying to pursue meaning, freedom and connection among my very ordinary demands of work, parenting and life admin.

Some days I pick my way gingerly across the brittle surface of my week, managing to focus on emails and booking dentist appointments and all the 'How are you doing? Fine! Good weekend? Lovely thanks!' small talk, pretending to be a normal person. But I keep putting my foot through the crust and dropping down into the deeper stuff, letting my intense, earnest self show through. Do you think about death? What is goodness? Why on earth, and I mean this sincerely, are we here? And I sense an increased appetite among the people I meet to go there.

This book is partly about how my faith helps with those kinds of questions but I don't assume you share it. You may be unfamiliar with the religious instinct, and possibly find it intriguing and off-putting in equal measure. If so, I'm glad you're here. The things I am addressing are deeply human, and (I believe) shared. Medicine for the ills of being alive pops up in all kinds of places. The offer of this book is a few more bottles for your shelf. Please see me as a travel writer, sending field notes – the weirdness of church, the intimacy of prayer, as private and as difficult to describe as an orgasm – from a far-off land that you may or may not ever actually choose to visit.

I am trying to break out the treasures from Christianity in particular, rather than religion in general, though I'll refer to other traditions where relevant. Part of the surprise at being back here, broadly aligned with one particular faith, is that you'd think my hungry soul would have gone mad in the sweet shop of religions. One of the most unattractive elements of Christianity for our current sensibilities is the insistence, in atheist philosopher Alain de Botton's words, that we 'eat everything on the plate'.[7] Despite all this, something about the rigour of internal coherence, and a suspicion that I might not be a fully trustworthy editor and synthesiser of centuries of thought, keeps me drawing mainly, if not entirely, on this one particular tradition, while noticing the resonances with other wisdom paths.

I also don't have the right to speak on behalf of other faiths, to appropriate their heritage for my own ends, adding a 'multi-faith' overlay to make it more palatable. I am a white Western woman. Christianity is not, of course, originally Western in any straightforward sense, but is so intertwined with the history of Europe that it is the closest thing I have to an ancestral tradition. I fully claim the right to speak as a pilgrim, not an expert, from my own path, but 'spirituality' can bleed in its worst forms into spiritual tourism. It is also because I think 'religion' is itself a bit of a bogus category (though I don't seem able to avoid the word) lumping together complex, ancient ecosystems of thought and practice into an indistinguishable mass of platitudes. It always reminds me of the film *Mean Girls*, in which Lindsay Lohan's lead character has recently moved back from that well known country, Africa. As my friend Nick Spencer often says, any label that can contain Isis and Quakerism is too baggy. Yes, these diverse traditions that come under the label 'religion' have things in common, but maybe less than we'd like them to, and once we get to that universalising level it's hard to hold on to the grit, particularity and power.

I know that seeking wisdom for now in this very old body of thought might sound bizarre. Honestly, some days the felt truth of the thing, the conviction that God exists and loves us, slides out of focus like I've got grease on my glasses, and for a while I can't remember what it feels like when it makes sense. This is just my best guess, my wager on what makes me feel most human, the strongest container I have found for the pain and love and longing of being alive. Even on the blurry-glasses days, though, something about these practices, ideas and communities feels healthy to me, like they are forming me in a direction I want to go. They help me resist the strong cultural tides always pulling me away from the person I want to become. That is why I think others who can't quite get the metaphysics to come into focus may find them steadying, comforting and liberating too. I hope that listening in to my quest helps you think about the values you want to define your life, the kind of person you want to be becoming, and whether you have what you need in order to do so.

I can't offer you certainty, then, but I will translate some treasure. This book will introduce you to themes, rituals and rhythms that I've found life-giving and which you might like to experiment with. I'll take you on a tour of these via my own life, because it is only in practice that they have come to make sense to me. I hope this book functions as an antihistamine for an allergy to faith, enabling you to get past the thorns to smell the flowers, but I am not here to defend the worst parts (and there are many). What I hope to do is help you understand, despite the abuse and bigotry and power-hungry politics that are too often the public story of my faith, what on earth I still see in it. Why I keep finding in it sign posts and support to become the kind of human that I think this world might need.

Hidden behind the heavy organ chords and dusty-voiced delivery, there is real, applicable wisdom in here. And the first one might look like a thorn, but I believe (handled well) it is in fact a flower: the concept of sin.

THE HUMAN PROPENSITY TO FUCK THINGS UP

I am unstacking the dishwasher, loudly. Every few plates I stop to check my phone and call my husband, who is not picking up. It is a glorious autumn day, the sun streaming like lemon curd through the windows, but I am full of rage. Yesterday we took our daughter for a PCR test, bribing her with marshmallows to endure the sneezes, the gag-reflex, the coldly clinical procedure in a shipping container in a local car park. Today is a school day and she isn't allowed in until we can prove that her ominously persistent cough isn't Covid. My husband booked the appointment, and so the results will go to his phone, and he is working elsewhere.

Five missed calls, six. I slam the mugs into the cupboard as if he, a mile away, can hear me jungle-drumming my feelings. I am absolutely sure she is negative, and that the results will have arrived already. I am equally sure that he, more able to focus than me, less vigilant, will have missed them. I'm supposed to be working and I can't get my head in the game until she is at school. All the weeks and months of this feeling – the thinly spread pandemic juggle, the scarcity of time and energy and space – are pressing down on my mood, causing me to huff and sigh and mutter under my breath. The cutlery is away, and the dishwasher filter is covered in gunk, and of course I will be the one to clean it, as always.

Eventually he messages. She is negative. The results arrived hours ago. Of course.

'Shoes on, time to go!' I bellow through to the lounge. My daughter, untimely ripped from an episode of *Junior Bake Off*, appears round the door, pale and hacking into her elbow. 'Can I stay home Mum? I'm really tired.'

'No. You have to go in. I need to work.'

'But it's weird to go in for half a day. I don't want to go in at lunchtime.'

My voice rises from brisk and harassed to forceful.

'Shoes on. No arguing. Let's go.'

I can see the stubbornness rising up in her red-rimmed eyes, the desire to watch TV and sleep and read *Harry Potter* for the day, because she has a cold and who doesn't want to do that when they feel rough? She is about to engage her considerable will and refuse to go to school. I could head it off with calm words and empathy and connection. I could problem-solve and chivvy and make her laugh and get us both through this, like I usually do. But today I don't have it in me. I am aggrieved, for all kinds of half-processed reasons, and she is the three-foot embodiment of all the things thwarting my will. The frustration and rage rise up in my throat, bitter as bile, and I shout so loud she bursts into tears in surprise: 'It's the LAW! Do you want me to be arrested by the police and sent to prison? Do you?' And then I slam the kitchen door on her terrified face and proceed to restack the dishwasher, stopping myself at the last moment from throwing a travel cup through a window. Plates, mugs, an encrusted casserole dish – I am waiting for her to come and apologise, because of course the sick seven-year-old, not the adult woman who has just invoked the force of a fictional authoritarian state to get her way, should be the bigger person.

I messed that up. I do that a lot. Please tell me you do too. Not (usually) in dramatic ways, the Obviously Bad things, like murder, and fraud, and adultery. Although even with those last two most of us have our grey areas. Our dubious choices show up most regularly in these private, banal moments. I don't think it's just me who lives among the attrition of tiny disappointments with myself: half-lies, broken promises, judgemental comments. Avoiding the eye of the homeless person, as if we might both believe they are not there.

Francis Spufford, who is Professor of Creative Writing at Goldsmiths, calls this tendency The Human Propensity to Fuck Things Up, or HPtFtu.[1] It is his attempt to rebrand the concept of sin, a word that has fallen far, far out of fashion. It's used now, if at all, jokingly. A slimming club's shorthand for calories, the name of a lingerie shop. It sounds like self-indulgent naughtiness, harming no one, the liberated opposite of Puritanism.

There are good reasons we shrugged off the concept. Alongside the sillier usages (Magnum ice cream had a 7 Deadly Sins range, the Vanity flavour including crunchy silver cake-decorating balls embedded in champagne-flavoured coating), we can trace a darker side. Church teaching on sexual sin has created shame around entirely normal human urges, and in some periods and denominations riddled people with terror of hellfire for the smallest misdemeanour.

Despite all this I'm going to use it, because without the word, or at least the HPtFtu alternative, I don't know how to speak honestly about the moment of fracture between me and my daughter. I am seeking a deep life of connection, and moments like these keep getting in the way. This language gives me a way of talking about all these fractures, large and small, the twig-snapping crackle-glaze of human interactions. Sin, theologically understood, is nothing to do with enjoying sensual pleasure. It is a relational concept, about the threads between us and others, us and the natural world, and, yes, us and God.

I've been sparing with my use of the G Bomb, so far, because it does need handling with bomb-disposal-team levels of care. It is present in the background of everything I am going to say, of course, but my hope is that those of you who are cautious or outright allergic to God talk will find much that is thought-provoking or useful anyway. If you are interested to read my attempt to address the subject more directly you can flip ahead to the final chapter. Until then, I'll mainly use [God] to remind us that this is perhaps the most semiotically dense three letters in our language, and that we will all be dragging our own associations into the space between those two brackets.

Meanwhile, sin, barely recognisable now in the cultural cipher it's become, is tragedy. What Kant called the crooked timber of humanity, the tendency to break things, accidentally and deliberately, that just seems baked in. I like Spufford's use of Fuck because its fricative-plosive helps us hear the brutality. HPtFtu is all the times we choose withdrawal, self-protection or attack. When we centre ourselves, not as part of a healthy rhythm of receiving and giving in a web of relationships, but because we're terrified no one is going to meet our needs but ourselves. I see my sin (which, I should say now, needs meeting with grace, not judgement), as a bundle of my self-destructive tendencies. HPtFtu shows up in lashing out, hiding, numbing behaviours that close down the possibilities of intimacy, with myself, others and the beyond.

HPtFtu also makes me feel less free. This is counter-intuitive.

Religion is associated with restriction, and rebellion against it with liberation. But this is one of the many places where my experience goes in the opposite direction to what I was led to expect. Free is a big word for me. It is what I pray over my children as they sleep, tracing a cross on their peach-smooth foreheads: may they be free, resilient, joyful, brave. May they never doubt they are loved. I think I use freedom in a slightly different sense than many though. I am not especially bothered, for myself or my kids, about being free from governments, useless as they often seem (though I'm sure I'd think differently if I'd lived under actual tyranny). I find the tin-hat individualism of many libertarians off-puttingly unrelational. The freedom I long for is something more internal. I want to be, want them to be, liberated in mind. The Bible talks about sin tangling us up and slowing us down, and it feels to me like lies. The lies I believe about myself and other people. The lies about what actually makes us happy. The seductive temptation of disconnection. Those, I want to be free of.

Fully aliveness, for me, is summed up in connection, and my definition of sin is everything working against that. Jewish theologian Martin Buber is something close to a patron saint for me, and his short, extraordinary book *I and Thou* as close as I get to a secondary sacred text. His thesis is that humans function in two modes, I-it and and I-thou. We can treat other people functionally as objects, symbols, supporting roles for our main character arc, or we can treat people as a 'you'. These are I-thou moments, when two people connect properly and really see each other. They are, for Buber and for me, what life is all about. 'All living is meeting,' he says, and these moments between us are all that is 'really real'.[2] He thinks an I-thou posture is the only way to really know the world, the only way to really experience the present.

'Being, lived in [I-thou] receives even in extreme dereliction a harsh and strengthening sense of reciprocity; being, lived in [I-it] will not, even in the tenderest intimacy, grope out over the outlines of the self.'[3] Buber's book is oft-quoted for interpersonal models, but the last third is about a connection with [God], and worship as the ultimate I-thou.

This relational understanding of sin changes how I read all sorts of things. There is a terrifying Bible verse, beloved of sandwich-board-wearing street preachers, which says 'the wages of sin are death'. You can definitely conjure 'angry god' from it, scratching our misdemeanours into a heavenly ledger. If though, as in my understanding, fullness of life is in connection, then every time I connect with myself, with the natural world, with other people and with the divine I am moving lifewards. I am groping out over the outlines of the self into the really real. Each choice I make moves me towards life and connection, or towards disconnection, and therefore death. That verse becomes more like a summary of natural consequences, a sat-nav's warning.

I find this deeper, older sense of sin – prone to disconnection, in need of help to move towards life – a label that is not psychologically crushing, but liberating. It seems healthier to have language to explain what happened when I deliberately terrified my sick child. To have a name for the tangles I'm trying to cut off.

Because if it's sin, my worst choices are not my identity. I don't have to move from 'I did a bad thing' to 'I am a bad person'. This older moral universe allows me not to be surprised by the darkness I find in myself and others. I don't need to hide it or explain it away. Like the twelve-step programme, which draws heavily on theology, it teaches that the first step is admitting we are powerless. My faith says I can't just *#dobetter* through my own will. Two thousand years ago, a highly educated, competent and privileged Roman citizen called Paul said, 'I do what I do not want to do, and I can't seem to do the things I want to do.'[4]

That day with my daughter, a shamefully long time later, when I'd calmed down enough to realise I was in the wrong, I didn't need to marinate in shame and regret. I knew what would help. There will almost always be mitigating circumstances. Sin language doesn't need to be in competition with the other helpful frames I can use to understand myself – my awareness of my psychological health, my childhood scripts, my attachment model. It's not irrelevant that I was hungry, and tired, and I don't think I am a monster for snapping at my child. What the sin frame does acknowledge is that, even with all this understanding, my choices matter. There is dignity in being responsible for my actions, even while acknowledging the systems and other people who may have made my mistakes more likely. They are also responsible, but it's not *my* job to judge them. I've got enough going on over here.

You can call this acknowledgement a confession, but it doesn't have to be in a booth. I try to look calmly at my actions, and – with compassion, not attack – acknowledge what I did. That day I prayed 'forgive me,' apologised to my daughter, told her that it wasn't ok, and we had a cuddle. Later, I told a few others in my community and asked for help keeping my temper.

The forgiveness bit is vitally important here. The concept of sin prevents me from explaining away injustice, including my own; forgiveness allows me to find a way through it. I once interviewed Katharine Birbalsingh, an educationalist known as 'Britain's Strictest Headteacher', for my podcast *The Sacred*. She admitted that although she is not a Christian, she believes in something close to 'original sin', the deep brokenness of humans, and it drives her philosophy of education. This worries me. If the only bit of theology that gets culturally transmitted is sin, disconnected from forgiveness, you land somewhere very bleak. It's grace, the possibility of healing I did not earn, that keeps me sane. Because I believe in cosmic-level forgiveness, I am learning to have more grace with others, and with myself. If sin is the rupture of relationship, forgiveness is repair. Fuck up, tell the truth, say sorry, ask for forgiveness, be open in community, ask for help, fuck up again, but maybe, just maybe, slightly less badly. It's a rinse-and-repeat cycle that stops me despairing, even while I'm forced into deeply uncomfortable awareness of my shadow side on a regular basis. It feels like growth.

I also think sin-and-forgiveness is helpful beyond the personal. Collectively, I worry that in excising sin we've also abandoned forgiveness. We have ceased to believe that people can really change.

Our sinless society, which promised liberation from the psychological harm that externally imposed guilt brings, has begun to feel a bit suffocating. No one is really responsible for anything, but neither can anyone really be forgiven. Two seemingly incompatible moral universes have meshed in a toxic brew. On one hand, the ways we hurt each other are simply social conditioning. We might be able to unpack the triggers through therapy, but it's a tragic project of entanglement in trauma. On the other, there are certain beliefs and identities that function like unforgivable sins – and these will be unique to your tribe. Some days the whole world seems high on self-righteous rage, locating evil conveniently outside ourselves and our group. I regularly feel tempted to performatively avoid causing offence, signal my moral purity or publicly align myself with whoever the right tribe is that day. It doesn't leave much energy for actually becoming more loving or more just.

Christianity – and believe me, I know this is not the public perception – should be radically non-judgemental. It's one of Jesus' most famous sayings – don't judge others, or you'll be judged. Why are you worrying about the speck of dust in your neighbour's eye, when you have a plank in your own? It's why prison chaplains will readily sit with paedophiles and murderers. This older moral universe says some actions are heinous, but no person is irredeemable.

Even as I write this I can feel the objections bubbling up. It's too neat, too easy. Forgiveness has gone out of fashion partly because it's been misused. Everyone has heard an insincere, PR-polished apology and rolled their eyes. Forgiveness without real regret, real repentance, is jarring, and dangerously open to abuse – I can't swallow the sour taste in my mouth remembering that Jimmy Savile went regularly to confession. Did he think it acted like a heavenly get out of jail free card? Honestly, forgiveness in this context sounds like an obscenity. A large part of me does not want child abusers to be visited by a prison chaplain with kind eyes. Except many of those abusers were abused too. Perhaps we are tempted to reject the Christian moral universe because we think we don't like sin, but deeper down it's forgiveness we can't swallow. Some things should be unforgivable, shouldn't they? But who gets to decide?

Rather than a rigorous, ethically thought-through conclusion, when I get stuck in this maze I land on what feels liveable. I can't change other people. A default posture of non-judgement and a willingness to forgive when people repent is frankly less exhausting than being angry all the time, and leaves more energy for trying to become more alive, more connected, myself.

Unexpectedly, I have found the seven deadly sins to be a helpful way forward. Few ideas first conceived by desert monks and kept alive in a dusty branch of academia called patristics feature in so many LinkedIn posts. The seven deadly sins of bulk email fundraising! The seven deadly sins of year-end accruals!

Before they were a click bait trope, they were a list of eight 'bad thoughts' or 'temptations' written by Evagrius of Pontus in the fourth century.[5] His list was gluttony, lust, avarice, sadness, anger, acedia, vainglory and pride. The desert monks were pursuing an extreme ascetic lifestyle, with long periods of solitude and fasting, and Evagrius observed that these eight tendencies pulled focus from prayer and contemplation. It seems that, even when stripped of normal social structures, humans struggle with the same things. Vows of poverty do not fully prevent an acquisitive impulse, nor chastity lustful ones. Evagrius's list cropped up in various iterations over the following centuries, with pride and vainglory being combined, sadness (harsh!) dropping out and envy added. They eventually settled into the seven we might recognise today, though different lists are extant.

The medieval heyday of the sins has long passed. They are rarely taught now in churches; most Christians know them more from the aforementioned Magnum range than the pulpit. I'm on a mission to unearth them, not as a comedy concept but as a genuinely helpful framework for self-reflection. I've found them an astute taxonomy of disconnection.

They are helpful partly because our moral language is so shrivelled. Where we used to have a complex palate of vices and virtues, contemporary moral tastebuds are trained on thin gruel: harm reduction. Beyond that, there are now few places to talk about the kind of people we want to be, and all the tendencies that make that difficult. *New York Times* columnist David Brooks writes about the difference between résumé and eulogy virtues:

> The résumé virtues are the skills you bring to the marketplace. The eulogy virtues are the ones that are talked about at your funeral – whether you were kind, brave, honest or faithful. Were you capable of deep love?[6]

He argues that, even though we all know that the eulogy virtues are most important, it is the résumé virtues – the skills we need to earn more money – that we spend vastly more time and attention on. When I look at the non-fiction shelves in my local bookshop there are titles focused on how to reduce the harm we cause (how to be anti-racist, for example), but none on how to be someone who keeps their promises, loves their enemies, even lays down their life for their friends. My guess is there are more books telling you why growth involves the opposite of these things, because they are seen as 'emotional labour'. The tiny section focused on character is dwarfed by the shelves of books telling me how to make more money and project success.

I want to get beyond the 'résumé virtues', and even beyond 'harm reduction', great baseline that it is. I want, for the sake of the world, my kids, myself, to be better. (Even now, I have to resist my own internal cringe, because cringe is a terrible indicator of what is actually important.) Our moral vocabulary is so allergic to anything that sounds judgemental that it's hard to know where to start. I don't think I can overcome my darker self just by upbeat positive thinking. I don't believe that denying my tendency to Fuck Things Up helps, but injecting something a bit more robust into my life really has.

Though led by the 'sins', the following chapters will also unpack their opposites. I find change happens more easily when I have something to be moving towards, not just something I want to avoid. There is an established set of alternatives within church tradition, the 'Heavenly Virtues' of humility, patience, chastity, kindness, charity, temperance and diligence. I wish that list didn't make me yawn but it does. The Bible also offers a list of the 'fruit of the Holy Spirit' that should be growing in any believer's life: love, joy, peace, patience, kindness, goodness, faithfulness, gentleness and self-control. Ditto – great things but hard to get a hold of, partly because they feel so. . . nice. Therefore, knowing how easily distracted I am, I am working instead on a very unorthodox, non-theologian list of my own:

Wrath (from polarisation to peacemaking)
Avarice (from stuffocation to gratitude and generosity)
Acedia (from distraction to attention)
Envy (from status anxiety to belovedness)
Gluttony (from numbing to ecstasy)
Lust (from objectification to sexual humanism)
and
Pride (from individualism to community)

All these things bleed into each other of course – greed is tangled up with envy and pride, gluttony and acedia are closely related. I am not attempting a watertight analysis of my weaknesses. But these seven different lenses have helped me see disconnection – and what might actually make connection easier – in a fuller, deeper light. Along the way, I'll give you a (piecemeal, personal) impression of the broader theological landscape of Christianity, and, if you want it, finally address the G bomb directly right at the end.

Is that antihistamine kicking in yet? Then let's go.

WRATH: FROM POLARISATION TO PEACEMAKING

When the UK voted to leave the European Union in June 2016 I was in the middle of a difficult second pregnancy. I have an autoimmune condition that gives me unstable joints, and have had periods of significant impairment in the use of my hands. Can you brush your teeth using your elbow and do the Big Shop pushing the trolley only with your belly? I can. That year, the weight of a baby added to my pitifully weak wrists a pelvis that did not want to stay together. Walking made my pubic bones grind against each other like a tiny miner was drilling under my muff, and not in a good way. We lived in a small flat up two flights of concrete stairs, and the battle to get myself, my belly, all our bags and our toddler up those stairs at the end of a long day at work and nursery became increasingly traumatic. So I noticed Brexit was divisive, but my mind was elsewhere. At the start of November I gave birth, and decided that since the world was so angry I would take a step back during my maternity leave. I summarily signed out of all my social media accounts, deleted my news apps and retreated into a milky bubble of nappies and exhaustion.

On 9 November Donald Trump was elected. Definitely a good time to take some time off from the news cycle. I predicted that by the time I came back to work the spike in polarisation would have blown over and we would have remembered how to live together.

I don't have to tell you that's not what happened. My break prevented 'boiling frog syndrome', where we don't notice things getting worse because it happens slowly. The difference between 2016 and my return in 2017 was stark. Contempt was in fashion. It's not that public conversations had been all Kumbaya before, but it seemed any social censure for dehumanising your opponent had gone. In fact, the more withering, rage-full and sarcastic you could be, the more you were lauded. I have always had friends from different tribes but now I feared inviting them round for dinner together. Everyone seemed triggered all the time. I was appalled.

I racked my brains for a project we could do at the think tank I was running that might help. I came to the conclusion that while we could track polarisation, provide data and analysis the most meaningful thing I could do was learn and model a countervailing approach. I started *The Sacred* podcast with my then colleague Hussein Kesvani, himself no stranger to online controversies, with the aim of understanding better the various divides. On *The Sacred* I speak to individuals from different tribes, from communists to Conservative MPs, Brexiteers and Remainers, social conservatives and the former head of Stonewall. I try my very best not to argue with them, but to listen with openness and curiosity to why they believe what they believe. I am naturally nosy, fascinated with how people tick, but I also had a bodged-together peace-building theory bubbling underneath. A little while after I started *The Sacred* I read this from Barack Obama, a veteran of community organising, describing the methodology they used.

> Just going around and listening to people. Asking them about their lives, and what was important to them. And how did they come to believe what they believe? And what are they trying to pass on to their children? I learned in that process that if you listen hard enough, everybody's got a sacred story . . . And they're willing to share it with you if they feel as if you actually care about it. And that ends up being the glue around which relationships are formed, and trust is formed, and communities are formed.[1]

This echoed what I was learning. You could add 'the glue that sustains democracies'. Relationships where we practise trust and respect across divides are vital for us to be effective citizens, especially in times of crisis, but no one teaches the skills you need to do it in school. *The Sacred* began as an experiment in me teaching myself. And I found Obama was right, that my guests were willing to share their moral reasoning if they felt I 'actually care[ed] about it'. If I listened with curiosity and respect rather than defensiveness and rebuttal. If I gave them the gift of sustained attention. I interviewed people who held positions completely incomprehensible to me, some of which felt offensive to my very identity, who I had to force myself to stay in a room with and talk to. Over the course of an hour of concentrated listening they transfigured from a symbol of a tribe to a whole, complex, usually even likeable human being. By repeatedly forcing myself to tolerate the discomfort that difference and disagreement brings, I was learning to resist what I have come to understand as wrath.

Wrath is not the same as anger. The words are used interchangeably, but traditions around the seven deadly sins imply that wrath is one way of being angry. One of the New

Testament letters offers what sounds like a command: 'be angry, but don't sin'[2]. Jesus got angry himself, at the oppression of the poor and the misuse of religion. Not all anger is to be avoided. It's possible to be righteously angry at systems and events, and even to be healthily angry at a person, if we are seeking to remain connected to them throughout and the anger is expressed in the service of the relationship. Theologian and Professor of Africana Studies Willie Jennings told me when he came on the podcast that his Pentecostal church has a policy: when you're angry with someone, tell them, but hold their hand while you do so.[3] Anger itself is not necessarily an enemy of aliveness; indeed it is sometimes required.

Wrath, though, disconnects us. Like many of these temptations, it initially feels good. Media content creators know the sad secret of the human soul – wrath, in the form of self-righteous rage and contempt, is a compelling, borderline pleasurable emotion. Historian Noel Annan wrote in his 1990 social history *Our Age*: 'for many more people than we care to admit, moral indignation is the supreme joy in life'.[4] How much more so now. At least compared to fear, or guilt, or overwhelm, the feelings I am often trying to stuff it down with, it is delicious. Wrath allows the tension of balancing in complexity to dissolve in the joyous free-fall of certainty. It is akin to a sugar high, and as addictive.

It is also not new. In his book *Fractured* Jon Yates unpacks what evolutionary psychologists call 'homophily' and Yates calls PLM: People Like Me syndrome.[5] We are more likely to marry, buy from, befriend or vote for people like ourselves. Birds of a feather all get houses in the same postcode. And on one level PLM is fine and even useful, creating small networks of care and solidarity. If a parent didn't pay more attention to the needs of their own children than others we would think something was wrong. Loyal love of your friends, your own community, even your own nation, is no sin. But at its worst, as Yale professor Amy Chua succinctly puts it, 'the tribal instinct is not just an instinct to belong. It is also an instinct to exclude.'[6]

Yates argues that, while PLM syndrome is a constant across history, societies have always created norms, institutions and rituals that check its worst excesses. Our PLM tendencies need places where we spend time and have common cause with those I call Not Like Me (NLM). Yates labels these institutions, norms and rituals a 'common life', a set of threads that keep us connected beyond PLM, and it is these which we have seen rapidly eroded in recent generations. Demographic shifts have led to what sociologists call the 'Big Sort', leaving us less likely to encounter NLMs in the shops, in our workplace, in a congregation or union or social club.[7] We spend more and more time with PLM. Algorithmically driven information tech like social media means we are only shown aspects of NLMs that are likely to enrage us, and we don't know any of them IRL so we can't check the narrative we are being sold.

Once you start seeing the world through the lens of PLM it makes a lot of sense. Not just of the Obviously Bad stuff like racism, but also the weirder tiny tribalisms we tolerate in ourselves. Yates recounts how repeated studies show football fans are more likely to stop and help an injured person if they are wearing the shirt of the team they support.[8] We can be manipulated to band together against others over characteristics as arbitrary as eye colour. We feel rapidly warmer towards strangers if we can find something, anything, in common with them. Honestly, it's embarrassing. Reading

Yates and others, I became more aware of how I (and, social science would indicate, you too) scan the world like Narcissus, looking for fragments of my own reflection.

I find sugar a useful metaphor here. These deep-seated instincts (to band together in tribes, to eat sugar) are both helpful in survival situations. Sugar provides quick calories, tribes help protect us. However, both of these responses need containing. When our desire for sugar is not checked, but instead exploited, nutritionists call it an 'obesogenic environment'. It's hard to stay a healthy weight when multinational profits rely on your overeating. I think what we now have is a 'conflictogenic' or indeed a 'wrathogenic' environment, when political and technological forces benefit from amplifying our worst instincts. Even though we all know we are being played, that we are more likely to click a link or watch a programme if it makes us feel outraged, we still do it.

Fun though it might sometimes be, that feeling rots our teeth and is driving us further apart. Since we started the podcast in 2017 things have continued to get worse (you mean a podcast didn't fix tribalism?!). Movements like *#metoo* and Black Lives Matter that started with such promise and have delivered much progress have also provoked backlash and become things to disagree on themselves. Whether it's trans rights, colonialism, vaccines or good old-fashioned politics, we keep finding new and better reasons to hate each other.

Have you also noticed other people becoming more annoying? Yes, there are myriad stupid people out there. They say ignorant, obviously wrong things. They are often sexist, and racist, and politically deluded. My goodness, they are deluded. Also they can't spell. Or punctuate. Or use correct grammar. Or they are patronising spelling and grammar pedants. They jump on bandwagons. Or they are self-consciously contrarian. They virtue signal and self-promote and snip and carp and complain. The human animal, especially online, is infuriating.

And so, I fear, am I. I am so tempted to focus on how to fix them, the NLMs. To expose their delusions with my evidence, to call them out and shame them. I want to bitch about them to the PLM, to know the thrill of a synchronised eye roll, a shared snide remark. As I'm becoming more conscious of these dynamics, though, the brutal truth is that I tend to be judgemental of others but very quick to let myself off the hook. Wrath disconnects me from myself as well as other people because I use it to cover up what I'm really feeling and to disguise my part in the conflict. Wrath covers over the deeper desolations of fear and hurt. It can make me feel alive because it gives me a rush of adrenaline, a sense of power and agency, but, if death is disconnection, it is really death in disguise.

As part of my attempt to uproot wrath from my life, I started keeping a record in my journal of the moments when I felt warmer towards people I had something in common with (PLM) and hostile towards those I didn't (NLM). It became obvious that I carried absurd granularity in these categories. After a while I started applying this awareness in how we functioned as a team at work, and then began to be asked to help other groups with it. I usually start with a simple exercise to force our tribalisms into our consciousness. You can try it.

Write two lists, one titled 'types of people or groups I feel instinctively comfortable with' and the second 'types of people or groups I feel instinctively uncomfortable with'. A helpful test is, how does the thought of going to a party filled with this kind of person make me feel? Start with the obvious maybe, political tribes, beliefs, social types, but you can get a lot more granular than that. Personality types. Interest groups. Just get it all out, and don't stop until you have at least ten on each list.

Then attempt to fill in a second column for each marked 'Why?' The challenge is that your reason has to be about you, not about them. So instead of 'Remainers are smug and superior' you could write, 'The one Remainer I know makes me feel lectured and I've always been allergic to that.' If you feel a weird soft spot for Hells Angels, it might be that your dad was one. Or even that you once read a novel with an incredibly likeable Hells Angel as the lead and it opened up some empathic space for them in your imagination. Unless you are some kind of highly enlightened anti-tribalism ninja, it is likely your first list contains lots of PLM and your second is mainly NLM.

When I did this it threw up some curve balls. I realised that, on first meeting, I am instinctively more comfortable with tall than with small women. Next to a petite female, particularly a blonde (I'm brunette), I tend to feel like Captain Hook next to Tinker Bell. Although my adult brain now fully endorses Captain Hook as a style icon (*opens new eBay tab for 'scarlet steampunk pirate jacket'*) part of me is still intimidated. The List helped me realise that this is because I was teased at school for being a giant by a group of small blonde girls. I didn't get into Oxbridge, or go to private school, so people who did tend to make me feel intimidated, and thus slightly shoulder-chippy, to begin with. Both these things are mildly embarrassing to admit. I'm giving you my lowest-stakes examples. Even so, if you're a short blonde woman, or Oxbridge educated, please keep reading. You may notice that you now feel less well-disposed to me and what

I've got to say because I've admitted to being initially less comfortable with you. That is normal. I've just given you a tiny tiny dose of the threat reaction we will unpack in a minute. Try to just be aware of it rather than immediately reacting to it. We can get through this. We can stay connected.

If your list isn't slightly painful, you're probably not being honest. You don't need to show it to anyone. Just let it make you more conscious.

Understanding the PLM theory helped with this growing awareness of wrath in myself. I wanted to learn more, and it was becoming a parent that helped me understand the role my fight-or-flight reactions were playing. I knew vaguely about this shared human response to threat before I had kids. Like most of us, I had picked up that when humans are in danger our amygdala triggers pre-conscious reactions to keep us safe – giving us the energy to either fight back or run away (or, less commonly, to freeze or fawn[9]). It was only when I really saw it in the form of out-of-control toddler meltdowns though, the screaming, stubborn, banshee behaviour, triggered by any small thwarting of their will, that it became salient. Rich Bartlett, an expert in group dynamics and decentralised organisations, uses the metaphor of demon possession for fight-or-flight in adults.[10] When presented with what did feel, in a blackly comic way, like demon possession in my child, I noticed my reaction to it was uncomfortably similar. If I let it, my frustration and rage would build until I would lose my rag and shout. We frequently both ended up in tears. I once poured a whole bottle of water over my child's head in the park in a crazed attempt to snap her out of it. It didn't help.

Desperate to find ways to navigate these deeply unpleasant tandem meltdowns, I read child development studies to try to understand what was actually happening. It is easy to overstate how much we understand the brain but, in very simple terms, the fight-or-flight threat response is driven by our limbic system. This is one of the seats of emotions, along with the entirely automatic brain stem, sometimes known as the reptilian brain (because it's the only brain a reptile has). In contrast, the prefrontal cortex (known as 'The CEO' and one of the last brain areas to develop in children) is implicated in decision making, empathy and moderating social behaviour. In fight-or-flight, the prefrontal cortex is largely inactive, ceding control to automatic functions. We are therefore less likely to take properly considered decisions or care about the other person, so can find ourselves doing stupid things like pouring water on a child, or worse. Survival mode, by its very nature, is pre-rational. It is designed to help us scan the world for potential threats, and so it makes me more likely to interpret events or comments in negative ways, turning everyone into an enemy. It makes intimacy or connection almost impossible, because for those we need vulnerability, and vulnerability is danger.

When I'm in fight-or-flight, I really am in one sense possessed, not fully 'myself', or at least my best self. I don't make conscious decisions, can't summon empathy or patience. Everyone makes me angry, even those trying to help me.

The key piece of the puzzle for me was understanding that this survival system, in many of us, doesn't differentiate between actual physical danger and perceived social threat. It's why stage fright can make me throw up. I am in fact safe, but my body, twitchy with an overload of adrenaline and cortisol, very much does not feel it. It's the same when someone disagrees with us in something important to our identity, or just presents as different from us in ways that grate against our PLM preferences. Most adult brains develop safeguards and systems so our meltdowns become less visible than a toddler's (mainly by growing a prefrontal cortex) but we still very much have them.

Learning about fight-or-flight in these tiny intra-familial conflicts with my child helped me become more conscious of when my threat reaction was being triggered. I noticed that I feel it first in my fingers: I tense up, and start talking faster and more forcefully. When I begin to feel pissed off and aggrieved I can sometimes now stop, breathe, walk away before anyone gets wet or ends up in angry tears. I wonder how your body reacts, if you start to notice it more.

As I saw the difference in my parenting that this understanding made, I became fascinated with the way it plays out in adult situations of polarisation or disagreement. This was all happening alongside starting the podcast, and I could see how my discomfort with staying in the room with someone NLM was low level fight-or-flight. I noticed that when I'm triggered by adults I react the exact same way, easily ascribing malign intent to what are usually misunderstandings or thoughtless moments. My own misconceptions and insensitivities become irrelevant to the important task of winning. If I'm in a tense conversation with you, my own threat reaction tends to trigger yours. We will likely both emotionally arm up, withdraw and disconnect.

I now see this pattern of mutual triggering happening everywhere, without any accompanying pressure-valve practices. It's there in marriages, work teams and even societies. Fight-or-flight really accelerates our PLM tendencies. When our body is telling us we are in danger, we want the safety of a group where we belong, to bond over shared contempt. The parts of us that might be more naturally collaborative, which care about the common good rather than just our own self-interest, are bypassed and we more easily believe lies or stereotypes of whoever it is who has triggered us. It becomes a vicious cycle, making connection more and more difficult. Sociologist Fathali Moghaddam calls this 'mutual radicalisation'.[11]

So far, so sadly recognisable in our current political dynamics. But what on earth has it got to do with theology?

The explanatory neuroscience was a way off in first-century Palestine, but the Jesus portrayed in the New Testament seems to not just to have understood these facets of human nature, but to offer real pathways to resist them. He knew what a temptation polarising wrath could be, and set out to demonstrate a different way of being in the world. Becoming more conscious of my wrath and the form it took in others was helpful, but these forces felt so strong I needed something more robust with which to challenge them.

Whatever you think about Jesus' claims to divinity, his teachings have demonstrably been central in conflict resolution down the centuries. They are often packaged up as 'non-violence', a form of peaceful but far from passive resistance to injustice. They offer a recipe for tempering our PLM temptations and interrupting the fight-or-flight vicious cycle of mutual triggering, disconnecting and othering. They have been used by Christians like Martin Luther King to shape the revolutionary Civil Rights Movement, and many who would not call themselves Christians, like Mahatma Gandhi, who used the Sermon on the Mount as his model for resistance in India. The effectiveness of Jesus' blueprint in these intense scenarios, and myriad other post-conflict countries, is well documented, but I have seen how it can transform conflict in much more everyday situations.

First though, what are those teachings?

Disrupt the tribes

The first one is not so much an explicit teaching (though it was fleshed out later in the New Testament letters by St Paul and others) as just the way Jesus conducted himself. In the Gospels – the books of the Bible that record his life – Jesus attracts a lot of attention and criticism. Most of it is driven by flagrant, repeated, seemingly mischievous fraternising with people others deemed NLM. First-century Palestine was as divided a society as ours is, as riven with spoken and unspoken in and out groups. The big 'out' group from the perspective of the text was the colonising Romans, but even within the people group we'd now call Jewish there were divides. Followers of Rabbi Hillel hated followers of Rabbi Shammai, the Essenes hated the Zealots, the Sadducees hated the Pharisees and vice versa. Then you have tax collectors (collaborators with empire), women (often unclean, definitely less than), those disabled or unwell (ditto) before you even get to Samaritans and Ethiopians. All jostling, criticising, oppressing and being oppressed. In a society that was as obsessed with tribal purity as ours, Jesus just ignores all these invisible lines. While I spend longer than I'd like relationally triangulating a retweet, trying to shake off the dread of guilt by association, Jesus never seems to calculate who it is safe to be seen with. I picture him when I'm reading a Gospel, walking nonchalantly into a scene, giving a *Fleabag*-style wink to camera, then making a beeline for the lowest-status, most outsider person in the place. A woman caught in adultery. A woman who is haemorrhaging from her vagina. A leper. A widow. A woman who dares to touch his naked feet. A Roman soldier. A money-sucking tax collector. A blind person. A person who can't walk. He basically only spends time with, pays attention to, holds whole conversations with people he shouldn't.

If you're old enough to remember the shock waves Princess Diana sent when she held the hand of an AIDS patient you have a tiny glimmer of what the reaction must have been like – but with more anger. These were real and serious transgressions of established social norms. Jesus doesn't seem to care what people think. When I've been criticised for having guests on *The Sacred* who others believe are beyond the pale (communists and Conservative MPs both get a lot of mail, as do trans people and 'TERFS') I remind myself that Christ's puckish attitude looks more interesting than just sticking with PLM. I find that these labels and signifiers are just one tiny part of the person in front of me anyway, and they rapidly cease to be relevant. And if comparing a podcast to Jesus sounds grandiose, it absolutely is, but I'm attempting to pattern my life on his and I have to start applying the principles somewhere.

Stand your ground

Turn the other cheek, like many phrases from the Bible, has become so familiar that we cease to really hear it. I find this paraphrase helps:

'Here's another old saying that deserves a second look: "Eye for eye, tooth for tooth." Is that going to get us anywhere? Here's what I propose: "Don't hit back at all." If someone strikes you, stand there and take it.'

These verses, taken from the Sermon on the Mount, are probably the most demanding and rigorous ethical teaching the world has ever known. They still make me uncomfortable every time I read them. When people talk about Jesus being a great moral teacher they are often, consciously or unconsciously, referring to these verses.

I used to have no idea how to apply them. I don't think I have ever been hit, let alone in the face. I failed to see the relevance until I started learning about the way our threat response easily kicks in not just when we've received a blow, but when we've been insulted, or ignored, or just disagreed with on something that feels important. The injunction suddenly makes practical sense. To apply it today to situations of interpersonal discomfort is to avoid letting fight-or-flight rule. Turning the other cheek, in its original context of physical violence, would involve overriding the strong bodily instinct to either fight (hit back) or flight (run away). It would mean standing your ground. It would have been, and still is, a surprising thing to do. A powerful statement of inner peace, resolve and control. I use the phrase 'Stand your ground' as shorthand for maintaining eye contact or keeping the conversation open, not as a cowering victim, but someone committed to connection. It takes courage and enormous intentionality. The civil rights campaigners in the US, inspired by Dr King's preaching around these verses, practised role-playing situations of threat in advance. They acted out their response to attacking police officers and baying crowds, building the muscles that would allow them to stand their ground in the heat of the moment.[12] Extinction Rebellion have used the same kind of training to equip activists to stand their ground under abuse and attempted arrest. Hundreds if not thousands of other campaigns have used this practice too. It's difficult, but worth pursuing because it's a non-violent manoeuvre that flips the expected dynamics of a situation. It creates space for fresh thinking and fresh solutions to emerge. It shoves a stick in the spokes of the vicious cycle.

It is also, obviously, not always the best course of action. If you are in real physical danger or subject to abuse, listening to the instinct to flee or fight back is where wisdom lies. Peacebuilding doesn't (except in exceptional circumstances, if chosen) require us to sacrifice ourselves.

But in many other situations, it can be hugely effective. I am under no illusions I'd be much use in a situation of physical threat, and am in awe of campaigners who can apply this practice under those conditions. I have however seen how it can play out in my small experiences of social conflict and be transformative in these more private battles.

A few years ago, I was asked to attend a gathering of progressive political activists from across Europe, meeting in tepees, festival style, for talks and panels but also 'ritual experiences' and open sharing. The pitch was that spirituality might help the left have more traction in a moment when the alt-right was in the ascendancy. And not just spirituality, but maybe (whisper it) actual religion. Several other publicly religious people had been invited, but had all turned the invitation down, probably because they felt tribally uncomfortable: they didn't want to walk into a gathering of NLMs. I had a friend who was going, so there would be at least one PLM, so I said yes. I was at the end of maternity leave, itching to get back to the world of ideas, and more and more distressed at the divided state of our common life. I was still breastfeeding, so agreed to go on the basis that I could bring my son, and my husband for childcare, and our three-year-old daughter as well.

As it turned out, we were the only people with children. We drove into the car park to be greeted by a woman wearing antlers, face painted blue with what I later learned was actual woad. All the food was vegan, which would have been manageable for us but didn't go down well with the three-year-old, who proceeded to eat nothing but bread. By the time we'd settled into our ramshackle tepee and got a cup of herbal tea, I was already dreading the session, which had been dressed up as something cuddlier but was clearly that dread word, 'networking'.

At first it went ok. I was in a promising conversation with a small, groomed woman whose clear-framed glasses took up half her face. She was exactly what I had expected a Silicon Valley entrepreneur to look like. She had been sharing stories from Burning Man – at least half the participants at this festival-cum-conference had just flown back from there, I was gathering. It sounded fun, and we'd been laughing together at the tech bros embracing desert defecation, and then the question came:

'So what do you do?'

There it was. The face.

People have strange reactions when you say you run a religion think tank. I'd got used to polite if wary smiles. To sometimes abrupt questions. I'd learned how to handle hostility online, in emails and articles, but most people cover it well in person.

This group was different. The word 'religion' seemed to act as a trigger for a bodily reaction. Like a pair of magnets pushing away from each other, withdrawal was instant. The delicate dance of initial human encounter – the sizing up and elevator-pitching and groping for connection – all brought to an abrupt halt. She needed another cup of tea. In my next conversation, at exactly the same point: Would I excuse him, but he needed to find the loo? In one case, a lean man in neon with pupils the size of five-pence coins just walked away without another word.

By the time the session was over my boobs ached, and the left one was leaking. More than that, I was angry. I could feel it in my body, in my lips and fingers. The whole place, which had seemed quirkily charming, now looked shoddy and try-hard.

Seeing something you care about provoke distaste, on repeat, can't help but feel like low-level emotional assault. By the time we got into our (freezing) tepee that night, after wrestling our kids away from the psychedelic-driven dancing and skunk-haze, I was in full-on fight-and-flight mode. My husband listened while I ranted in a whisper about the prejudice of the self-proclaimed open minded. I paced, absurdly, hunched under the canvas roof. They didn't want me. I didn't feel welcome. I was out of my tribe and it sucked. Their fear and suspicion, driven by who knows what personal baggage, had met its opposite in me. Reject me? Not if I get there first. We would pack up and go that night.

Wise as ever, my husband talked me down. Still trying not to be overheard by those completing some kind of mirror-and-fire ritual noisily outside, he argued that things would feel different in the morning, that we should give them a chance.

He was, of course, right. My threat response wore off overnight. I woke feeling more able to stand my ground in that place, to walk back into the sessions baring, metaphorically, my other cheek.

I made myself sit in sharing circles. I breastfed my son while speaking on a panel, from necessity, which gained me some credibility with the feminist faction. I morphed from NLM to something like PLM. I confessed to feeling like a fish out of water, to feeling afraid of their judgement. The group had a chance to get to know me as a person, not a walking cipher for homophobia, and it turned out most of them weren't just rude, they were also on a Burning Man come-down combined with jet lag. I was calmer, and less defensive, less likely to read every interaction as a battle. And, as is often the case, these people who looked like the enemy, who perhaps saw me as an enemy, turned out to be walking worlds of meaning, bruised and beautiful and as endlessly fascinating as humans always are. Many people sidled up to say that they were in fact pretty interested in religion, they were just put off by the institutions or the perceived political positions. The kids had more fun than they had in months, dressed up like dinosaurs and fairies, dancing to ever present drums. The three-year-old even ate some hummus. And many of those people are now dear friends.

The things that I had forgotten, as my brain flooded with cortisol and my spirit with self-righteousness, turned out still to be true. Real human encounter across difference takes time, and trust, and the letting down of guards. Our first reactions don't have to define our relationships.

That weekend showed me my own response to difference and it was sobering. I wasn't being faced by truncheons or attack dogs, just very mild social discomfort, but I'd been possessed by my own threat reaction. I'd let wrath take me over. I decided that being more conscious was part of my plan to try to stop these tantrums happening so often. I now go into new experiences and tribes *expecting* to feel uncomfortable. I remind myself to look out for the signs, the twitchyness and tight hands, the phrase 'these people' showing up in my thoughts, the rising contempt, and to resist it. To give the person or group who have triggered the response time to look less like the enemy, not make decisions or statements until my more rational self is back in control. I now see these encounters as an opportunity to have a bit of an adventure, to expand my horizons. Because as one of my favourite poets, Elizabeth Alexander, says, 'are we not of interest to each other?'[13] I am nosy about people, want to understand them, but I can't if I'm letting my wrath disconnect me.

This attempt to stand my ground has become habitual, and it doesn't have to be in person. A few years ago I tweeted something that felt very innocuous and a novelist, someone that I know slightly, replied with a long and pointed attack thread. He accused me of being duplicitous as a 'religious leader', of not really understanding my own faith. He insinuated that I'd just not read enough books or got my head round the important ideas. With icy civility, he implied I was ignorant, lazy and a liar.

I wish I could say I took a deep breath, remembered that this 'type' (highly educated male atheists) features on my List, let my stress hormone wear off, and went straight into using empathy, curiosity and vulnerability, but I didn't. I felt winded, and a bit sick. I was angry and hurt. I drafted a long, withering thread in response that included the phrases 'mansplaining my religion to me' and 'arrogant patronising arsehole giving good atheists a bad name'. I pointed out his errors in understanding of the books he'd quoted at me, and his failure to locate them in recent scholarship, and everything else I could think of to make him feel as I felt – stung and small. And then I deleted it and called my husband and asked him to change my Twitter password as a matter of urgency and under no circumstances to let me have it back.

Evagrius, our desert father guide to the original

understanding of the sins, wrote as if he could see into my experience: 'boiling and stirring up of wrath against one who has given injury – or is thought to have done so. [wrath] constantly irritates the soul . . . seizes the mind and flashes the picture of the offensive person before one's eyes. Then there comes a time when it persists longer, is transformed into indignation, stirs up alarming experiences by night.'[14]

He was right. This time one sleep wasn't enough. I just dreamed about revenge. The threat response was so powerful it took me four days to calm down. I've also had death and rape threats online, but weirdly this was worse. The thread had pressed on some deep insecurities about my intellectual abilities. He had accused me of something (being disingenuous) that felt like an attack on my identity, because I strive for honesty. I needed to regroup. And so, after days of arguing with him in my head on bike rides, once I'd calmed down enough to do so I made myself pray for him. The wrath drained out of me. When it finally felt safe to go back on Twitter, I was able to respond with calm, honesty and vulnerability to his accusations. I invited him to dinner, and we've since spent more time together. I have come to see what's driving his questions, his incomprehension, even his anger, and we understand each other much better. We might even end up being friends.

One of the most persuasive writers of the last century, James Baldwin, knew how powerful this approach can be. He was a black bisexual man living in America in the lead-up to the Civil Rights Movement, the son of a preacher and the grandson of a slave. The blows he received were not minor slights like mine. He, like millions, knew what it was to be both literally and metaphorically hit in the face by the reality of racial oppression. His 'Letter to My Nephew' begins with a stark confrontation of the facts: 'you were born into a society which spelled out with brutal clarity and in as many ways possible that you were a worthless human being'. Baldwin burns with the injustices heaped on Black people, but he has a steely commitment to neither fighting back nor running away. In *A Hard Kind of Courage*, written on an uncomfortable tour of the American South, he visited a recently desegregated school. After meeting a stoic, dignified and high-achieving Black mother and child, he talked to the white principal, who still believed in racial segregation. Rather than lambasting him (Baldwin could be bitingly sarcastic when speaking in general terms), or closing the conversation down, he listened to the man's concerns. He kept the conversation on an empathetic, if politely challenging, footing, standing his ground. The principal, presumably feeling the automatic decrease of fight-and-flight hormones in the face of such apparent understanding, was able to be honest, open and vulnerable about his position, and how shaped it was by 'how things have always been'. Baldwin demonstrated he had listened to the man's desire to be a 'good man' by saying, 'I should think . . . it's very hard for you to face a child and treat him unjustly because of something that he is no more responsible for than you are.' The act of staying in a conversation with a man he profoundly disagreed with and must have felt personally insulted by took 'a hard kind of courage', but paid off in a real change of heart. The account ends with the principal facing his own intellectual and moral dishonesty, and Baldwin staring at 'a man in anguish'.[15]

Baldwin, like his fellow civil rights campaigner Dr King, turned the other cheek consciously and repeatedly in political conflict after awkward conversation after outright attack. They did it for slightly different reasons – though steeped in the Bible and drawing strongly at certain points on a deeply Christian sensibility, Baldwin was no orthodox religious believer like King was. But while Dr King was motivated by Jesus' non-violent ethical teaching partly as an expression of his faith, both were pragmatists and knew how strategically effective it could be at short-circuiting conflict.

Because fight-or-flight is not only relevant when we are thinking about our own reactions to situations of social threat and discomfort. It is almost always driving the other parties' reactions to us. As we have seen, an excess of circulating stress hormone cannot help but make people defensive, liable to lash out and blame. It temporarily suspends or represses the functioning of the part of the brain that makes more considered rational judgement, weighs arguments and solves problems. If our cause is correct and our position is right (and we are genuinely seeking to persuade rather than just playing to the gallery of our own side) then we have a vested interest in helping the other person or group get out of fight-or-flight. We need their whole brain on the subject, not just their defensive reptilian attack mode. It is incredibly difficult to persuade anyone to change their minds or their approach if they feel threatened and destabilised. Contempt is like kryptonite for real change. It can only harden us into our pre-existing positions. Turning the other cheek by remaining open, calm, curious, even vulnerable gives our perceived adversary the best chance of feeling safe enough to listen. If you need another reason to try this approach, try it because it works, and because we are going to need it.

Love and blessing

Love your enemies and pray for those who persecute you. It's such a hard thing Jesus says. Even as I type it out, it sounds like madness. The counter-intuitive nature of the response Jesus invites me into means it requires enormous concentration. It never, ever comes naturally. My experience is that the second half of the command helps with the first. In my Twitter spat with the patronising atheist, what really changed my outlook was praying for him. I didn't feel at all loving towards him. I was mainly motivated by how unpleasant the acidic wash of resentment and rage was to carry around inside me. The temptation to attack was strong, but I held out no hope it would make me feel better, so I tried prayer. Through gritted teeth I prayed he would be blessed, he would be safe, he would know love. I prayed that, whatever the unknown context for such an outburst had been, he would find comfort. I can remember the rapid physical response. The relaxing of my shoulders, the releasing of my clenched fists. I honestly think it is impossible to pray for someone and remain full of wrath. It might take more time, depending on the size of the offence (perceived or real), but it brings relief. Resentment doesn't seem able to coexist with blessing. Empathy, the necessary precondition of love, sneaks through the crack in the wall and spreads like hot honey.

I don't think you need to be a Christian to pray for someone. My Buddhist friends use loving-kindness meditation, which seems to have a similar effect. You also don't need a rigorous theological framework to bless someone. Quakers, even atheist ones, call it 'holding [someone] in the light'. If you are holding resentment and rage towards a person or a tribe, and you'd like to be rid of it (rather than feed it, as we are all tempted to do), just turn your thoughts towards them, and ask for good things for them. Keep going and I bet you will find, despite yourself, that you mean it.

I don't think Jesus is asking people to feel fluffy warm feelings towards their enemies. Love in theological terms is rarely about feelings at all, but about action. Praying a blessing over someone I hate is an act of resistance to that hate, to the wrath I find in myself. It orientates me towards the possibility of love. It feels like hacking off the clinging tentacles of an invasive plant to give the tree I actually want room to grow.

When it is too hard, when the craving for the clean burn of contempt calls to me, I go back to James Baldwin. He had all the reasons in the world to be righteously angry with white Americans, but he instead implores his nephew to love them:

> There is no reason for you to try and become like the white man and there is no basis whatever for their impertinent assumption that they must accept you. The really terrible thing, old buddy, is that you must accept them, and I mean that very seriously. You must accept them and accept them with love, for these innocent people have no other hope.

Baldwin's startling commitment to understanding his enemies, to seeking empathy with them, is incredibly challenging. He goes on:

> They are in effect still trapped in a history which they do not understand and until they understand they cannot be released from it . . . many of them indeed know better, but as you will discover, people find it very difficult to act on what they know. To act is to be committed, and to be committed is to be in danger. In this case the danger in the minds and hearts of white Americans is the loss of their identity.[16]

The astute psychological insight here is one of the reasons Baldwin's writing has endured. He sees how the fight-or-flight response is triggered by destabilising change. He knows fear makes it easy to cling to power and privilege, and how only love and acceptance create space for people to do hard and necessary things like face their own sin. He loves his enemies and prays for people who persecute him and, if he can do it under his radically more challenging circumstances, surely I can in mine.

Interrupt the cycle

The possibility of forgiveness is the central doctrine of Christianity. It's been an underground river in the culture of the West, shaping our politics and justice system for twenty centuries. It sometimes seems like the river is drying up. Many commentators have noted that forgiveness is now seen as suspicious, legitimising injustice, and too heavy a burden to put on victims. There is little social permission for forgiving NLM people and groups, let alone encouragement or help to do so.

I don't know how to fix this. I'm also not going to try to persuade you to forgive people who have wounded you. I don't know what scars you carry. I'm obviously a fan of forgiveness, receiving and giving it, but the deep stuff is too personal, too tender for a stranger's opinion to have any legitimacy. In my own life it has required many years of stumbling spiritual practice. I have needed a determined rooting in a story that reminds me how much I, too, need forgiving to make it even occasionally possible for me to forgive the people who have harmed me.

What I want to offer instead is something more achievable – a way of short-circuiting conflict in the moment. A willingness to say, 'Can we just start again?' has sometimes worked to interrupt the wrath cycle in my own life. It's forgiveness-adjacent, but less demanding.

I live in south-east London, in an area with no Tube, and navigating myself and two tired children around the crowded bus system at the end of a long day of school, nursery and work has been one of my most regular frustrations. A few years ago, I got onto a mercifully empty bus and settled both of them into their own seat. An older woman got on, behatted and glamorous. Despite there being free seats both behind and in front of us, she snapped, 'Move your child!'

In response to her command, I indicated the many empty seats, but she just repeated, 'Move that child! He doesn't need a seat to himself! I want to sit there!' Fuming, I dragged his eighteen kilos onto my lap, and in an icy and superior tone said, 'There is no need to be rude. A please and thank you would be nice. I am trying to teach my children manners.' This snide comment clearly didn't fit into her model of respect for elders because she sat next to me for the next five stops, loudly muttering about disrespect. Anyone who has had an uncomfortable human encounter on public transport will know the unique torture of being forced to stay sitting in close confines with someone you are finding unbearable.

There is a detail in this story I am tempted to leave out, because I am ashamed of it. The woman was Afro-Caribbean, probably in her sixties. Where I live in Peckham, I have had previous encounters with older Black women on buses whose behaviour struck me as unnecessarily opinionated and forthright. I'd been told off for various misdemeanours and instructed to 'Put a hat on that baby!' several times. It doesn't take much for our brains to make a story out of a few isolated incidents, to generalise to a whole group of people. This is how prejudice works. I'd probably also unconsciously internalised the stereotype of 'angry Black woman' that so many women of colour have to deal with.

All of this baggage, this tribalism, this bundle of cognitive shorthands and stereotypes and, let's just name it, racism, was at play in me that day. I wasn't seeing a full human person, and I was riled.

I am admitting this detail because the things about ourselves that are unmentionable become unmanageable. Part of my journey away from wrath has been noticing and bringing into the light these dark corners of my own soul. I don't believe we can become more free, more loving or more just unless we are able to name the things in ourselves we want to change. Given that research into PLM syndrome shows we all carry ridiculous, irrational prejudices, confessing one of mine, as long as I am not condoning them, shouldn't be controversial. But in our current febrile public debates, it is. We want racism to be in a neat box occupied only by Bad People, rather than something we are all tangled up in to different degrees. We want to deny that all these PLM prejudices are there, often lying dormant until we are in fight-or-flight and therefore looking for a reason to resent someone. But we can't overcome the wrathful tribalism and work on this stuff unless we get a bit more honest.

Obviously, I rehearsed withering rejoinders in my head as I sat there, my shoulder squashed against my unwelcome seatmate, trying to stop the squirming toddler on my lap kicking her. That week, I'd been reading in a parenting book about 'do-overs', the technique of stopping in the middle of a row or power battle with your child and resetting from the beginning. I'd started sometimes going out the front door and coming back in again, pretending the whole fraught previous encounter hadn't happened. It seemed to make us laugh and break the tensions and had proved surprisingly effective. It reminded me of similar techniques in peacebuilding. Asking to start over doesn't require forgiveness on either side, just a willingness to draw a line and look to the future. It doesn't wipe out past wrongs or hurts, but it can, sometimes, make it possible to move on and stop negative cycles. And so, mainly to get out of the awkwardness of having to sit next to a vocally hostile person for an unknown amount of time, I took a deep breath, turned to my neighbour, stuck out my hand and said, 'Shall we start again? I'm Elizabeth, what's your name?'

I have never experienced a situation turn around so quickly. She smiled, then laughed, then introduced herself. We went on to have an enjoyable conversation about our shared love of the area. I'm sure I had presented as – let's be honest, had acted like – one of the entitled white women who'd recently moved into the gentrifying area that had been her home for decades. I remembered the aunties I go to church with, who can present as gruff and stern (and, given the struggles most of them have lived through, understandably so) but are in fact fiercely kind, who can be bossy about other people's kids because they raised theirs in a more communal culture, not the isolated, atomised parenting we do now. We both felt our grumpiness wearing off. I learned she was on her way back from King's College Hospital, and was suffering from joint pain. We compared notes on our joints, becoming more PLM to each other. When I asked Cole Arthur Riley, creator of Black Liturgies, how to avoid falling into 'the white gaze', she said, 'Unapologetic particularity'. The antidote to our scripts and stereotypes is curiosity about the unique person in front of us. In my request for a do-over, and her gracious acceptance of it, we'd found enough space to really see each other.

By the time we'd been chin wagging for a while, the bus had filled up considerably. When someone else started having a go at me about the positioning of my buggy, my new friend stood up and actually defended me. When we got off the bus a few stops later we waved goodbye with real warmth and she blew my kids a kiss. And I thought to myself, what is this, magic?

I realise this sounds painfully utopian. I've seen it work personally, but can it work elsewhere? A low-stakes awkward encounter on a bus isn't geopolitics. But I wonder what would happen if Brexiteers and Remainers, still carping at each other all these years later, could go, 'Ok, enough, let's dissolve these categories, put a moratorium on using them and begin again.' If any group of culture war combatants could get in a room with a crate of wine, or see some comedy or do a salsa class together to burn off all that stress hormone, might it be possible to decide to make a fresh start? To let go of the slights and hurts they have caused each other? Not, necessarily, to forgive, but just go out the front door and come back in. Maybe. I believe in the power of the unexpected, the flair of the person confident enough to try something new, to be the first to put their verbal gun down and say, 'Could we just have a time out? Do we really want to be doing this?'

I don't want my life defined by wrath, to spend it clenched against the wrongness of others. It feels like death. Forgive us our sins, as we forgive those who sin against us. If I want more tender compassion and second chances for my own mistakes, the deal is I have to give that to others. I have to wean myself off the high of self-righteous rage, the hit I get from finger pointing, and stand my ground instead, look the other person in the eye, refuse to let my mental image of them collapse into stereotype, maybe even try to bless them. I am far from free of the temptation to wrathful contempt, but I'm free-er, and the spaciousness I'm finding in the quest smells like life to me.

AVARICE: FROM STUFFOCATION TO GRATITUDE AND GENEROSITY

My grandma, my dad's mum, was part of the wartime generation who never completely forgot the years when a teaspoon of sugar was a longed-for luxury. She made-do-and-mended holey socks and worn-through sheets, and thought an egg yolk in shortcrust pastry an extravagance. They didn't struggle financially, but she wasted nothing. At Christmas she sincerely rejoiced over a pair of woolly bed socks. She was frugal, and also one of the most content people I've ever met, with a sharply sarcastic sense of humour and a mischievous flash in her wrinkle-framed eyes.

It's helpful to remind myself that contentment and simplicity can coexist. What scares me about tackling my greed is that I might end up in scarcity. The line between Grandma's joyful frugality and joyless austerity is too fine for my liking. I have put off addressing my avarice because I am scared of making my life a grey trudge devoid of treats. I love treats. I love things to look forward to. The monastic discipline that comes easiest to me is celebration – I want to pop the fizz, order the pudding, book the holiday. I have associated fully aliveness with abundance, and maybe material abundance at that. As I write I can recognise the layer of fear underneath the visible healthy freedom.

You don't need telling that material abundance is not, in any direct or lasting way, the path to fullness of life. Though if you are currently struggling to pay your bills or buy food this sounds like a cruel joke, and you should skip this chapter, dear heart. You have quite enough to be dealing with.

I'm talking here not about having enough, but about having more than we need, which may apply to more of us than we think. Oliver James published *Affluenza* fifteen years ago, putting a name to a condition that we intuitively recognise. He defined the 'Affluenza virus' as 'the placing of a high value on money, possessions, appearances and fame'.[1] The middle and upper classes have, until quite recently, enjoyed steadily increasing living standards, normalising access to goods and services that were unimaginable for their parents and grandparents. But we're not happier. In fact, we have seen correlated rises in emotional distress. James' argument is that there is a causal link. He apportions blame for our growing misery to 'selfish capitalism', which drives inequality and overconsumption. He believes that 'most emotional distress is best understood as a rational response to sick societies', and the sickness is, in my language, avarice, the insatiable desire for more than we need.[2]

You might not need reminding *intellectually* that accumulation does not equal happiness, but that doesn't mean any of us know how to live that truth in practice. We live and breathe and have our being in a system that relies on us ignoring that truth for its own survival. If endless growth is the only way an economy can function, and people's actual needs have been met, then false needs must be created, and relentlessly advertised. An unfortunate aspect of human nature is that we quickly adjust to our circumstances, which means we get used to each new possession or level of comfort and start craving the next. Psychologists call this the 'hedonic treadmill' and it acts as the crank on capitalism.[3] The possibility that material accumulation might bring satisfaction is the carrot, always just slightly out of reach, to motivate us to keep climbing.

Even the high priests of economic theory acknowledge this noble lie, the con hidden in plain sight. John Maynard Keynes saw it as essential to his economic model, designed to deliver a wealthy planet where all could have leisure. He thought our avaricious desire for more than we need could be redirected to bring universal prosperity. Once that had been achieved, he wrote, people would be 'free, to return to some of the most sure and certain principles of religion and traditional virtue – that avarice is a vice . . . and the love of money is detestable . . . We shall once more value ends above means and prefer the good to the useful. But . . . Avarice and usury and precaution must be our gods for a little longer still. For only they can lead us out of the tunnel of economic necessity into daylight.'[4]

Must be our *gods*. Keynes wrote this in 1930, and anticipated 'at least another hundred years' before we could wake up from our self-induced (economics-induced) delusion and return to our natural state of contentment with just enough. We're less than ten years from his expected deadline, and universal wealth and a fifteen-hour working week still seem a *little* way off.

Keynes wasn't completely wrong – capitalism has driven many (though not all) of the reductions in absolute poverty globally that we've seen over the last century.[5] It's just also often associated with rampaging inequality. For those of us who have benefitted, we have more goods, but too often feel crushed underneath them. James Wallman termed this 'stuffocation', which I felt in my body when we recently tried to move house.[6] We were literally weighed down by the sheer amount of crap we own, hiding in drawers and cupboards and under beds. When our house chain fell through after we'd given notice on our rental and we were left without an address for three months, we had to find a storage container at speed. We spent more time and money than I care to remember storing and shuffling our stuff around until we eventually landed in a home. All these things I'd been seduced by, that had once been shiny and distracting, I now longed only to be rid of.

Soaring living standards have been accompanied by less, not more leisure. The average time we have to do 'what we will' with, as unions demanded in their campaigns for limits on working hours, has gone down since the 1980s.[7] Many of us have too little time and too much stuff and we're not even enjoying it.

James frames affluenza as a uniquely contemporary phenomenon, but the temptation to accumulate more than we need (and find ourselves mysteriously unsatisfied) is as old as scripture. The biblical book of Proverbs, from ten centuries before Christ, urges, 'Do not toil to acquire wealth; be discerning enough to desist.'[8] Alexis De Tocqueville asked in 1835 why the Americans he observed were so restless and discontented in their prosperity, cursed with a 'strange melancholy. . . in the midst of abundance', dreaming 'constantly of the goods they do not have', pursuing wellbeing (wellness?) with a 'feverish ardor' but 'constantly tormented by a vague fear of not having chosen the shortest route that can lead to it.'[9] It is all depressingly recognisable. De Tocqueville's subjects didn't waste hours of their life reading online reviews, agonising over every purchase, but when I do I also feel 'tormented by a vague fear' of getting it wrong.

It may not be new, but my guess is that recent decades

have made the con of avarice even harder to resist. Ivan Illich, the radical priest who wrote so much about the scourge of growth-obsessed, globalising societies, received a letter from a Mexican friend who had visited West Germany in the seventies. They reported that 'most Germans act like destitute people with too much money. No one can help another. No one can take people in.'[10] Destitute people with too much money. This phrase has haunted me. The perception of scarcity in the midst of abundance makes it hard to share, to give freely. Illich was much influenced by Karl Polanyi, a mid-twentieth-century economic historian, who argued that many pre-modern societies deliberately avoided situations of scarcity, knowing it drives envy and dissatisfaction, which are bad for social cohesion and happiness.[11] Our societies, our businesses, do the exact opposite, manufacturing scarcity to keep us all on edge, constantly hoarding and acquiring to avoid missing out.

As well as artificial scarcity, recent generations have had to deal with the increasing psychological acuity of marketers and advertisers. Many of them draw to impressive effect on what sociologist René Girard termed 'mimetic desire', our tendency to want what other people want. Girard wrote, 'Man is the creature who does not know what to desire, and he turns to others in order to make up his mind. We desire what others desire because we imitate their desires.'[12] We are interdependent, interconnected people play-acting at being free individuals. Mimetic desire is why groups of teenage girls often wear variations on the same outfit, why middle-aged men all end up with the same coffee machine. It's the premise of the entire advertising industry. We can fail to know a consumer good even exists, then see someone we admire with it, and suddenly it's a 'must have'.

Mimetic desire is also one of the founding principles of social media. 'Connecting people' on free-to-join platforms doesn't seem like an especially lucrative business model, but once you add 'social advertising' you get the wealthiest companies on the planet. The vast majority of our material desires, once our need for shelter, warmth, food and safety is met, are learned – caught, even – rather than innate. This social aspect of consumerism is related, obviously, to envy, status anxiety and the struggle to feel enough. Donella Meadows, one of the early voices to warn against rapacious growth's effect on planetary health, wrote, 'People need identity, community, challenge, acknowledgement, love, and joy. To try to fill these needs with material things is to set up an unquenchable appetite for false solutions to real and never-satisfied problems. The resulting psychological emptiness is one of the major forces behind the desire for material growth.'[13]

Theologian Eve Poole summarises three main components to consumerism: insatiability, novelty and subjectivity.[14] My childish desire for better leggings, new serums, nicer stationery, fits all of these criteria. I never reach a point of satisfaction, I always want something new, and I want, not exactly what everyone else has, but my own, personalised version. I am shaped by mimetic desire but also want to maintain the fiction of my own autonomy and authenticity. I want to be part of the crowd, but also stand out from it. It is, now I think about it, a bit pathetic. At the time of writing I am wearing silver hoop earrings, not gold like everyone else's this season, and red sneakers as a rebellion against the ubiquitous white ones, but they are still hoops and sneakers. I am like Andy in *The Devil Wears Prada*, thinking I am above the trends of the herd and yet clothed in them.

Marx famously coined the phrase 'commodity fetishisation' to describe the way we value some objects beyond their actual usefulness. Consumer goods, especially 'luxury goods' (and what brand now does not aspire to at least pretend to be luxurious), come equipped with social currency. Our associations with fetish now are mainly cheap PVC gear and stiletto-sniffers, but the word is older, meaning an object with protective powers. Think an amulet or charm to ward off evil spirits. Those blue glass evil eye bracelets sold in parts of the Mediterranean and Middle East count, technically, as fetish wear. Fetish in this sense helps me understand a bit more the psychology of my accumulation. An undeveloped part of me must really, deep down, believe in the protective powers of all this stuff, or why else would I keep buying it? Protective against what, I'm not sure. Social censure? Scarcity? Boredom? Come the apocalypse my earrings and leggings will not save me.

Multiple theorists would say that, deep down, what I think my goods are protecting me from is death. 'Terror management theory' argues that many of our least rational behaviours are driven by a desire to distract ourselves from the fact of our own demise, a pathological refusal to acknowledge the finitude of human lives. I might one day be going to die, but I'm going to die stylish, and not before I've tried hot yoga. I can't be this simple. Can I? What if my avarice, when I'm indulging in disconnected, mindless consumption, is actually a search for symbolic immortality?[15]

Honestly, my top-level response to all this theory is grumpiness. I know, I know, I know, my brain mutters, sitting here in expensive leggings, typing into three different Apple products. FFS. My serums are not about death. They are about. . .

looking like I am less close to death. My brain scrabbles for a reason to discount it all. Facing up to the reality of cultural and personal avarice is so depressing. I don't want to be lectured about what I buy or own by people who also buy or own things, so I dismiss them. I also don't want to be lectured by people who move to the woods and ferment their home-grown crops (making it look beautiful on Instagram) because they seem like distant weirdos with unattainable ideals. Also they are probably hypocrites too, I comfort myself. I bet they fly to foreign holidays and don't post *those* pictures. I think we all feel stuck, knowing something isn't working about how we are living, mired in resentment and our unrealised principles.

That doesn't mean, unfortunately for my grumpiness, that these principles aren't important. That my quest for fully aliveness doesn't require a reckoning with my avarice, a fight to get out from under my stuffocating consumption. I want to call time on Keynes' delusional project, to join those long sounding the alarm. You can't call 'foul fair and fair foul', as he said we needed to, for very long before it's difficult to go back to the original definitions.[16]

Avarice is just a fancy word for greed, but specific to material possession and money, as distinct from gluttony. If sin is disconnection, the sin of avarice disconnects me from the world, from what I *really* want and need, and from other people. Because of our rising levels of misery in relative abundance, the fraying of the social fabric driven by inequality would be problem enough, but we have a much more urgent one. We are also stuffocating our only home.

My desire to uproot avarice from my life is driven, most urgently, by my climate anxiety. This is a hard subject to think, talk and read about, which is in itself part of the problem. I don't want to tip you into panic (can you feel the uncomfortable feelings rising? The desire to skip this bit?) but neither can I swerve this cold hard fact – our climate, our world, is in clear and present danger, and it's our fault. Rather than steward the incredible gift of this glorious, unlikely habitat, taking what we need and sharing the abundance that really does exist, we've asset stripped it. We – and I very much include myself in this – have been so reluctant to accept the smallest limitation on our comfort and convenience that we may well have rendered huge swathes of the earth uninhabitable for the very near generations. On my blackest days I find bitter humour in the idea that our flight from death into possessions is in fact literally killing us.

Breathe. The scale of the threat is indeed existential, but I've learned the hard way that blind terror is unproductive. I have relatively stable mental health, but the times I have been closest to actively unwell have been around this, a creeping black dread about how to explain to my children just what we have done, what we have left undone, out of ignorance, weakness and our own deliberate fault. God have mercy.

What helps me move through the threat response is prayer – prayers of confession and repentance, prayers for help, prayers of surrender. I cry about it in church quite a lot, and find whole books of lament in scripture, which help. I try to locate myself in the story my scripture sings – one where the world as we know it was never going to last forever, never promised a life of comfort or safety, but invites me to press into the love of [God] and the beloved community and find in them enough grace, courage and resilience for whatever is to come. Once I have processed my feelings as healthily as possible, I am then able to work out what, in fact, I can actually do to help. My friend Dougald calls it 'getting to work in the ruins'.[17] Another friend, Vanessa Zoltan, asks 'What kind of people are needed at the end of the world?'[18] What kind of people do I want around, do my kids need around, as we navigate the fruit of our avarice? I think we will need capable, generous, grateful people, not avaricious ones hoarding resources and compounding the problems, and so I'm seeking the practices that will help me with that.

There is another reason I want to uproot my avarice. As well as laying waste to the earth, I've concluded that societies in which we take more than we need harm our relationships. Andy Crouch says, 'This is the power of money: it allows us to get things done, often by means of other persons, without the entanglements of friendship.'[19]

I sort of miss my twenties when all my friends were renting and so always moving, the showing up for each other to lug boxes up and down stairwells. We'd sweat and laugh and rub our aching biceps, packing late into the night, or sharing a takeaway in IKEA-bare rooms. Now we're older, many of us with kids in tow, most of us with at least a bit more money, we pay movers. You don't make memories with movers, don't weave a net of reciprocity, of shared need and shared generosity. If 'a friend is someone who will help you move', and I never need help moving, how do I know who my friends are?

I do know, of course I do. They provide other kinds of non-financial help, and I provide for them in turn. I can't be the only one who found friendship easier in my twenties though. I assumed what had changed was just less time as we all worked more, less proximity as we scattered from the city, but I now think part of it is more money and therefore less need of each other.

We're also less equal. If I'm honest, friendship is very

slightly trickier over great gaps of wealth, because the way we want to show love is so often by help. It's part of the delicate semaphore of affection. It's less awkward, at least early in a friendship, to offer to pick up someone from the airport or water their houseplants or lend some tools than say aloud, 'You are an important person in my life.' That moment of contact, of giving and receiving, builds connection and weaves a thick basket of reciprocity. It's the stuff of community. Helping others makes us feel good. Knowing we have been helped, if we can deprogramme ourselves from the shame of vulnerability, feels good too. For those who can pay to outsource everything they need, it takes a bit more creativity and perseverance. It's far from impossible. I have precious friends who are both a lot higher up and a lot lower down the income ladder. But I can see how, without attention, I could let the centre of gravity of my life end up being with people who have roughly equal levels of vulnerability and agency, which sadly often equates to roughly equal amounts of money. It's another way in which we prefer PLM.

Christian scripture, as we will see, is pretty stark in its warning about the effects of wealth. I wonder if this is part of the reason. If you never need material help, it is harder to become fully knit into the tapestry of community. You can give, sure, and that is good, but no one wants to be in a relationship long term that is all one way. That's not community, it's patronage. When seeking to live more connected lives, we need to keep an eye on power, and money and power usually go hand in hand. Unless the rich also receive, have parts of their lives in which they need others whom they are not paying, and value the help they receive, shared dignity is hard. I think the very rich, who are able to access abundance without dependence,[20] who want for literally nothing, must be quite lonely.

If you are materially wealthy, this is not me judging you. I am too, compared to most of the world. As with sex, money is a touchy subject, tending to make us defensive or insecure. Finger pointing, blaming or shaming is almost never conducive to connection, or to actual change. I'm just trying to become more alert to the dynamics in my own life that make me feel less fully alive.

So what helps? Well, taking the problem seriously for a start.

Take the medicine

Oliver James acknowledged that religious ideas and practice are one of the things capable of 'inoculating someone against Affluenza' because they repeatedly 'encourage satisfaction' with what people already possess.[21]

Consumer society immerses us in a powerful narrative machine. I may know, in theory, that more stuff won't make me happy, but in order to listen to a podcast, walk down the street or read the news I have to consume messages trying to shape my desires in the other direction. It's relentless. It's why I try to also expose myself to Christian teaching on money, which now feels more like bracing medicine than moralising buzzkill. It may taste unpleasant, but I need the antidote, the strong counterweight to the narrative universe I'm usually shaped by.

And it is unpleasant, honestly. In thinking through this subject I have been struck again by just how uncomfortably challenging the Bible is about money, and how focused on it.

The number of scripture verses about sex are outnumbered many times over by verses about money, which you wouldn't necessarily get from media coverage of the Church. In the whole Bible there are around 500 verses on prayer and over 2,000 verses on money. It's almost as if the whole thing is spiritually important. Jesus in particular seems more interested in money and what we do with it than almost anything else. His teaching is so direct I can only look at it out of one eye, on a day I am feeling calm. Do not accumulate treasures on earth, but treasure in heaven. No one can serve both God and money. Guard against greed, because *life is not in the abundance of possessions.* (That one feels like it's speaking directly to me.) And, most challenging of all, he responds to a question about how to 'inherit eternal life' from one who 'owned much property': 'If you would be perfect, go, sell what you possess and give to the poor, and you will have treasure in heaven.'[22]

Eeeeeesh. Even writing this makes me tense up; I am so far from the ideal. I can feel myself getting dismissive and defensive. Philosopher Phyllis Tickle in an essay on greed sums up the response of most Christians to these most-difficult-of-verses: 'Whether the . . . believer assigns responsibility for his or her failure in this regard to necessity, to other and honourable responsibilities, to a more palatable [reading] or to outright personal failure, he or she is always aware of being, thanks to greed, just a little bit less than truly Christian in the fullest . . . sense of things.'[23] Phyllis sees me.

The thrust of the Church's teaching on money is that it is a useful tool and a terrible master, but it's a tool that will always have ambitions to rule us. It's not just bad for greedy individuals though. We should keep an eye on greed because it enslaves us while promising freedom, but also because our greed feeds endemic injustice. It enslaves others.

The most challenging sermon I have ever read is from a fourth-century Turkish cleric called St Basil, who came from wealth, gave it away and devoted his life to the poor. He directly links our greed and others' poverty:

> Who are the greedy? Those who are not satisfied with what suffices for their own needs. Who are the robbers? Those who take for themselves what rightfully belongs to everyone. And you, are you not greedy? Are you not a robber? . . . The bread you are holding back is for the hungry, the clothes you keep put away are for the naked, the shoes that are rotting away with disuse are for those who have none, the silver you [have saved] is for the needy. You are thus guilty of injustice toward as many as you might have aided, and did not.[24]

It is such an uncomfortable thing to face up to, this. Christian thought claims that I am complicit in economic injustice. Poverty is not an accident or the fault of an evil few, but has something to do with me. It's related to this other hard fact, that climate change is not just down to fossil fuel companies, but driven by a culture of insatiable desires in which I have played my full part.

Honestly, I am going to stop soon because none of us are enjoying this. I don't know what to do with challenges like these. Am I supposed to make myself and my kids destitute? Give away all our savings? I'm making myself look at these verses, write these quotes, because otherwise I will forget that this, perhaps of all the temptations to disconnection, is huge for me. I want to stay angry at how hard it is to live the thing I know to be true, but I'm also a little bit glad it's hard because it gives me an excuse not to. In a throwaway line in the Parable of the Sower, Jesus tells how the good seed of the Gospel (life, and freedom) is often choked by weeds, which metaphorically stand for 'the cares of the world and the deceitfulness of wealth'. Yes! Wealth *is* deceitful. It's a big, beautiful, charismatic liar. It's a sexy seducer I always want to snog, not realising it's sucking the life out of me in the process. I need help calling bullshit, resisting its siren song. The love of money can be for me like Devil's Snare, the plant in *Harry Potter and the Philosopher's Stone* that sneaks up and twists around and suffocates people to death. Jesus' radically counter-cultural teaching on the love of money acts, sometimes, like the spell Hermione uses to bring light and heat and force the killer weed back into the darkness.

I want to break the enchantment. I don't want to wake up when I'm ninety and find I'm a well-dressed, well-accessorised, lonely slave to Mammon. Past a certain point, continuing to date a charming liar, no matter how sexy, is foolishness. I don't want to be an obedient drone to the culture and miss what it is to be fully alive because I was too busy buying things from Instagram and fretting over my bank balance. I want to really live, and, even if I take only one small step in this direction, it's better than giving in.

So let's move on to something that feels a bit more achievable than giving away all my possessions to the poor.

Gratitude

Gratitude is definitely easier than voluntary poverty, but that doesn't mean it's easy. Introducing the extremely well-evidenced practice of gratitude journaling, essayist and creator of *The Marginalian* Maria Popover begins: 'You'll need pen, paper, and a silencer for cynicism.'[25]

I do need a silencer for cynicism. Thanks to the work of Martin Seligman and other researchers in positive psychology, we now all know what religions have always taught: gratitude is good for us.[26] The trouble is that like most virtues, most things that are good for us, it has low cultural capital.

Gratitude sounds so nice. So polite and ineffective. Children are grateful, and I don't want to be infantile. The great Maya Angelou might preach an 'attitude of gratitude' but even from her I cringe at the rhyme, at the peppy wholesomeness of it. Gratitude grates on the bit of me that still wants to be cool, detached, one ironic eyebrow cocked at the bin-fire of the world. Keynes foresaw a return to the honour of 'the delightful people who are capable of taking direct enjoyment in things', but we are not there yet.[27] The wise-cracking fatalist will always be more attractive than the gushing princess, delighted by the twittering of the birds in the trees. For many of us, sarcasm and cynicism are our best defences against existential terror.

Also gratitude sounds a bit weak. 'They expected me to be grateful,' we spit, as if inherent in gratitude is humiliation. In some contexts, this makes sense – enforced gratitude from refugees, people of colour, anyone receiving charity in place of justice, *is* humiliating. It's also not real gratitude, and I don't think that's the only reason we are too often mildly repelled. Gratitude is connected to interdependence. We can't be grateful for things we (at least believe we have) made or earned or worked out ourselves. We can be puffed up, but not grateful. Gratitude is unavoidably relational, implying we have received help, or a gift. It acknowledges need and need equals vulnerability. And given that the self-made, self-loving, authentic independent individual is held up as the ideal, that is always going to be a bit uncomfortable.

Uncomfortable, and important. I am learning that all the important things are uncomfortable, which is annoying. In order to change for the better I am required to repeatedly choose against the grain of my cultural formation. I want to surrender to this. Resistance is self-defeating. Gratitude is the only thing that seems to help me step off the hedonic treadmill. It's a tonic for my restless acquisitiveness.

The practice of gratitude is a form of attention training. It builds my ability to keep seeing the things familiarity has veiled from me. So much that I now take completely for granted was longed for and hoped for. Gratitude helps rebalance my negativity bias, reminding me not to just scan for threats and problems to solve, for the next thing to covet, but to notice the gifts in front of my face. There is a prayer I pray over and over: 'God, help me receive the gifts I have already been given.'

Anything that trains my attention makes it easier to be grateful. Poetry, that magnifying glass on the world, helps a lot. Poets notice what the rest of us overlook.

I also sketch, badly, into my journal, taking a few minutes to really look at the shape of leaves on a plant, or the quality of light on my cup of tea. It makes me contemplate the world instead of my phone for a moment, stare at the contingent creation, which is 'a given' in the sake of being a gift, but not 'a given' in the sense that it had to be here, like this. Contemplation turns the volume down on my tendencies to exploit and consume. It helps me see a thing, or a person, as an end in themselves, not just a delivery mechanism for my satisfaction.

Relatedly, paying more attention to what and how I consume has helped, slightly, with my climate anxiety. Part of what's hard is helplessness, and so taking some, any, agency calms me down. 'Conscious consumerism' is in no way a solution to avarice (or indeed, the climate crisis) alone and the market is riven with greenwashing. I'm aware how futile buying less and buying better sounds given the scale of the challenge, and how much I want to outsource the hard job of changing my heart to the ever-adaptive market. However, given that there are some things I *do* need to buy, it makes sense to try to find more ethical versions. At its best, properly attentive consumption connects me back to the raw materials, energy and chain of people involved in creating the thing I'm buying. It surfaces what avarice wants to keep hidden – their lives, the real costs – and asks, is this thing worth it?

As so often, the steps I take to uproot sin in my life, which look like they will be punitive, turn out not to be. When we moved into our intentional community house we made a commitment to try to furnish it entirely second hand. It was partly pragmatism – it's not as if we had enough money to go on an interiors binge – but also for climate reasons. I love making rooms look beautiful, and had carefully curated Pinterest boards ready to go, so resigning myself to lowering my aesthetic standards didn't, initially, bring me joy. But it's been a delight. When people heard our plan, they started offering things. Often solid old furniture passed down from relatives that they wanted to find a good home. These forged a tiny link of love. Lots of it was beautiful. We sourced various key items from the streets of Peckham, coming home triumphant at our scavenged treasures. A dear friend who'd been in crisis and spent a lot of time at our previous house offered a sofa, too big for the lift, and the evening spent carrying it down eight flights of stairs from his flat was a hilarious bonding experience we might never forget. Every time he visits, which is a lot, he sees the sofa he contributed, a visual reminder that he is part of us.

When you live in a community with a strong ethic of hospitality, you need a big table, and all of my Olio, Gumtree and eBay stalking was drawing a blank. Then a friend of a friend offered a twelve-seater that had been sitting out in their garden for a year, and we took it as a temporary fix. It had been painted an ugly blue and was peeling from the rain, and when it arrived the shabby hulk of it made me wince. Underneath, though, we discovered it was sturdy, old-style IKEA. I borrowed an electric sander and – in my first ever solo DIY project – sanded it back to the wood in three weekend-long stints. I covered the kitchen and filled my own mucous membranes with blue dust, but the steady circles of unveiling, the rhythmic vibrations of the task, became deeply, soothingly satisfying. It will never be a fancy table, but we can squeeze eighteen people round it. I know its every knot and joint, running my hands over the indestructible yacht varnish as I wipe up Weetabix. It's the table Liz built, the one with a story. I pay attention to it, the prerequisite of gratitude, in a way I would not if I had worked for it less.

It's the same with clothes. Horrified by the environmental impact and human cost of the fashion industry, I stopped buying new clothes, cold turkey, three years ago (the expensive pandemic leggings were the last thing). For the first time in my life, I feel stylish. Old clothes are better quality and more interesting, force more creativity to the surface because I can't, even if I wanted to, just wear this season's trends. New clothes seem boring to me now, flat and story-less, icons of restricted choice. When I find something amazing in the racks of a charity shop, I feel like an explorer of old, and no plastic ASOS package ever gave me that. It's another tragic trick of the human brain – when things come too easy we struggle to give thanks for them.

And of course, my faith reminds me to give thanks. Gratitude is a major ingredient in almost every church service. I go in, too often, grumpy and distracted, mentally gnawing at my to-do list of problems and desires. Church is a sort of zoom-out function for me, a way to raise my gaze off my graspy self for a minute.

The forms of prayer help too. It's not always followed, but I was taught to pray according to a structure, moving through worship, confession and thanksgiving before getting to requests. This last 'asking for stuff' part of prayer is probably the most familiar and attractive, and it's a very valid form, but by putting it at the end of a list I find my soul has settled a bit by the time I get there. I have surrendered some of the clenched and compacted desire through the other steps. I'm often able to tune in, a little bit, to the longing underneath the presenting craving, to notice what is already in my hands, not just what I am missing.

If you're not involved in a congregation, how could you create some trellis for gratitude in your life? Start small. I find 'habit stacking', like stopping to notice food before eating, reflecting in a moment of silence on all that it took to get nourishment onto your plate, can be easier to adopt than whole new habits. You'll know what helps you turn your attention to what you've already received.

Generosity

I know I said we'd move away from the discomfort of the 'sell all your stuff and give it to the poor' theme, but generosity can't be avoided altogether if I want to be fully alive. Because while I am clearly committed to resisting the radical generosity that Jesus, at least in a plain text reading, is inviting me into, my compromise is trying to grow in generosity in smaller ways. Maybe I'll work up to the 'vow of poverty' stuff. Maybe.

Generosity feels, like many of these practices, a form of resistance. It's a crowbar for the hard crust of stuff I'm always attempting to armour myself with.

In our community house we have a rule that visitors should never leave empty-handed. It sometimes seems silly and is almost always socially awkward. People have had Tupperwares of leftovers and jars of jam thrust into their hands. One housemate in particular who is further ahead than me with generosity will have listened attentively to the person. They will choose from the house something that will bring our guest lasting joy. A houseplant for example, which I've carefully tended. Repeatedly, a beautifully bound volume of Celtic daily prayer. It's only available in hardback, and has four brightly coloured ribbons to mark the place in the readings and time of the year. These books are things of beauty as well as oft-used tools in our house. Buying them was my suggestion, and I love them. More times than I can count when we've had people join us for prayer, they've remarked on the book and my husband has said, 'Please, take it.'

I always feel a pang of irritation when he does this. The psychological chain between me and the thing I believe I possess tugs as it departs. It is a step onwards from Marie Kondo. The prayer book sparks joy, but that's part of the reason to let it go. It will (we hope) spark joy elsewhere, the gesture communicating love when the person uses it. It's not that I am totally deprived by this practice. The joy of others does give me a glow. Academic consensus is that giving or buying for others ('prosocial spending') does actually make us happier.[28] It is better to give than receive, said someone. So far we have had enough money to replace the books that leave, or we've been gifted some in turn. It is a tiny attempt to participate in what theorists call 'the gift economy', the idea that hoarding creates scarcity, but generosity builds momentum, allowing what is needed to flow and move, bringing abundance for everyone. The hope, even with these basic acts of giving, is that it short circuits the acquisitive scripts. Our tiny acts of generosity are a way we can participate in a chain reaction, encouraging 'paying it forward' and normalising open handedness. The gift economy is not directly reciprocal, with balanced debts and credits of generosity, but more circular. We're supposed to willingly give and willingly receive without totting things up too much. My guess though is that we have received at least as much as we've given away. It's certainly more relational than individual producers and consumers meeting their own needs only through the market. As Charles Eisenstein says, at its best, 'The gift economy represents a shift from consumption to contribution, transaction to trust, scarcity to abundance and isolation to community.'[29]

Christianity, like almost all wisdom traditions, teaches me to also give money away. One of the most illuminating moments of living in community was when we needed to share financial information with our housemates. We were applying for a mortgage and needed to work out joint income and spending for the bank's affordability checks. Our housemates were, it turns out, giving away a lot more money, proportionally, to charity than us. It was a helpful kind of peer pressure. We are such social creatures, so responsive to norms, and surrounding ourselves with generous people changes us.

Tithing works similarly. Many churches interpret the Hebrew Bible's practice of the tithe, which was initially giving 10 per cent to the temple, as meaning Christians should now give 10 per cent of their income to church. It sounds like a con right? It's been massively misused by televangelists financing their BMWs but I increasingly feel lucky to have this baked into my practice. Ten per cent sounds a lot, but because of hedonic adaptation you get used to it fast. Tithing shouldn't be a legalistic thing – Jesus is incredibly acerbic about the religious leaders who even weigh out 10 per cent of their herbs to give to the temple and then ignore the poor. The point, I think, isn't so much the number but the practice. Giving should be enough to break the chokehold of money, not just an afterthought out of surplus but built into budgets and finances and put aside first. It is another psychological middle finger up to the lie that accumulation will save us.

It is also a way of having a stake in a community. Our tithe pays for the practical things we need as a church – leaders' salaries, maintaining the building, covering the bills. It also helps fund the parents and toddlers group, the debt advice centre and the food bank. Some goes towards a local knife crime prevention charity and refugee support. We give to charity individually as well, but the practice of giving *as a community* feels important. It makes it less about me and my virtue and more about a family, a household, trying to be oriented outward. We feel a collective sense of ownership to this thing we're all supporting, and, because it's in theory based on percentage not amount, the poorest are doing their part just as much as the richest.

What tithing does is it forces me to keep an eye on the

expansionist tendencies of my concept of 'need'. The very uncomfortable St Basil sermon I quoted above is called 'I will tear down my barns'. This is a reference to the parable Jesus told of a rich man who built bigger and bigger barns, but died before he could enjoy any of the contents. If avarice is taking more than I need, and doing it mindlessly, with neither gratitude nor related generosity, then how I define 'need' is important. 'Need' can be an ever-growing barn, gobbling up everything and leaving nothing over to share.

How much do I really need? More than my grandmother did. A dishwasher feels like a need, and a comfortable bedroom, and several bottles of wine a week. I 'need' nice sheets. It is hard to go backwards down the hedonic elevator, to return to a lower standard of living (which might previously have felt luxurious) if we've experienced more.

John Wesley, the founder of Methodism, was clear-eyed about this. The story goes that he made sure his 'disposable income' stayed static throughout his life, while the proportion of giving went up, rather than the other way round. The money he had to spend on treats and luxuries was the same in his twenties as in old age, and as his income went up he just gave away more. He prefigured the Effective Altruism movement beloved of tech bros with his principle 'Earn all you can, give all you can.' He became a wealthy man through his books and preaching and ended up giving away 98 per cent of his income.[30]

Needless to say, I have not done this. I buy more expensive serums now than I did in my twenties, spend more on high thread count sheets. I don't want to go backwards, but I wonder if it might at least be possible, psychologically, to stick here, to not let my standard of living drift up to the point when I can't enjoy cheap wine or budget holidays because fancy has become my normal. I don't think I'm actually at risk of that (I'm a writer married to a philosopher!) but it's all relative, and the principle is a good one. It might at least encourage me to give a bit more away.

You probably don't tithe, but my guess is that if you are reading this book you already give money to charity. I heard a sermon that advised looking at the percentage you are giving away, and trying to up it by 1 per cent every year. I haven't always stuck to it, but it means I give more than I would have. If you're someone in the kind of job that gets yearly pay rises, then taking those small, inflation-linked rises and putting the extra directly into giving, before you get used to spending it, is another way I've found helpful in curbing this tendency in myself.

These kind of small, almost laughably entry-level acts of generosity with 'my' possessions and 'my' money feel like clearing out my gutters, pouring weed killer on the Devil's Snare. The practice is at least as important for me as for the person receiving. In fact, I find it most helpful to focus on what it does for me, partly because I'm still selfish enough to need that motivation, but it also protects me a bit against saviour syndrome.

Gratitude and generosity are strong bulwarks against false needs and the treadmill of ever-increasing comfort and convenience. They are steps towards the things religion and social psychology show *actually* make us happier, towards being fully alive. They are not, of course, foolproof. The formative power of a consumer society is usually stronger, coming at us all day every day, even if we puncture it with moments of giving thanks and giving away. Enough filthy-rich Christians exist to make me question whether these teachings really can break the spell of seeking more than we need, but that is just me judging. I don't know how much they give, how they live, and it's not my business. It's not my story.

My story is one of realising just how tangled up I am. I am scared of Jesus, of the level of challenge, but I am (or want to be) more scared of what our collective avarice is doing to us, to our world. I'm applying this call in my life in such small ways, and the siren song of the culture is so ubiquitous. As quickly as I cut back the weeds, more seeds are planted. Sometimes it feels like the only way to uproot avarice from my life permanently is to go full hermit, detox from all the malicious messaging for more. Writing this chapter has made me surprisingly envious of the monks and nuns who do choose the nuclear option, selling everything and taking a vow of poverty. It feels so clean, like an alcoholic going cold turkey. Unless I'm able to opt out in that way (and probably even then) I can't avoid money. I have to find peace with it, and have compassion for my hungry, childlike heart. And I have a hunch that the world that is coming, the world we have created with our avarice, is going to force many of us to let go of the things that used to be luxuries but are now necessities. And enforced simplicity, a stripping back to basics, might not be as terrible as I fear.

Gratitude and generosity help, but with this temptation, more than any other, I feel in need of stronger medicine. I promised I'd leave most of the direct [God] chat to the last chapter, but it would be remiss of me to not at least gesture to the deepest, strongest antidote for avarice offered by theology. Thomas Traherne, a seventeenth-century poet and cleric, wrote of the snackish search for satisfaction that drives the pursuit of more money and things. He, and many religious voices, believed that this hunger was in fact a gift designed to point us towards the divine. His poem 'Desire' calls it 'restless longing, heavenly avarice', something within him 'that did incessantly a paradise/Unknown suggest, and something undescribed/Discern', an urge that can't be satisfied in 'dead material toys'.[31] As William Schweiker puts it, 'the love of God can limit the desire for acquisition precisely because what is desired exceeds objectification'.[32] Now I've faced up to the scale of the problem, it is this that feels like it has the potential to really change me.

But that's for later.

ACEDIA: FROM DISTRACTION TO ATTENTION

When I was twenty-two I went skiing and shattered my left leg, coming home after a helicopter rescue and five days in a French hospital with twenty-one pins in my tibia and three in my fibula. Four months into my first six-month BBC contract, I was facing a long recovery period with no idea whether I'd still have a job at the end. I couldn't weight bear at all for months, and so washing myself, shopping for food or carrying cups of tea from one room to another were impossible. After two days of sobbing alone in my flat with a caffeine withdrawal headache, I moved back home with my parents.

It was a record-scratch pause in the *Sex and the City*-soundtracked film montage in my mind. My London friends carried on going to the theatre and out for drinks on the South Bank while I watched back-to-back episodes of *America's Next Top Model* in my magnolia childhood home. My recovery lined up coincidentally with a flurry of family funerals. None were for people I was very close to, but I was struggling to look after myself, so had to go along. Wheeled into churches and crematoria by my parents, blurry with pain and frustration, I observed the strange rite from a distanced, anthropological perspective. Whereas most people in their twenties can go years or decades without hearing a eulogy, I listened to a decent sample in the course of a few weeks.

David Brooks is right about eulogies. They are a distillation of our philosophy of the good life. The things people choose to say (and not say) about a dead person seemed, through my opiate haze, to be telling me something important. No one spent much time talking about jobs. A brief factual list, but mainly in reference to what the person had meant to colleagues. If their work had left a legacy of compassion or creativity it might get more than a mention, but only rarely. Some of the dead were successful, some ordinary, some attractive, some not, but these things did not crop up. The focus of the eulogies was relentlessly relational. What was left of a person was their imprint on others, as a friend, child, neighbour, colleague, parent, partner, community volunteer. How much they cared, how they showed up. How well they loved.

After the third funeral, I sat in an armchair with a Thermos of tea that I'd made in the kitchen and crutched through to the lounge in a backpack, and wrote in my prayer journal: 'I don't want to get distracted by ambition and being impressive. I want the focus of my life to be relationships.' I hope I'm not the only person who fantasises about their funeral, and the packed cathedral of devastated loved ones. It was partly a self-interested realisation that loving well would make that scene more likely. It also, though, felt like a real spiritual challenge – did I believe a life defined by love was a good life? If my accident had been worse, and I was never able to achieve my ambitions, did I still believe that loving [God] and loving people was all that really mattered, in the end?

I'm still grateful for that day. I got a dose of what many only receive later, with a cancer scare, major bereavement or similar brush with mortality. I had a clear-sighted moment of knowing what I wanted my life to be about. These moments thin the fog temporarily, puncture the delusions and distractions that keep us from that sight. Consequently, I have tried to live as if my relationships with others and the divine are the main thing, where I devote most of my attention. This has taken a lot of pressure off all the other stuff. I think it makes me happy. However, in a competitive, individualist world, deluged with technological toys, the fog of distraction is always threatening to steal this focus.

When I pine for my phone, I can feel it on my skin, a tingle akin to a lover walking into the room. Patricia Lockwood calls it 'the portal', glowing with the promise of significance and connection.[1] Smart phones act like the enchanted Mirror of Erised in *Harry Potter*, which shows us what our heart desires, but never allows us to reach out and take it. Dumbledore tells Harry, after he's sat up all night gazing at it, 'Men have wasted away before it, entranced by what they have seen, or been driven mad, not knowing if what it shows is real or even possible.'[2]

Perhaps I am especially susceptible to the lure of technological connection, unusually weak willed, because I have sometimes felt like I am being driven mad. I have two young children and all too regularly have a phone in my hand when they are trying to talk to me. It always feels like something important, worth the moment of disconnection, but at a distance I can see that I am often just scrolling listlessly and restlessly. I have social media blockers on all my devices, which worked well until I discovered you could switch them off easily. They invented a locked mode, I learned to delete the blocker app. Now I download and delete my blockers multiple times a day, like an overeater hiding food from themselves and repeatedly opening the cupboard. I have been known to stare at my phone, after I've taken it down from the highest shelf where I've 'hidden' it, and quote *Brokeback Mountain*: 'I wish I knew how to quit you.' I am embarrassed by this (especially when a housemate catches me talking to a digital device like a cowboy), but I know I'm not alone.

You might not associate this endemic distraction with sloth, but, before there was sloth, there was acedia. Acedia is both the Latin word we now translate as sloth and for many centuries its precursor. It's not simple laziness but a richer, more capacious concept, difficult to translate. I also think it is endemic, the unnamed temptation of our times.

John Cassian, a monk writing in the early fifth century, described brothers with acedia experiencing

> Bodily listlessness . . . as though he were worn by a long journey or a prolonged fast . . . Next he glances about and sighs that no one is coming to see him. Constantly in and out of his cell, he looks at the sun as if it were too slow in setting.[3]

Listlessness, distraction, apathy, restlessness. A monk never called it this, but I recognise it most in my own life when I'm faffing. Failing to settle to anything, craving something, trying to sate a snackishness I'm only semi-conscious of. Time feels either baggy or tight. The opposite of flow.

Etymologically the Latin word comes via Greek, and joins the negative *a* 'without' to *kedos* meaning 'care'. Carelessness doesn't quite cover it though. The list in listless comes not from to-do lists but the Middle English *liste* meaning pleasure, joy or delight. So joylessness is in there too. The monks who first coined acedia called it the 'noonday demon', the post-lunch slump when all the focus and energy of the morning has worn off. It wasn't originally seen as a sin in itself, more a state of mind to be avoided. Chaucer, in gloriously juicy Middle English, said it 'for-sloweth and forsluggeth' anyone attempting to act.[4]

Mid-January, as half the country resignedly gives up on their resolutions, might be peak acedia season. Boredom is a key component, both an unwillingness and inability to attend to what is important. John of the Cross thought it was part of the 'dark night of the soul', less glamorous but no less dangerous than despair.[5]

Non-monastic thinkers have recognised acedia. Aldous Huxley blamed the Romantics for it becoming a fashionable pose for aspiring poets and artists. He despaired that in his time (as in ours), many creatives and intellectuals put on acedia like clothes, adopting ennui, cynicism and languor as part of their personal brand:

> The sense of universal futility, the feelings of boredom and despair, with the complementary desire to be 'anywhere, anywhere out of the world,' or at least out of the place in which one happens at the moment to be, have been the inspiration of poetry and the novel for century [sic] and more.[6]

Acedia leaves me pinging around like a pinball, a 'forsluggish' one sometimes, but also like the monk popping restlessly in and out of her cell hoping for a visitor, or a notification. Too many of my days are lived in this scattered state. Acedia neuters my ability to do good in the world, or even just properly enjoy it.

I don't want to be a pinball. I want to be a plant.

With a concept this broad, there isn't one opposite, but I've come to believe that the antonym of acedia is attention. The etymological root of attention is stretching toward something, moving intentionally closer. Ideally, I would decide carefully what warrants my attention, what people, ideas, objects or projects have sufficient meaning and value for me to spend a part of my fleeting life attending to them. I would stretch towards those things that will help me be kinder, freer, more just. Things that bring me genuine joy. Primarily, for me, people and relationships, but also meaningful work, meaningful play, beauty, real rest.

We all know that we are living in what has been termed the attention economy. It feels more like the acediac economy. No matter how many articles I've read about how tech companies manipulate us with dopamine hits and our Pavlovian response to notifications (articles I've found via social media), it's easy not to see the full danger of it. We are so seduced by the convenience and gloss and repeated tiny emotional rewards for compliance that we don't recognise the opportunity cost. How rapidly our lives are passing with our minds resting primarily on matters only pixel deep.

Philosopher and later Catholic martyr Thomas More wrote: 'Many things know we that we seldom think on. And in the things of the soul, knowledge without remembrance little profiteth.'[7]

In other words, the things I 'know' but fail to train my attention on do me little good. I wanted to live primarily for relationships, but the war on my attention means I am often failing, forgetting to remember what I know. When I stop to notice it, I feel actual rage. It is hard enough to live a good life, to do the work, to grow, without a context that is actively working against those things. I have to remind myself that learning to attend to what is important has always been a part of wisdom paths, distraction always a hurdle to overcome. Monetising and mining our attention has accelerated, but isn't brand new. Dorothy L. Sayers summarised the messaging of advertising in 1933 as:

> Whatever you're doing, stop it and do something else! Whatever you're buying, pause and buy something different. Be hectored into health and prosperity! Never let up! Never go to sleep! Never be satisfied. If once you are satisfied, all our wheels will run down.[8]

Sayers' exclamation marks help me recognise the artificial urgency, to feel in my body the way the messaging of our culture is fracturing my relationship to time. Go! Go! Go! Do! Do! Do! Shiny! New! Over here! Take your eyes off the people in front of you and keep moving. Don't stretch steadily and intentionally towards the most important things, but ping around responsively, because this whole engine is running off your distracted, restless hustle.

My culture is telling me, in a million different ways, to never be satisfied.

I want to be satisfied.

I want to stop pinging around and put my roots down deep. I need to learn to draw nourishment from the gifts I have already received, the relationships in front of me. I am taking my time and my attention back.

It was only in my thirties that I began fully recognising the powerful resources my tradition offers in this quest. I have come to the conclusion that training attention and structuring time are the hidden genius of religions. Yes, they give ethical guidance and existential comfort, but the centuries-honed tools they offer are a pragmatic, applicable and sane response to the madness of distraction and hurry.

The Rule of St Benedict, the urtext for monastic thought,

implies that it is precisely a well-ordered rhythm of days that keeps distraction at bay. Acedia is presented as a disruption of rhythm, a bum note in the song of the hours. I love Abraham Joshua Heschel's term for disordered time: 'the screech of dissonant days'. I react badly to the idea of a schedule but a rhythm sounds inviting. When I'm living in rhythm time feels less like a quarry or an enemy and more like a dance partner.

Monks ordered their twenty-four hours starting from the belief that in each day there is enough time – enough time for prayer, work, community and solitude. We of course see echoes of this in productivity culture – colour-coding your Outlook calendar and constantly iterating your schedule to 'find' more pockets of time. These are faint echoes though, because under the monastic approach was the assumption of abundance, not scarcity. Time hacks can be useful, but too often the things we are repeatedly encouraged to find time and attention for are narrow – work (output) and health/appearance (input), the second implicitly framed as a way to keep servicing the first. Time is money and money never sleeps. Time, like many things previously conceived of as gifts, is now a commodity, subject to the voracious logic of the market.

Monastic rhythms, often codified in individual communities as a Rule of Life, protect time for a wider, wiser range of activities. Different orders have different rhythms, but they always include hard work that contributes to the community (monks are the opposite of the turn on, tune in, drop out communes of the sixties). Work, though, is kept in place as one important focus among others, with the life of the soul the lodestar. When it's time for prayer, community or hospitality, work stops.

A few years ago I decided that if St Benedict was right then ordering my time is part of how I tend to my soul. I've been attempting to beat back my endemic acedia with a range of spiritual practices (you could call them spiritual technologies) that the Church has used for centuries, and to do it not in a burst of enthusiasm that I then lose a few weeks later, but over years. Much to my annoyance, repetition seems to be the key. Our novelty-obsessed culture is allergic to repetition, associating it with dullness and scarcity, but that is a problem. Research on neuroplasticity and the power of habit only confirms what religions have always taught – the repeated, committed choices we make day after day are the sum of who we become. This means our own Rule of Life, the way we structure our time (whether by accident or design), is one of the most important choices we can make to influence what people will say about us at our funeral.

All these practices, as I learn to use them properly and regularly, feel like a trellis. They are helping me train my attention on the connected relationships I say I want to define my life. I feel saner, calmer, more focused. Spiritually alive.

Daily rhythms: prayer and contemplation

It is 6.30 a.m., the devil's hour. My alarm is going off but the bed is warm and womb-like. I fight my way out, muttering, wondering why I ever thought living in community was a good idea, and pile jumpers and coats and slippers on over my nightie. In the kitchen someone perkier than me has left me a cup of tea, like an offering to an angry domestic deity, and I take it gingerly down the dark and frosty garden to the concrete slab garage we have converted into a chapel. It has a tin roof and no electricity so we gather by candlelight as the dawn slowly lightens the corrugated plastic roof panel, huddled over our prayer books in Puffa jackets, looking like a particularly brutalist Caravaggio. I yawn. In the name of the Father, Son and Holy Spirit. We begin.

I detest mornings. My family and housemates give me a wide berth before 10 a.m., and I vigorously reject exercise, green drinks or any other 'power-hour' activities before noon. People who come to stay in our community guest rooms who know me already are often shocked at the monosyllabic, blank-eyed creature that greets them before coffee. I do, despite all this, try to start the day with some kind of prayer. I can't pretend to live a full monastic rhythm every day, though I do try – and usually succeed, now – in keeping reasonable boundaries around work and making time for rest and hospitality. It's the commitment of part of my morning to prayer and sacred reading though, despite all my natural instincts, that has been most transformative. Several times a week it is with others in the chapel. Other days prayer might just be journaling my thoughts vaguely heavenward in bed. Often, alone, with our community or with the kids over breakfast, I use written prayers from a modern monastic community based in Northumberland.

One line lifted from the Psalms always stops my distracted thoughts in their tracks: 'Teach us, dear Lord, to number our days, that we may apply our hearts unto wisdom.'[9]

A modern paraphrase might be: Teach us to take our lives, our time seriously. Help us apply our hearts, turn our attention, orientate our desires to wisdom. Help us to really live.

Saying the same things regularly has the effect of writing and overwriting the words onto my consciousness, reminding me of and reorienting me to what I want this day to be about.

Usually when I am spending time in prayer in the morning my body does not want me to be. I'm either half asleep or, if the caffeine has kicked in, full of adrenaline, ready to crack on, my to-do list winking seductively at me in the corner. The latter can feel like driving with feet stamped on both the accelerator and the brake at the same time. These lines from the Psalms give more power to the foot that is on the brake. Just stop for a minute, Liz. Number your days. Notice *this* day. Nested within the practice I am using to structure my time and train my attention is the justification for why I'm doing it. 'Number our days' is a stark reminder that I don't have forever, that this day is one of a finite total that will eventually run out. One day I will die. What am I going to do with this wild and precious life?

Practically, I almost always either say aloud or write these prayers down. Internal, silent prayer is definitely also a thing, but I'm bad at it. My mind wanders off. Externalising my prayers, as with my thoughts more generally, makes them concrete.

I realise prayer here sounds a lot like meditation or affirmation. And it is. For me, it's also a conversation with someone, a sitting in the presence of unconditional love. St Augustine prayed, 'You have made us for yourself, and our hearts are restless until they rest in you'[10] and it's that meeting which is the best acedia medicine I have found. I'll talk more about that later. For now, you can see prayer as something that might be helpful for anyone trying to take back their attention, no matter where you land on that ultimate question.

This is because neurologically, prayer is a type of meditation – repeated, focused attention – and this kind of attention is good for us. Multiple neuroscientific studies have found that people who pray regularly display beneficial changes in the part of the brain responsible for focus and willpower, and in the area that controls compassion and empathy. This in turn reduces responsiveness in the amygdala, which controls fear and anger.[11] Of course, brain imaging is an extraordinarily blunt instrument, and any repeated cognitive activity changes our brains – London taxi drivers who had to do The Knowledge showed changes in their hippocampus, the area related to navigation.[12] Given we know our brains are changeable, adopting habits that might make me more self-controlled and empathetic and less afraid and angry sounds like a good idea. In an age long before brain scans, the New Testament writers had a hunch that prayer might change us mentally and emotionally. Readers are told to 'be transformed by the renewing of your minds', by repeatedly focusing attention on what is good, true and beautiful.

As well as written and spoken prayers I have increasingly come to value the practices within what is known as contemplative Christianity, especially a form of meditation called Centring Prayer. This simply involves sitting in silence, with one's mind anchored on divine love, and surrendering every thought and feeling that arises to that love.

I'm rubbish at it, and practise only patchily, but I am learning from the mystics that, the more steady time and attention we turn towards the divine, the more our awareness will deepen. It reminds me of artist Jenny Odell's 'exercises in attention', which she prescribes as an antidote to the attention economy.[13] Exercising attention is one way we can overcome what science calls 'inattentional blindness'. Many people have seen the famous video in which, because viewers are asked to count the number of passes a basketball team makes, they completely miss the person in a gorilla suit walk through at the back. We see what we are looking for, not necessarily what is there. Odell argues that art helps us see afresh because we have permission to fully use our senses. The more we look, the more we see. In the same way contemplative practices train us to look differently, not letting our eyes slide over the world or, worse, miss it entirely because we are on our phones.

At the end of the day I sometimes use a practice called the Examen, which comes from the sixteenth-century founder of the Jesuit order, St Ignatius. Ignatius encouraged his followers to look back over their days in the evening, re-narrating the events to themselves, and to look for what he called moments of desolation and consolation. It sounds a lot like highlights and lowlights, and can be used like that, but the sense of desolation and consolation seems to me to be translatable to disconnection and connection. In desolation, we turn in on ourselves, away from divine love and other people, and in consolation, we know hope, joy, peace etc and move outwards. The Examen simply involves sitting with both these tendencies, holding them with grace, giving thanks for consolation and asking for help with tomorrow's desolations. I find it a gentle, helpful way to settle down for sleep.

Thanks to the work of Jon Kabat-Zin and others to translate the meditation he learned in Buddhist contexts into the more accessible mindfulness, it's easy now to get on board with the idea of prayer-as-meditation.[14] I've found even more explicit confession to be life-giving, though. This part of prayer still has extremely bad branding, all noir-lit booths and even shadier priests, but I find it freeing. Many of us are coming to the uncomfortable realisation that, as research also shows, we are a little bit racist, a bit sexist, basically a big bundle of half-conscious prejudices against people who are Not Like Me. A regular practice of confession acts like a medical check-up, catching problems early. If I look at it regularly, I get less freaked about the mess inside me. It's a sort of *#NormaliseSin* move. I have also learned that the sooner I get conscious of something the sooner I can do something about it. It's the shame and hiding that can feel like it's rotting me. Saying sorry is good for my soul.

I also love collective confession. Many church services include a prayer of contrition, said out loud and altogether. There is something amazing about a group of people admitting in unison that they messed up. The Anglican liturgy in its ancient strangeness really works for me: 'We have followed too much the devices and desires of our own hearts . . . We have left undone those things which we ought to have done, and we have done those things which we ought not to have done.'[15] It acknowledges we can sin 'through ignorance, through weakness, through our own deliberate fault', and the first two are an uncomfortable reminder that when I cause harm through ignorance or weakness the harm is still harm.[16] Crucially though, while confession encourages me to look my faults in the face, it also offers the possibility of restoration and a clean slate. It can feel as satisfying as squeezing a blackhead.

This year I asked a friend who has got cautiously interested in church to come to a service that happened to fall at one of the penitent times of year, and so included a lot of focus on sin and confession. I felt tense throughout it, because the service went so radically against the grain of a culture that tells us to liberate ourselves from guilt, that there is no real right or wrong, and that all we need is self-compassion (I think self-compassion is *one* of the things we need, FYI). At the end I started half-apologising, wishing I had found a softer way in for her, but she said, shining-eyed, that she'd loved it. It's so real, so bracing, she said. Can I come again?

Casper ter Kuile, author of *The Power of Ritual*, speaks about this relief of using confession and contrition prayers, for him outside of a traditional theological context: 'Finally! A chance to be honest, witnessed by the Great beyond, about what's going on and confront the way we want to show up in the world: braver and free.'[17]

I have several other dear friends who have started praying despite being very unsure if there is anyone listening. Novelist Elizabeth Gilbert writes a letter starting 'Dear Love' in her journal every morning, as her own private form of prayer.[18]

For me, prayer is a compass for my consciousness. When I start the day without it, the arrow of my attention spins wildly between other people's demands, tasks, and all the things the world is trying to sell me. Prayer, no matter how half-arsed or fleeting, reminds me of my true north, the deeper things I want to root in, and my day seems to lead into straighter paths.

Daily rhythms: sacred reading

I also read the Bible in the morning. It's my founding text, the narrative I locate myself in. Its strange oblique stories act as a counterweight to the cultural soup I'm swimming in the rest of the time. It never fails to provoke, inspire or infuriate me. If you're intrigued I'd encourage you to give the book of John or Ephesians a go in a modern translation. Yes, the King James Version is beautiful and cultured Brits show they are Radio 4 listeners by pretending to prefer it, but it's also heavy going. The crown-jewels sheen distracts from the original earthy, human punch of letters written largely to and from marginalised underdogs of empire.

I am currently reading the Bible with a group of friends for whom it hasn't been part of their life in any real way before. Not coincidentally, they are all writers themselves, drawn to the text for its stock of stories and vast range of genres. We call it 'wild Bible study' because in reading and chatting together we are not after one right answer, not seeking to solve anything. I used to try to read it like this, not least because many Bible study notes do make it feel like the text is a puzzle to be solved, its vivid and dense language in need of putting into doctrinal boxes. I found that approach boring, so stopped going to Bible studies. Now I don't worry that there are many things I don't understand, whole books and passages I don't know what to do with. I don't think either Bible reading or faith itself is about resolution. It is a lot more like poetry, drama or music, which any good teacher will tell you are not completely amenable to the question 'But what does it mean?' I want only to keep tasting it, turning it up to the light like a crystal to see just how much it holds.

However, you may not be drawn to reading the Bible. If not, the tools of sacred reading are entirely applicable to other texts you want to shape your life.

Vanessa Zoltan, an atheist chaplain, author and podcaster, developed an approach for treating different kinds of texts as sacred while studying at Harvard Divinity School. Unable to engage with the Torah, her tradition's sacred text, she began to read *Jane Eyre* instead using some of the practices Jews use for studying scripture. She committed to treating the text with faith (the expectation that the more attention you give the text the more gifts it can give you), rigour (reading regularly and with focus) and community (reading with others).[19]

Studying beloved novels in the same way you might study texts in a yeshiva, Bible study or madrassa initially sounded bonkers to me. Yes, I reread Dorothy L. Sayer' *Gaudy Night* regularly, usually when I'm ill, but treating it as sacred? Now, though, it makes complete sense to me as a form of attention training. By choosing one or a small number of texts that we want to be shaped by and learn from, and then reading and rereading them with faith, rigour and community, we take control of some of our attention, and thus our formation. I know I am being formed and shaped by the blur of my Instagram feed, the adverts on the Tube and the tenor of the news. Why not commit to being consciously shaped by a story whose values I aspire to, and spend intentional, communal time with characters who help me get clearer on the kind of life I want to live?

Weekly rhythms: sabbath

On Friday night, roughly as my work day ends, I turn off my phone, my iPad and my laptop and light a candle. It's a precious moment of peace. Then I jump up, hunt down a housemate, thrust all my devices hurriedly into their arms and ask them to hide them, and (this with slightly wild eyes), NOT give them back to me on pain of death for twenty-four hours.

Sometimes it works. Often it doesn't, because the way we have set up society means there is usually (what seems like) a very important reason to turn them back on. If I can't get said housemate to crack I just use my husband's phone. More recently, we've tried committing to doing this together, as a community, which has helped a bit. I still successfully manage twenty-four hours off devices only about half the time but the attempt every week feels important.

Tech sabbaths and digital detoxes, even half-arsed ones like mine, are a modern iteration of one of the oldest ideas in civilisation. In the second chapter of the Hebrew Bible, itself one of the oldest documents we have, [God] undertakes six days of creative work, and rests on the seventh. He blesses the day and declares it 'holy'.

Theologian Walter Breuggeman called the practice of sabbath an act of resistance.[20] The word conjures French fighters, stylishly sabotaging Nazi infrastructure while smoking Gauloises. Imagining myself in a beret with red lipstick really helps when I attempt to turn off my phone for a day. It's certainly a more attractive image than the grey, dull associations most of us carry. Sabbath sounds to us like the shop closing early just when we've run out of milk. It sounds like restriction. Which it is. But it is also (and this will be a theme) through restriction, liberation.

For most of the week, my value is in what I produce and what I consume. If I'm not careful my main goal in a day becomes being impressive and competent, subtly signalling my status with the things I buy, say and post.

Sabbath is the opposite. It is a line in the sand. Today I am just a person, and a person is beyond price. Sabbath is about valuing, fighting for and fiercely guarding rest.

I have had to learn to choose rest in a culture that only really recognises frantic work and exhausted, passive leisure, ideally consumed using the same screens we've been working on all day, produced by the same small number of global corporations. Despite being deeply convinced of my need for rest, sometimes the only way I can justify sabbath to myself is on a productivity basis. Jews, who have been persecuted and mocked partly for their observance of it, have had to do this over the centuries. The Romans (proto-neo-liberals?) were contemptuous of it, believing it revealed laziness to have a day off a week. Philo, a first-century Jew, made the case that his community was more effective and productive because of their day off: 'A breathing spell enables not merely ordinary people but athletes also to collect their strength with a stronger force behind them to undertake promptly and patiently each of the tasks set before them.' Rabbi Joshua Heschel though condemns this justification, saying, 'Here the Sabbath is represented not in the spirit of the Bible but in the spirit of Aristotle.'[21] For Jews and Christians, the Sabbath is not designed to serve work, because love, not work, is our ultimate end. It always moves me that the sabbath command was given directly after the Exodus, to a nation that had until recently been enslaved for generations. There is a tenderness in mandating rest and play for traumatised people who had only ever known enforced labour.

Mandated time to rest seems a foreign notion now. It's become one of the few clear political intuitions I have: that it shouldn't be. Breaking time, and people, into ever flexible units of production is one of the strongest drivers of disconnection that we experience. I have come to see sabbath as central for my personal project of connection, with myself, with my family and community and with [God]. It's a relational reset every week, a bulwark against the instrumentalisation of relationships and the commodification of time.

Sabbath is, it is important to underline, a deeply Jewish practice. It is no accident that I have mainly quoted rabbis in this section. Christians share a commitment to it in theory, and several denominations observe it strictly, but many others have been far less disciplined in practice, at least in the last century. It is not quite appropriation for Christians and others to adopt it, but I think it's only polite to acknowledge that sabbath is a gift from the Jews to the world.

Honestly, before I started being intentional about it, I thought I was pretty good at rest. Acedia is a temptation for me, and so is straight sloth itself, the desire to down tools and get in the bath with a book always lurking at the back of my mind. I have never been a workaholic, never found boundaries around work a problem, which feels more shameful than admitting to a niche sexual proclivity in public. It's almost encouraged. In writing that I don't suffer from this temptation, I fear judgement. What if someone reads this and decides not to hire me when I need a job? This push to be always performing productivity for imaginary future employers or clients is a large part of what makes rest so hard. It feels embarrassing.

As a leader of a think tank I tried to resist this culture, to make sure we had reasonable hours and people took their holidays, and we'd all go to the pub at four on a Thursday. I believed – and still believe – that it is possible for people and organisations to be effective and creative and strive for excellence in a sustainable way, without burning out, without the extractive pace that so quickly curdles work relationships. Then the pandemic hit, and trying to hold an organisation together over Zoom while home-schooling threw all my careful balance completely out of whack. The financial fear and the worry for my team, many of them isolated and clinically vulnerable, meant I worked harder and harder. I was determined that the organisation would not only survive but do it healthily and relationally. And we did, mainly. But I was not healthy. I had a persistent twitch in my left eye and back pain so bad I had to do most of my meetings lying down. Like most of us, I just kept going.

By January 2021, every time I prayed this phrase floated up in my mind: Stop and rest. Like an annoying fly, it just would not go away. It made me tut and mentally swat. Ha! Rest. Chance would be a fine thing. But it stayed, quiet and compassionate, sweet-smelling somehow, and I began to wonder whether, rather than just my wishful subconscious, it might be some kind of guidance from [God]. For context, I don't hear [God]'s voice at all clearly or regularly. I don't even know quite what I mean by that phrase. Characters in the Bible have angels appear to them, or vivid dreams, but when it happens for me it is much subtler and slower than that. A dawning sense in prayer that I need to do something, or in this case stop something, and a tug on my conscience when I try to ignore it. It had only happened this clearly twice before.

You are very welcome to explain it away. You might call it my intuition, or listening to my body. I don't think the explanations are mutually exclusive. Either way, by February I had conceded that this was something I needed to listen to, that it was time to leave my job, but I was full of fear. I was then the main wage earner in my family and we didn't know how to make the maths work. What savings we had were in the hope of being able to buy a community home, and we were renting with another family at this point, and already spending more than our income. Stepping away from a job I loved without a plan or a safety net felt scary financially and also a threat to my identity. Who was I, without something to say when people asked, 'So what do you do?' I had been a promising young woman. I didn't know if I wanted to be just a woman.

It was this phrase that I wrote in my journal that reminded me of all those funerals, so many years ago. The lesson I'd learned listening to the eulogies had, it seemed, worn off. And I needed to relearn it. I needed to stop and rest and trust that life is not a treadmill, that it is not, in fact, me that holds up the sky. We decided we would take the leap and hope that our past experience of following these leadings would be repeated.

So I handed in my notice and wrote a leaving blog that said, essentially, 'I don't have an impressive next job to announce or a flashy future project to share. I'm just stopping for a rest and I don't know what's next.' That short, off-the-cuff final piece has had more response than anything else I have ever written. I posted it on LinkedIn, headquarters of performing productivity, and had my inbox flooded with messages of support and relief. People shared it to their feeds and strangers messaged me saying that they didn't know you were allowed to say things like that in public without it being code for a politician having an affair. Three people told me I had inspired them to quit their jobs too, which seemed a lot of responsibility. It was a tiny version of the response Jacinda Ardern, Prime Minister of New Zealand, got a few years later when she stepped down, saying honestly that she was just too exhausted to do a good job. Everyone who heard it felt their shoulders relax a tiny bit. We all felt, suddenly, that it is ok to admit you're human, even when you're running the world.

And rest is, fundamentally, about being human. About recognising our limits when advertising tells us we are limitless. It requires intention, and working out what we do actually find restorative. It is going in the bath with a book for me (but not with an iPad), or gardening, or rollerblading, or pottering around charity shops without my phone. I need to not have access to the news or social media in order to rest.

It might seem counter-intuitive to prescribe rest as a medicine for the sin that is often known as sloth, but I think it's right. Proper rhythms of real rest rather than passive leisure consumption make focus easier when we need to work, make it more likely we will find joy and flow in it when we do.

Weekly rhythms: liturgy

Liturgy is one of those churchy-sounding words. It means the form of a public ritual, almost always repeated, and is often used to describe the written words used in a church service. It is worth pausing on the broader use though, because whenever we do something repeatedly in public we could be said to be performing a liturgy. And the point of a liturgy is to continually direct our desires. They are heart-shaping technologies and they help create our character. No formation without repetition, the saying goes; we are what we repeatedly do. Philosopher James K. A. Smith calls secular versions 'cultural liturgies', and names going to a football game or a regular trip to the shopping mall as examples.[22] Both involve their own rituals, buildings, offerings, even songs in the case of football. Smith also sees consuming advertising as formative social liturgy, the creators of which are not at all naive as to its power. Values and truth claims are covertly embedded in the images and repeated narratives used by marketing rather than through direct argument or evidence. Legitimate and pre-existing desires – for community, for the esteem of others, for adventure – are carefully associated with products that imply they will fulfil those longings (beer, an expensive watch, a holiday). New desires, for these products rather than experiences, are thereby incepted into us. 'This covertness of the operation is also what makes it so powerful: the truths are inscribed in us through the . . . instruments of imagination and ritual.'[23]

Smith's work has helped me see the power of repetition, ritual and image to form and orient me. It's made me more aware of how often I am mindlessly participating in liturgies that are shaping me in directions in which I have not consciously consented to go. And so I now see participating in church liturgy as a form of pushback, another little resistance. I am making a free(er) choice about what I want to shape me, what values and desires I want inscribed on my heart and mind. Every Sunday, I show up for a service that will contain, in more or less formal ways, the following ingredients: an opportunity to acknowledge where I've failed, a time to forgive and reconcile with others, a talk that locates my life in a bigger narrative, collective singing, prayer for people in need, a shared ritual meal (Mass or Communion) and an opportunity to practise financial generosity.

Particularly in a church that uses a small number of set texts again and again, as all Catholic and most Anglican churches do, the words can become deeply ingrained. This can sound dull and rote. Like most teenagers and young people, I spent a long season thinking only entirely spontaneous, 'authentic' self-expression counted, including in prayer, and that all tradition and structure was deadening.

However, as I age I begin to see the value of regular (even, whisper it, sometimes mindless) repetition. Some days the words come alive and feel deeply sincere, my thinking is stretched and enriched by their beauty, and other days I say them out of habit, but they are always forming me. Honestly, it's nice to have a break from innovation. Every week I give at least part of my attention to a ritual that reminds me of the things I am in danger of forgetting. I use my body as well as my mind, standing and kneeling and sitting and singing. I often have a dance around at the back and have stopped caring about the curious glances. During the various Covid-related lockdowns and restrictions it was this singing and dancing I missed the most. My voice is nothing special, but belting a song with a hundred other people can't help but sound beautiful. I often cry. For an hour and a half I don't look at my phone, and when I come out my thoughts feel saner and steadier.

Yearly rhythms: the church calendar

The acediac economy doesn't just make it harder to order our days and weeks well, but has flattened out the rhythm of the year also. Rowan Williams says 'undifferentiated time' is one of the hallmarks of secular, capitalist societies.[24] Largely detached from the seasons, time becomes a headlong linear rush of news cycles punctuated by the commercial breaks of Black Friday and Starbucks Red Cup Day.

As an alternative, Christianity offers the church calendar. The vestiges of it are still there in the post-Christendom West – we stop working for Christmas and Easter – but the rest has largely eroded.

In the church calendar, the year is a spiral, meaning

Christians return to the same stories, readings, songs and practices, the same fasts and feasts reliably year after year. By repeatedly returning to the same special days and seasons I discover new aspects of them, and of myself, bringing to them a slightly different person each time. I connect whatever is going on in my own life at that moment with the story we're in, deepening through the geological layers in myself and in the texts.

In 2022 it was Ash Wednesday that felt most nourishing. The war in Ukraine was raging, the threat of climate change ever more terrifying and a relational breakdown in our church had left me feeling a toxic emotional brew of bleak, sad and angry. I googled 'Ash Wednesday service, Peckham' and found one nearby. I walked in the rain to a church surrounded by estates, and joined a mainly black, mainly female congregation, who welcomed me warmly. The Ash Wednesday liturgy marks the beginning of Lent, a period where Christians are encouraged to sit with sadness, to acknowledge our brokenness, to look the bleak parts of life in the face. It's called Ash Wednesday because the palm crosses from the previous Easter are burned, and the ash used to mark the congregation's foreheads. It's very goth – a ritual meant explicitly to remind us of our own mortality, to create space to reflect on death and loss and grief. It isn't exactly fun, but this year especially it was exactly what I needed. It felt like an outlet, to pray these prayers with strangers-who-are-also-sisters, to walk into Peckham marked by the experience (and laugh with friends on the school run who kept trying to wipe off the smudge). It was healing.

Through marking the church calendar, time now feels neither straightforwardly cyclical (as in early agrarian societies) nor linear and accelerating (as in ours), but more like a deepening spiral of meaning. Once a year I go on retreat, usually in the sombre period of Advent, to spend time in silence and prayer and reflection. I look back on the retreat the year before, and wonder where I will be next year. At Easter I'm reminded of the psychological richness of those three days. I move with my community through a dark day to meditate on suffering and the brokenness of the world (Good Friday), a waiting day that represents the 'in between' of most of life (Holy Saturday) and a day of celebration and rejoicing (Easter Sunday)

Learning to observe the church calendar has made time feel less like a scarce commodity that I need to hoard and more like a gift. It is a rich and layered soil through which I am moving both forward and deeper, a source of nourishment.

The trellis of these anti-acediac practices is training my attention, making me feel less like a pinball. I am often pretty rubbish at them, failing and forgetting to do the things I know ground and centre me, but the gaps are getting shorter. Day by day, week by week, year by year, they are shaping my soul and my neurobiology, depending on which language you prefer. I like both. I am very much a beginner, but I see those who have been on the road longer, and how nourished and rooted their lives seem. A big part of the joy in them is that I did not invent them, and I am not practising them alone. Most of them have been developed over centuries, and I can feel the wisdom that time has polished to a gleam. I find joy in personal practices that connect me through time and space with millions of others, joining my one weedy note to a song that has been being sung since long, long ago.

If you're also longing to take back your attention, to order your days, weeks and years with your eulogy in mind, I would recommend writing a Rule of Life. What do you want to be being formed by, and how do you prioritise time for repeated attention to those things? Whether you want to experiment with the church calendar, living more in line with the seasons or the moon or some other structure, is there a community you could do it with? It is much easier to dance in rhythm if you're not doing it alone.

ENVY: FROM STATUS ANXIETY TO BELOVEDNESS

Envy has bad branding. The other temptations carry their own dark glamour – lust is sexy, greed might make you rich; even gluttony, read as a hedonistic pursuit of pleasure, sounds like someone you want at a party. Acedia is the languid pose of poets; pride, disguised as self-love, our defining social virtue, and wrath, especially in call-out culture, a quick route to acclaim.

Envy and its sickly companion, status anxiety, not so much. The cluster of emotions around them (shame, insecurity) all boil down to that most tender thing: a deep-seated sense of not-enough-ness. They are a small septic wound, an embarrassing and painful secret. The verruca of temptations.

I don't think envy is primarily about wanting what other people have. That's part of it, but wanting something *just* because it belongs to someone else is called covetousness. This *is* condemned in the Ten Commandments: 'You shall not covet your neighbour's house . . . wife . . . servant . . . ox . . . donkey or anything that is your neighbour's.'[1] Leaving aside the Commandment's failure to condemn coveting my neighbour's husband (loophole!), my read of this is that desire is not the problem, but the way loving our neighbour and coveting their stuff is hard to do at the same time.

Envy goes deeper than covetousness into our sense of self. That sour pang of longing is the symptom, not the cause.

We don't tend to envy those who are wildly different from us, pursuing a completely divergent life, but those quite close by. Most of us feel envy towards those who surpass us in things that feel central to our own identity. Envy is a clue to who we wish we were, indicating dissatisfaction with who we actually are. This painful status anxiety is therefore only possible because, for almost all of us, our sense of self is anchored in external, unstable comparisons.

It's unsurprising. Our society, perhaps all societies, function on unspoken rankings of human value, based on hierarchies of achievements and attributes. My guess is that it's worse now, though. The loss of a transcendent frame lands responsibility for our lot in life squarely on the individual. When you add a supposedly meritocratic, socially mobile society, what excuse might I have for not crushing it? We are obsessed with self-improvement, progress and goals, and, though we rarely say the quiet part aloud, it's at least partly because it feels good to be better than other people. No one wants to be left behind. No one wants to be overlooked. Everyone is in search of a gaze.

In the earliest moments of a human life a baby is searching for one thing – two eyes turned towards it. As writer Andy Crouch puts it, 'recognition is the first human quest'.[2] Those babies whose quests are not met with loving, reliable attention, whose developing brains therefore do not receive this elemental communication of worthiness, develop different neural pathways. Much as we may like to think we define ourselves, love ourselves, create ourselves, from our very first moments we are inescapably social creatures, looking outside ourselves to find our value. This is a deeply good thing, because it drives us outward into the loving relationships we need to thrive, but it is also our Achilles' heel. When our need for deep, unconditional attention and affirmation goes unmet (as it almost always partly will, no matter how good our parenting) we look to wider society to sate that hunger. Too often, the world meets us with what Virginia Woolf called its 'notorious indifference'.[3] Williams James wrote in 1890 that 'no more fiendish punishment could be devised . . . than that one should be turned loose in society and remain absolutely unnoticed by all members thereof'.[4] What in the Enid Blyton boarding school stories of my childhood was called 'being sent to Coventry', being ghosted by an online date, finding our messages unreplied to, our social posts unacknowledged, these moments of feeling unseen, unvalued, slipping unnoticed down the leader board, cut deep.

This search for status, and primarily comparative status, is braided into our lives like shot silk, but I find it helpful to consciously notice it. The noticing feels like part of the answer to breaking the spell.

I am writing this in a cafe where two women bustle about behind the counter. Within minutes of walking in it is clear who has higher status. It is partly actual age, but status is made clear by a million other tiny signals. Body language, tone of voice, what someone is wearing. The obnoxiously noisy table of men to my left, bragging about their ski holidays (Peckham really has changed), have a clear alpha in their midst. Look around you, if you can see a group of people. Do you know who has the highest status? I bet that after a short observation you can guess.

It reminds me of the improvisation game we played in school drama class. Each student was assigned a ranked number, and told to interact with each other depending on how low or high we were on the social status scale. There was no need to unpack the concept further for fourteen-year-olds. We'd never had a lesson on status as a sociological concept, probably never consciously observed the differences between the low-status and high-status members of our class, but we knew it in our bones. Philosopher Charles Taylor says it shows in our 'very deportment': 'the way we walk, move, gesture, speak is shaped from our earliest moments by our awareness that we appear before others, that we stand in public space and this space is potentially one of respect or contempt, pride or shame'.[5] As I sought to portray a particular status in class my posture changed, my tolerance for eye contact, my laugh. I remember the shock of discovery, like a spotlight on something that had always been there. The acted emotions also felt real. I knew for the first time the thrill of acting a high-status role, the swelling power of it. I felt the ominous looming humiliation as I picked a low card for round two, reacted to the 'high-card people' with a queasy mix of obsequiousness and hatred.

These status games persist into adulthood. The first question we are asked at a party is: 'What do you do?', the answer to which too often determines the tone and duration of the following conversation. It's not just this obvious stuff, job titles and house sizes and hotness. Depending on where we find ourselves, the status signifiers change, but they are always there. In an intellectual grouping, points are awarded for quoting obscure books, holding the right opinions and being scathing about the right people. In other settings it might be the person who most proves their social justice credentials, in another the funniest. As I'm writing, I am semi-consciously seeking to score status points with you, dear reader, because I know we rarely pay attention to people we perceive to be lower status than ourselves. Put bluntly, I need to impress you enough to keep you reading to the point where I tell you that my impressiveness level is – or should be – irrelevant.

Which means it's time for me to call in someone else's status to boost my own, by means of another quote.

Psychologist Abraham Tesser developed a theory around these fluctuating, comparative status games called the Self Evaluation Maintenance Model.[6] He argued that our sense of self (or self-evaluation, closely connected to self-esteem) is largely dependent on our interactions with others, and that in any human interaction we are driven by a desire to maintain or improve our view of our own value. Yes, it's another of academia's regular 'No shit, Sherlock' findings.

Tesser argues that maintaining our self-evaluation doesn't have to be by beating people, or feeling better than them. Other people's successes can reflect well on us and improve our own self-evaluation, because we get a little thrill being around what is 'eminent', as Thomas Hobbes put it.[7] It's as if the status points get shared. A million awkward celebrity selfies attest to this 'halo effect', adorably guileless attempts to shore up our own sense of self through others. Did you like my selfie with Hobbes?

Sometimes though, our status does feel undermined. There is a felt difference between this kind of selfie-seeking admiration, and envy. Admiration requires a level of self-forgetfulness. When we purely admire another in their success, they fill our whole gaze. At its best, we cease to care about the selfie, the association at all, because our own struggles and triumphs fade from view, temporarily irrelevant, and we are able to be fully happy for another. This is surely one of those virtues which is straightforwardly pleasurable. Shared joy connects us.

However, other people's eminence or achievements, if they are too close to things that we feel define us, can be not enjoyable, but painful. We feel lowered and bitterly resentful. The resulting envy, Kierkegaard thinks, is 'concealed admiration'.

When the potential threat to our own sense of self, the fear of scarce resources and finite amounts of honour, creeps into our admiration, it curdles it. 'Admiration is happy self-surrender', Kierkegaard continues, but 'envy is unhappy self-assertion.'[8]

I have been to parties thrown by media outlets and think tanks and publishing houses. The haste with which conversation partners seek to extricate themselves from me when I've admitted to 'taking a break' or 'looking after my kids', brightly, holding eye contact, is sometimes funny, sometimes painful. Despite my optical lock, their gaze slides over my shoulder towards someone who is flavour of the month, standing nearby. They twitch to join the other people awkwardly hovering outside that circle, seeking a moment to break in with congratulations and make a connection, take a (usually) metaphorical selfie. On my best days it brings out an impish spirit that sets out to test who will stay and who will go, and on my worst I leave early and meet someone I love in the pub instead. I think the mischievousness is my attempt to change the rules of the game, to not let the memories of rejection rankle and fester. Sometimes they do anyway. Some people feel their whole lives have been defined by this lack of others' esteem; are embittered, like Iago, by a sense of being overlooked, even when and if they achieve apparent successes. I don't want to give away that power.

I have also had a few periods of feeling comparatively interesting in those settings, having something impressive to say. When I do find myself the winner in the status games, the potential object of envy, it's initially delicious. My ego stretches like a happy cat, purring. At my worst, I crave it – the dopamine hit of a viral post, the compliments on an outfit, sharing the news of a professional success. I've noticed it doesn't last though, that high. My own sense of satisfaction in a job well done does linger, but the acclaim? It leaves me not content but wired like a child after a birthday party, heading for a crash.

I'm increasingly convinced that, whether we are winners or losers in the status game (and almost all of us, if we live long enough, will be both), we are all being played.

I believe, of course, that part of the problem here is that we are looking for affirmation in the wrong place, hoping a human gaze can satisfy a need designed to be met by something else. There is also a less metaphysical reason neither of these states satisfy us deeply: status differentials are distancing. When I played the status game in school drama class, I was quickly drawn to people of a similar status, for a sense of safety. Those below me were pitiable and potentially infectious, those above hateful and smug. The warm glow of sameness, of us against the world, is maybe fine in moderation, but it also drives our tribalism, it's why we sort ourselves into social-economic slices. It also makes shared status a premise of the friendship in a way that I suspect can't help but subtly undermine it. It becomes conditional, a lurking vulnerability to status changes.

Status is one of the many things that makes it hard to really see each other, to properly connect. Moments of true human encounter are rare across strongly felt distinctions in status. Those we pity and those we envy are hard to see, while in the midst of those emotions, as fully human. If a good life is defined by relationships, then I want to resist this tendency too.

*

The framework of the seven deadly sins is useful because it helps me see the areas in which I am particularly prone to disconnection, and which I struggle less with. Writing this chapter has made me realise envy is lower down my list. I don't often feel envious of other people's achievements or possessions. I feel anxious about my status occasionally, at the aforementioned networking parties, but it's not a besetting problem. Does that make me sound like a sociopath? I've left it until now to admit in case it does. Self-deprecating confessions are a useful trust builder, and in this area my struggles are small potatoes. I fear it may be that I am not paying enough attention to those around me.

It may also be to do with a more practical, contextual reality. We know envy is most prevalent when people succeed in areas that are closely intertwined with our own identity. Perhaps I don't struggle much with it because the things I am trying to do with my life are quite unusual. I have no idea how to describe what my job is, for example, so there aren't really other people to directly compare myself to.

It is possibly unconsciously performative. Much of my desire to feel fully alive is related to a search for stability, a sense of self anchored somewhere beyond the volatile markets of social status. The people I most admire and seek to emulate at least give the impression of being confident, free from over-thinking and at home in their own skin. Focused more on what they are curious about and the world around them than their own performance of status. I've wanted that for myself, envied it, ironically.

Honestly though, I have always put my low-envy, relatively stable status tendencies down to an incident in my teens.

I must have been fifteen or sixteen years old. Taller than almost every adult in the room, with inconveniently large breasts, wide shoulders and a smattering of spots around my hairline. I wore a stretchy skirt from H&M in a green paisley print over the top of bootleg, heel-chewed jeans and a boho-chain belt. My main priority with clothes was covering what I felt was my too-rounded stomach. I saw it like an ugly carbuncle attached to my front that I sometimes fantasised about slicing off with a knife. So many hours spent sucking it in. I still do the posture now, when I'm tired and distracted and getting dressed or undressed, before I catch the thought and consciously interrupt it: standing sideways in front of the mirror, running my hand over the abdomen that has never been flat, wondering what I'd look like if it was. You're too old for this Liz, I think, fruitlessly. In my teens it was a band called All Saints whose image I longed to see reflected back at me. Belly button rings and crop tops and flat, brown stomachs. There were girls at school who did look like future girl-band members. Emily, Sam and Hannah, all under five foot five and captains of sports teams, their clustered heads from behind a paint sample card of caramels. I envied them their cuteness, their social ease, the way they didn't tower over the boys. If they were All Saints I was an overgrown version of Daria the bespectacled heroine of an MTV series popular at the time – a lanky, bookish presence on the edges of several friendship groups. Not as funny or cynical as Daria, obviously, I mainly kept my head down, pretended not to like poetry, and waited for my real life to start.

When I walked into the church hall on a misty autumn evening I had recently become a Christian. It was all still strange to me, this deep sense of another presence. A multi-generational group from the church I'd joined were gathering to be prayed for and taught by a group of visitors. It was the era of the 'Toronto Blessing', when middle-of-the-road Anglican churches up and down the UK were experiencing what was described as 'an out-pouring of the Holy Spirit', causing people to fall over and speak in other languages and receive healing for illnesses and injuries. Compared to my occasional brushes with an ailing and ageing Methodist Church, it was like the *Wizard of Oz* transition from black and white to technicolour. The visitors were going to help us experience 'more of the spirit', to speak 'in tongues' as the teenagers in the cowshed had done so casually. We would also learn to 'prophesy', which seemed to mean receiving pleasant but vague mental pictures for people while praying for them. I see a waterfall, it's [God]'s love pouring over you, I see a beautiful flower, you are as beautiful and valuable as a flower, that kind of thing.

I was naive, certainly, and suggestible as all teenagers are. The pleasant but vague pictures often moved me even while part of my brain was scoffing at them, and occasionally someone would say something eerily insightful or astute. Twenty years later, with all I've learned of how easy humans are to manipulate, how our voices and words and music can create impressions and change moods, I feel I should dismiss all of it. At another, later, time, and in another church, a pastor prayed for me while pushing hard on my forehead, offering a little help in being 'slain in the spirit', so I pushed back stubbornly, planting my size-eight feet, until he gave up and moved on to the next person. There were clearly charlatans at large. I would, now, be more sceptical. At the time, though, on that autumn evening, when two people stood softly beside me, and asked for permission to rest their hands on my shoulders and pray for me, I simply held my palms up, ready to receive. I remember nothing about the man, not his voice or height or facial features, but I remember his words and probably always will: 'You are fully accepted and approved of.' He prayed that I would know this truth, which he repeated over and over – 'You are fully accepted and approved of' while I lay down on the floor (lino this time) and let the words rewire my tender, insecure teenage brain.

As with my conversion, I felt different afterwards. I started having more fun, laughing more. I felt freer, and the mischievous, adventure-loving part of myself that up until then only my family really knew about came out more at school. I took myself less seriously. Apparently humility is not thinking less of yourself, but thinking of yourself less, and there was maybe a bit of that. Funny that being told I was approved of could make me humbler, but I think it did, at least temporarily, in that it meant I could stop worrying about it. James Baldwin said about sex and money that when you don't have enough you think about them all the time, but when you have enough you forget them.[9] I wonder if acceptance works the same way. I felt, quite suddenly, like I was enough, like my self was secure, so I could turn my attention to other things. Not unrelatedly, I became visible to boys my age for the first time, and not long after got my first boyfriend. Probably some of this was developmental, a shift in hormones, but I don't believe it all was.

It is entirely possible that I'm wrong to locate my security in this event. I had excellent parenting. My early search for a steady gaze was, I assume, successful. Attachment theory tells me that I am simply living the precious legacy of an extremely present, responsive parent. Securely attached people tend to feel more at home in their skin, to need less affirmation in order to feel valuable. My memory of that moment in my teens when I was told I was 'completely accepted and approved of' may have been emotional, but perhaps nothing really changed.

Or maybe the two things are connected. Some schools of therapy seek to provide an 'unconditional positive regard', a non-judgemental acceptance of their clients, as part of the healing process. The phrase comes closest to describing my encounters with [God]. I think I received it in my earliest childhood, from my parents, and I experience it again during these repeated ecstatic encounters with (what felt and feels like) divine love. My hunch is that, because I had been well parented, the news of a kind of cosmic parent who loved me unconditionally didn't sound so ludicrous. When I was told 'You are fully accepted and approved of,' my brain could accept it. Could risk believing it.

This isn't true of everyone. I hesitate to write about feeling well parented, securely attached. I'm realising how rare is the person who can say that, how smug and spoilt it might sound. How it might provoke, in fact, painful envy. Abusive or neglectful parents leave a life-long legacy. Even many loving parents cause completely unintended scars and wounds, never *despite their best efforts* communicate the worthiness their children need to hear. I feel ice-cold, some days, with the fear I am one of them, dashing into my kids' room late at night to whisper into their sleeping soft-shell ears, 'You are loved. You are loved. You are loved.'

I probably shouldn't overstate these effects, either of my parenting, or of the 'acceptance and approval' moment. Like everyone, I want to defend and define myself. I want the people I meet to have a certain bundle of half-conscious associations about me; in my case smart, warm and wise. And attractive, obviously, because I'm a woman and 'hot' as a legitimate goal was incepted into my brain by years of women's media. It sits, still, like a toad on a lobe of my mind. I've tried to euthanise it, to no avail.

Against the grain of some of these desires, my life has in many ways been downwardly mobile. I shot out of university into the BBC, but left a promising career there after five years to run a then tiny religion think tank. Having led it for ten years, I left without a plan and only a sense I needed to rest or risk burnout. Now, I am not sure what I am doing with my life. I keep failing to pursue the high-status, well-paying jobs recruiters occasionally call me about. When people ask me, 'So what are you up to now?' I can feel the social script glowing, the desire to tell them of a new and more impressive role, a cool project, and see them look admiring. Instead, I am trying to pursue a bundle of activities that feel vocationally important and hard to describe. I am practising hospitality in our tiny commune, helping with the church's poverty project, picking my kids up every day, after years of my husband being lead parent. I am writing this book because it feels like it needs writing, but I'm fully aware that only a handful of people might read it. I am learning to garden, often in the middle of a week day, and am teaching myself to rollerblade, just for the joy of it.

This season of focusing on hidden, relational and local things shouldn't feel like it takes courage to choose. Rollerblading is not exactly the Battle of the Somme. When you've spent fifteen years in the competitive fields of media, policy and academia though, choosing not to compete does take a certain weird bravery. But I want to do meaningful, lasting work, the work maybe only I can do. I want to be some use to the world, to the people around me. To do that, it felt important to drop out of the race for a bit, to actively practise caring less how I am perceived, to stop performing myself and start just being myself. To maybe even forget myself. And for that, I've found theology useful.

Secular, individualist, supposedly meritocratic cultures may leave many of us with an unstable sense of self, but religion is a counter-intuitive place to look for firmer foundations. The popular conception of particularly Roman Catholic Christianity is that it gives adherents an abiding sense of guilt, an overdeveloped awareness of every minor moral failure. The doctrine of original sin, after it's been through the distortions of cultural transmission, seems a recipe for self-loathing. Other subsets of Christianity can present the opposite problem – giving people a framework for their own superiority, from which (in direct contravention of Jesus' command) they can judge and finger point at others. In-group feeling is a powerful antidote against status anxiety, and religion as good an excuse as any to assuage a fear of worthlessness by joining a gang. Gangs of arrogant religious people may be the worst kind.

Despite this, my experience is that Christianity helps. Its story-logic paints humans as made to be in communion, not competition with each other. It both affirms my individuality and locates it in a web of relationships. Scripture allows me to claim that I am more than an invisible node in an indistinguishable mass of humanity. It affirms my particularity, makes it possible for me to believe myself to be seen and known, with a specific part only I can play, but it also humbles me. I can only begin to make sense as part of something bigger, an organ in a living body, a daughter in a family. It invites me into a story that I don't need to construct, in which I can both lose myself and find myself, and so reduces my tendency to strive.

You can read parts of the Bible as a sort of what-to-expect-when-you're-expecting care manual for owners of a self. When in possession of an unruly, fragile, longing soul with a hunger for affirmation, what to do. How to protect it from the all-too-pervasive shame so many of us feel, or avoid turning into an egomaniac.

Embedded in the complex library of genres that make up the Bible are some themes and concepts that I find enormously helpful. When I need to settle my status anxiety I remind myself that I am seen, that I am in some strange way an image of the divine and so equal with all human beings, to avoid idolatry and that I am, ultimately, beloved. I think you are too, and I wonder if these concepts are potentially accessible even for those who don't know what they think about the [God] stuff.

Equality

Comparative, ranked human value is a poisoned chalice, a nonsense game we all want to dissent from and yet continue to play. It's pragmatism, a way to get things done. You try getting a job, or completing a collaborative project, or finding a partner without indulging in some of the silent status-semaphore we all use. I'm worth your time, we signal. Look who I'm with. See my rosettes, my professional scout badges. Notice my medals, my brands, my broad shoulders, my wrinkle-free forehead. Deeper than that, in terror of the bottom we play in the hope we might come out towards the top.

It is also not that easy to make an honest intellectual case against endemic status rankings. It is not self-evident that we are equal. That is the whole problem. The reason we compare and compete and crave for status is that non-equality presents as an intuitive reality.

Larry Seidentop, the historian of democracy and liberalism, has argued: 'Christianity changed the ground of human identity . . . By emphasizing the moral equality of humans, quite apart from any social roles they might occupy, Christianity changed "the name of the game."'[10]

Most ancient societies, of which we know most about the Greeks and Romans, did not believe all humans were equal. It was the claim of the tiny nation of Israel, and later the steadily spreading Christians, that painfully, centuries-slowly, via myriad personal and institutional fuck-ups, embedded the idea that being a human was the baseline measure of value. It has become utterly foundational in many civilisations, to the extent that its origins are now largely invisible. The French and American Revolutions may have claimed it to be 'self-evident', the authors of the International Declaration of Human Rights may have excised the religious underpinnings, but they were building on a framework laid by medieval monastic scholars interpreting scripture. Seidentop concludes that 'The Christian conception of God became the means of creating the brotherhood of man . . . that both required and justified the equal moral standing of all humans.'[11]

Secular humanism, while it has made a land grab for the brand, is actually a cousin of Christian humanism, drawing deeply (and often wisely) from Christian anthropology. Even though there may be family squabbles, and some secular humanists could be accused of stealing the family silver, I'd want to say, like the Bishop in *Les Misérables* to Jean Valjean, take it.[12] Take it all. Spread it. Use it. I don't know how you ground a belief that all humans are equal outside of some kind of faith, but that's ok. The belief is so important and so liberating I just want more of it in the world.

Because what these ideas offer is an exit route from the

status game. Atheist philosopher Alain de Botton in his book *Status Anxiety* acknowledges that this audacious claim can act as a counter-narrative, even an antidote. The claim is not only are status games ultimately empty, pointless shadow posturing, but that if any hierarchy exists it is upside down.

There are many threads in Christian thought that underpin this commitment to human equality, but the key ones are the *imago dei* (the idea that all humans are made in and called to grow into the likeness of [God]), and the teachings around 'the first will be last'.

Imago Dei

In Christian tradition, humans are *imago dei*, made in the image of [God]. Not [God] ourselves, at least not in a straightforward way (though different bits of the Church argue over this) but related to and reflective of the divine. A spark from the great fire. Philosopher Terry Eagleton links this to the proscription in the Second Commandment against 'graven images', saying 'if there can be no humanly fashioned icons of Yahweh, it is because the only authentic image of him is humanity itself'.[13] Humans are icons, both in this strictly religious sense, and also in the sense we have adopted in computing – something that stands for and also links to something else. Though like the floppy disk for saving and the curvy handset for phone, the original semiotics are easily forgotten.

What the idea of *imago dei* means in practice is that when I feel myself perceived by Love, I think Love sees a family resemblance. Importantly, this applies to all humans, whatever we do or believe. We come from the womb as image bearers, and we go to our grave still sparking, still reflecting. Neither low status nor suffering nor physical or mental limitations can change that. Counter-intuitively, they might actually make the image clearer. Theological anthropology argues that this image-bearing is what makes us human, slightly different from, though deeply connected to, the rest of creation. This idea has its dangers of course (specifically in our posture to the natural world), but it also has its gifts. It undercuts our desire to be special, which is really a desire to be better than. When Dash in *The Incredibles* is told by his mother, 'Everyone is special, Dash' and replies 'Which is another way of saying no one is,' he is saying something profound. We have been taught to value ourselves in comparison, and the idea of the *imago dei* is an invitation to resist that. It is possible to be entirely loved, and entirely unremarkable in being so. When I sit with this thought, my ego feels abraded (a big part of me wants to be special, as in better than) but that eventually gives way to relief and a sense of deep connectedness.

The first shall be last

In the body of thought I am trying to learn from, if anyone has more worth, dignity and status it is the opposite of who we might expect. Scripture claims that 'the first shall be last'. Blessed are the poor, the meek, the persecuted. 'God has chosen those who are poor in the world to be rich in faith and heirs of the kingdom.' In the story of the sheep and the goats, we are told that those who feed the hungry, clothe the naked, visit the prisoner and welcome the wanderer are doing it for Jesus himself, and those who fail to are directly rejecting him.[14] Children, migrants, widows, orphans, the diseased and limited, the rejected and minoritised, in the biblical narrative these are the jewels in the crown of humanity. The logic is unclear, except a sense that a pursuit and possession of status somehow blinds us from seeing reality, while vulnerability keeps us close to wisdom, close to Love.

Many churches and especially monastic orders have taken this and codified it as 'a bias to the poor', their motivation for billions of hours of poverty alleviation and advocacy work.

This framework for seeing dignity and value in the people most often crushed at the bottom of the status pile is maybe why in many countries those groups are over-represented in churches. The early church was seen as a 'slave religion', spreading fast through the untouchables of the day. It might not be that those with low status are more credulous and irrational, but that they find in church what the world denies them: honour, value and affirmation. Jesus aligns himself with them. Marx's famous quote reads differently in its full context: 'Religion is the sigh of the oppressed creature, the heart of a heartless world, and the soul of soulless conditions. It is the opium of the people.'[15] He might have thought it a poor consolation prize for justice (the Bible is also harsh on those who oppress the poor) but he acknowledged the source of comfort. Nietzsche wrote most perceptively about this facet of Christianity, despising its centring of those he saw as weak, cowardly and sickly, stealing the honour of the strong.

Jesus himself was, of course, many of the things Nietzsche despised – poor, powerless, the victim of a brutal empire. Black theologians especially have claimed the suffering body of Christ on the cross as their own, finding in these stories a [God] who stands in solidarity with them. Theologian

Mary Shawn Copeland says that 'beauty', rather than being about hotness or status, 'is living up to and living out the love and summons of creation in all our particularity and specificity as [God]'s human creatures made in [God]'s own image and likeness.'[16] Because she, particularly and specifically as a Black woman, a descendant of the enslaved Black women who were whipped and lynched, is made in the image of a [God] also whipped and lynched, she can claim her own beauty from those who would seek to deny it.

It bears repeating, because this idea has been so woven into our culture that we nod along with it, and yet it still cuts radically across how most of our social structures are set up. It shows up elsewhere, yes, but historian Tom Holland has argued that the original source is Judaism and Christianity.[17] Whether or not it's a unique claim, it's a powerful and distinctive one: that every human life is already of value. That you, I, the homeless person camped outside little Sainsbury's, the weary refugee, the spotty fat kid at school, are already immeasurably beautiful, unchangeably loved, pulsing with dignity. Human value is not something we can ever earn, and our attempts to do so are laughable and actively corrosive. That rather than legitimising an existence, wealth, power and fame may actually work against our ability to really live, and steal our freedom.

I worry our culture is moving further away from this anchor. In recent years we have seen an increasingly visible transhumanist philosophy, not least among the libertarian tech bros who wield such disproportionate financial and cultural power. Transhumanism argues that humans can evolve past our current psychical and mental limitations with the help of technology. At worst, it carries with it an implicit hierarchy of the human. Strength and intelligence are valued, everything else is not. I can hear troubling echoes of Nietzsche, whose ideas have fuelled inhumane and authoritarian regimes. These stories are poison to our ability to treat each other with dignity. We absolutely need to believe that the desperate refugee, the mentally disabled child, the homeless person, those who have nothing to offer at the altar of productivity and power, are dignified, valuable and unutterably precious.

Idolatry and worship

Christianity doesn't just offer me alternative frames for thinking about my value, it offers a warning against playing status games. It implies that seeking my worth in others is idolatry, and actively dangerous. Idolatry means worshipping things not worthy of our worship. One reading of the Hebrew Bible is that [God] is a jealous and petty lover, demanding our worship out of their own unstable sense of self. It is possible to assemble an argument for that. I think a better, truer read is that [God] warns against idolatry because [God] knows it will harm us.

You possibly don't think of yourself as someone who worships. It might sound like an insult. It does sound a bit abject and degrading, at odds with our view of ourselves as post-Enlightenment creatures who have thrown off the shackles of superstition. Worship is not just singing praises like some dead-eyed cult member though. If we think of worship as the act of focusing on and seeking to move towards something (one translation of the Greek word for worship is 'to come towards, to kiss'), we all end up doing it. It is a cousin of attention. As novelist and essayist David Foster Wallace writes: 'In the day-to-day trenches of adult life, there is actually no such thing as atheism. There is no such thing as not worshipping. Everybody worships. The only choice we get is what to worship.' He goes on, unexpectedly, to argue that:

> the compelling reason for maybe choosing some sort of god or spiritual-type thing to worship – be it JC or Allah, be it YHWH or the Wiccan Mother Goddess, or the Four Noble Truths, or some inviolable set of ethical principles – is that pretty much anything else you worship will eat you alive. If you worship money and things, if they are where you tap real meaning in life, then you will never have enough, never feel you have enough. It's the truth. Worship your body and beauty and sexual allure and you will always feel ugly. And when time and age start showing, you will die a million deaths before they finally grieve you.[18]

We will come back to some of these other idols elsewhere, but for now you can see how worshipping, or over-focusing on, the opinions of other people sets us up for misery. Wallace's typically vivid phrase 'eat you alive' echoes the Hebrew Bible's warnings that a person who worships idols 'feeds on ashes; a deluded heart misleads him'.[19] Wallace, and scripture, warn that whatever we focus our attention on and seek to move towards will shape us – we will eventually look like our idols. We are formed by what we rest our attention on, what we consciously or unconsciously move towards, so we should probably make sure it's something or someone we really want to end up like.

Belovedness

I summarise a cluster of poetic and overlapping theological concepts to myself with the phrase 'belovedness'. If I ever get another tattoo after a disastrous experiment in my teens, it might be 'beloved'. I am beloved, and so is every person I meet. [God] is love, the Bible claims. [God] loves us first, and our human loves flow from that. If we love one another, the divine is somehow at work within us. And love does not suffer from status anxiety.

If you have ever attended a church wedding you will probably have heard 1 Corinthians 13. It's so familiar that the de dum de dum rhythms of nervous wedding-guest Bible-readers bob past our consciousness, as much part of the furniture as the pastel suits on the mothers of the bride or the strictures on where confetti is allowed. It's a sleeper cell of a text though, a life-key hidden in plain sight. It defines love as trenchantly non-competitive. It says, explicitly, that Love does not envy. It does not boast. It is not self-seeking. It is not bitter or resentful. If sin is what distances and disconnects us, Love is what restores. I read Love in these verses both as an entirely legitimate synonym for [God]and an invitation into the kind of person I want to become: a steadied, free, resilient self, opting out of the status game because I know myself to be loved.

In a brutally honest and moving essay on her writerly envy of her partner Jonathan Franzen, Kathryn Chetkovich asks, 'What are we here for, others or ourselves? Grandiose and overstated as it sounds, doesn't it come down to that?'[20] She senses in her own envy this toxic choice, between grounding herself in the evaluations of others, or seeking (I would say fruitlessly) to create and judge herself. Theology challenges the premise of the question by introducing a third option. We are here neither, primarily, for ourselves or for others, but because Love wanted us here.

Being seen

I once heard a singer called Jon Guerra, who has helped score Terrence Malick movies as well as writing devotional songs, describe the experience of his conversion. It was while listening to music and he said, very simply, that he had a sudden and undeniable sense of being perceived. I love how spacious that concept of perception is, how it holds both the sensory and intellectual. It implies a resting of steady attention combined with deep understanding. US Poet Laureate Ada Limón in her poem 'Sanctuary' speaks of her need to be 'made whole/by being not a witness/but witnessed.'[21]

Those first conscious moments searching for a gaze, scanning for the attentive eyes of a parent, mirror our search for the gaze of others throughout life. Receiving attention and affirmation from the people around me is a lovely thing, but making it the ground for my sense of self is dangerous. I can find myself playing roles in their stories, as well as they in mine, and their own search for a stable identity colours our relationship. In our recent increase in identitarian politics, which has brought a lot of important awareness and progress, you sometimes see this playing out. The temptation is to project simplistic fixed identities onto others as waymarkers for navigating our own.

Rowan Williams expresses more eloquently (as usual) what I feel, that grounding my sense of self as a seen, known and loved creature is a relief. It's a way out of the 'fearful and cautious negotiation of my identity' because 'God alone is beyond the precarious exchanges of creatures who need affirmation. With God alone I am dealing with what does not need to construct or negotiate an identity, what is free to be itself without the process of struggle.'[22] This gaze, being seen in this way, feels hugely liberating.

When I'm wrestling with status anxiety, fearful that in attempting to follow my vocation my career has become downwardly mobile, viewing my silver hairs and rapid-onset wrinkles as a problem, not a glory, I want to feel seen. I want to know that I'm not going to disappear if I'm neither successful nor hot, if no one, in the end, reads this book. I need to know that my frustrations and longings, and even my petty failures and spectacular fuck-ups, are seen, that I am known, that I am held in a gaze that is not panicked or surprised, but steady and kind. I still want that unconditional positive regard. Maybe I'm too childlike, and real adults grow out of this. Maybe it's another one of those things about atheism that I'm just not robust enough for, not clever or free or strong enough to tolerate being unseen. But I don't want to grow out of it. I'm very happy singing, as the old hymn goes, 'His eye is on the sparrow, and he watches over me.'

'Very well for you Elizabeth,' you might say. 'Sounds nice to feel seen by your sky fairy, but what about us?' I'm sharing these foundational concepts with you partly to help you understand the deep emotional appeal of Christianity, the solid psychological ballast it has given me. However, part of me hopes you can use these concepts too. I believe they are also true for you, no matter if you find the concept of [God] such laughable, self-evident nonsense that you are reading this as a noble anthropological safari, or if you are currently holding the possibility just outside your vision, not letting your gaze stray in case you see empty space, or are blinded.

I don't know if it's possible to move from envy to feeling seen, equal and beloved without knowing what you think about [God], but I think it might be possible to practise what Simone Weil calls 'experimental certainty'.[23] To try this posture on for size and see if it fits you better than you expect. I have friends who are recovering addicts, who tell me that this kind of 'experimental certainty' is often necessary in recovery. Surrendering to the awkwardness of 'God, however you understand them' as an intrinsic and unavoidable part of the twelve-step process. Just try it, new joiners are told. You don't need to get your intellectual ducks in a row, or even really believe. Just behave as if you do. Pick something beyond you and see if it will take your weight. Because you can't do this alone.

Maybe what I'm suggesting is adjacent to affirmations, popular since the self-esteem movement of the sixties. Affirmations acknowledge that resting our sense of worth on the opinions of other people is a trap. Honour and esteem are addictive drugs, and like lab rats we can spend our lives performing for another treat, or broken by the lack of them. The move to locate our worth within ourselves makes intuitive sense: I love myself, I am brilliant, I am beautiful. As a way of counteracting the often poisonous scripts with which we speak to ourselves, this seems all for the good. A bit of self-compassion can be enormously helpful. The affirmation of 'I am enough, I am loved' is like an incantation, a spell to hold back the dark tide of judgement. The conditions for believing these things, however, are hostile. The trouble is that, when we already fear our value is low, making ourselves an arbiter of our own value is a difficult cognitive trick to pull off. If I don't think I'm enough to start with, why should my own judgement mean anything? Monk Sebastian Moore in his book *The Inner Loneliness* argues that humans are such inescapably social creatures that the task is impossible – that identity itself is a relational concept. Even when we try to contemplate ourselves we do it by projecting the standpoint of another, perhaps someone imaginary but more likely a hybrid of all the people whose opinion we care about.[24] I can only judge myself on the bases other people have given me, the knowledge of myself others reflect back.

In any case, many studies indicate that decades of affirmations-based interventions to help raise self-esteem have done little good, and may even have done harm in increasing levels of narcissism and decreasing compassion.[25] We either don't trust our own judgement, or trust it too much and become monsters.

What I'm suggesting instead is that it might be possible to affirm something different – I am seen by something beyond myself. Whatever this beyond is, it calls me equal with all human beings, and they equal with me. I am loved. I don't know if this feels different, or even possible, because my certainty isn't experimental. It's not certainty either, really, just a reasonably peaceful hunch. I do know that I find it psychologically helpful to locate my worth outside of myself because I am inescapably relational. I want *someone else* to reassure that raw fragile part of my heart that feels unworthy that I am enough. Given other people are fickle, and rarely unconditional in their appraisal, I prefer to leave that judgement up to [God].

Some of my friends say their conception of [God] is close to this, the voice inside them, their deepest self, which says: this thing is self-evident, you are enough. Others feel perceived by The Universe. Maybe a deep divine self, or our intuition, will suffice. It's possible you can find the unconditional positive regard in the natural world – that is where Ada Limón goes with her desire to be not just 'a witness/but witnessed'. Wherever you find it, an anchor for a sense of self that is not reliant on the fashions of the moment, marital status or financial stability, professional success or public profile seems essential to sanity. To resisting the corrosive sting of envy that separates us. To becoming fully alive.

GLUTTONY: FROM NUMBING TO ECSTASY

If envy is the most socially shameful sin, gluttony has got to come in second. We're still fatphobic as a society, despite the gains of the body positivity movement, so those who visibly overeat are usually characterised as stupid and bullying or timid and deferential. I've always had a soft spot for gluttony though. My associations are with bon viveurs, the people who grab life's pleasures with two hands. Keith Floyd, the eighties television chef who always had a huge glass of wine in his hand. Nigella Lawson, picking from the fridge in a silky robe, clearly much more fun to be around than a size eight clean-eating guru. It looks adjacent to being fully alive, probably because it can be. Just as anger is not the same thing as wrath, I think eating and drinking, even a lot, can be done in deeply connected, even playful ways, remaining present to our bodies, emotions and other people. Feasting and celebration are part of the church calendar, the rhythm of any good Rule of Life. Life-long abstemiousness sounds like death.

I have, however, another model of what gluttony might mean.

My other grandmother, who I called Nanny, was a cockney. She was born within the sound of Bow bells, one of the eight children of an East End policeman. In the war she was evacuated to the countryside and stayed, becoming a nurse and then a ward matron. She raised four children of her own, doing her best on very little money (my grandad was a market gardener), taught her kids to love books, took them camping, held up the sky.

By the time I knew her all that had retreated. On our visits she stayed wedged into a brown velour armchair, draped in a polyester kaftan the size of a small tent. She chain-smoked shiny purple packets of Silk Cut with endless pots of teak-dark tea. She always seemed to be eating or brushing crumbs from the folds of her kaftan onto the floor for the dogs. Soaps played loudly on a loop, and she shouted at my brother and me if we walked in front of the television or spoke above a whisper.

I learned later about epigenetics and generational patterns in addiction, about how the children (particularly daughters) of alcoholics are 50 per cent more likely to be obese, as well as more prone to addiction and depression.[1] My great-grandfather, that East End bobby, was an alcoholic who drank his wages, leaving his family always short of food. It marked Nanny's whole life, that empty belly, forging an association between food and love, food and comfort that never left her.

It never left my mother either, nor her siblings. Nanny didn't grow up into an alcoholic – I only ever saw her drink one Snowball at Christmas – but her poison was food and fags. She loved herself and loved her kids with food, making sure her family would never go hungry as she had. In my memory her beige Formica kitchen sides were always piled high with primary coloured, plastic-wrapped cakes, biscuits and crisps. My mum remembers waking up distressed in the night, and Nanny, rather than asking what was wrong, telling her to think about (turn her attention towards, meditate on) her favourite party food. All of Nanny's daughters became obese.

Nanny developed diabetes in her fifties. She would prick her finger to take her bloods, then hitch her kaftan to reveal legs entangled with violet and teal varicose veins. Inject insulin directly into the thigh, chase with a garibaldi. I was transfixed by the ritual, the little black machine that beeped out the reading, the casual jab of a woman who'd given injections all her life as a nurse. When I was in my early teens she got cancer, but ignored doctors' advice to quit smoking. She loved her cigarettes more than her husband or her children, she told my mum when she was tearfully begged to stop. The chemo would make her sleepy, and, as she always had a fag in her hand and dressed entirely in flammable fabrics, there were several brushes with premature cremation. I remember taking part in a family production line making roll-up cigarettes for her, because they go out quicker than the shop-bought ones. At the end, the velour chair was surrounded by bowls and saucepans of water so whoever was passing could douse the fire quickly when she nodded off, leaving her steaming and swearing.

Nanny wasn't a bon viveur, she was absent. She wasn't savouring life's pleasures but self-medicating. For her generation then, and class even now, therapy was not really an option. She had no one to teach her to be present with her emotions, no easy access to mindfulness. She stuffed her traumas down with gammon and chips and shop-bought Battenberg, and who can blame her? Food is the cheapest drug. It works, at least in the short term, to overwrite hard feelings. It disconnected her though. The fags and the food and the telly built an impregnable wall around her, made it hard for others to reach her. I don't think, now, that I ever really met her, and I grieve it.

I have come to believe that gluttony is on the same spectrum, in the same family as addiction. My great-grandfather's alcoholism – and, most likely, the addictions of the generations that came before him – are in my DNA as well as in Nanny's. The curses roll down the generations until someone gets aware enough, awake enough to stop them.

My mum stood in that gap. She acted as a bulwark against the worst of the harms, giving us other methods of comfort, weakening the link between food and love for her children in a way she hasn't ever quite managed for herself.

I'll never forget getting caught stealing food. I was sitting on the toilet behind the brown MDF slab of door with the round gilt handle that all housing estates built in the seventies seemed to have. The loo seat was cool on my thighs as I shoved contraband prawn cocktail crisps into my mouth. The hot shame as Mum opened the door acted like a photographic developer on memory. I'd been sucking the neon pink shards so she couldn't hear me crunch, so I needed to swallow the whole soggy mass before I could reply to her question: 'What are you doing?' I was seeking to numb out after a horrible day at school, was the answer, wanting the salty blankness of a full mouth and full stomach. I don't remember what I actually said, but I remember her response – scared, initially, at seeing her own struggles reflected so clearly back – then compassionate and calm. You don't need to hide, sweetheart, she said. You don't need to steal food. You probably just need a cuddle.

I occasionally still eat dysfunctionally. After a very stressful day I might find myself cramming crisps into my mouth like it's a compactor, revelling in the sensation of vinegary spikes pressing outward against my cheeks, chasing that feeling of fullness to the bottom of the bag. More often it's spending too much time imagining the frosty bottle of white wine waiting in the fridge, the first cherry-dark mouthful of red. I have to watch my alcohol intake closely.

Realistically, aside from giving me a stubborn spare tyre, neither of these habits is on a scale to make them especially harmful to my health. The bigger danger to my fully aliveness is when I actively use them to disconnect – from myself and my feelings, from the moment I am in, and often, as a result, from the people around me. I become, like Nanny, functionally absent.

Addiction

I've come to believe that gluttony is not the same thing as over-indulgence. It's subtler than that. My definition is about numbing and distraction, when I'm seeking to use food or drink to escape the full experience of my life. I'm intrigued by the phrase 'alcohol abuse'. It's a bit out of fashion now (Alcohol Use Disorder has replaced it) but we've all heard the term, the shorthand. Are you using or abusing alcohol, using or abusing food? It's a strange phrase because we don't generally think of inanimate objects as victims of abuse. It's not the gin or the ice cream that gets hurt when I misuse them, it's me. My liver, my microbiome. But the ordering of the phrase helps me understand gluttony better. It is possible to eat and drink healthily, and that most often looks like receiving these things as a gift. I can consume carrots and kombucha or Sauvignon Blanc and Kettle Chips with attention, savouring the textures and the smells, and I do feel fully alive. When it's unhealthy I am instead deliberately *not* paying attention or taking time. I cram and chug in search, not of the substance itself, but the numbed-out feeling it can give me. What I want is escape. I'm intent on disconnection from myself. If an inanimate object *could* be abused, it would surely be in the same way as the rest of us – by being treated as a means to an end, not an end in itself, worthy of attention. I don't think I can hurt the feelings of food and booze, but it does now seem sort of disrespectful to use them mindlessly.

Neuroscience helps me understand what I am seeking when I am in binge mode. The dopamine system should orientate us to the things that actually make us feel fully alive, through reward prediction. Explicitly addictive substances like alcohol, cannabis, tobacco and cocaine hijack and amplify this reward system, while suppressing the part that learns how poor a solution for the problem of emotional pain they really are. While our more socially acceptable addictions might not be as powerful in their hijacking of our neurobiology as drugs, everything from disordered eating to gambling to social media can, and indeed is often designed to, have the same learning-resistant effect. I do the same thing again and again expecting a different result. Maybe this time my crisp binge/hours of doomscrolling/unnecessary online shopping will actually make me feel better.

I am absurdly intolerant of uncomfortable feelings. My low-level addictive behaviours are as often a response to boredom, or the anxiety that precedes writing a tricky email, as they are a way to escape distress. I go looking for a little treat, something to jolt me forwards through my day. Many of those in recovery speak about the process revealing how addictive our wider societies are. Almost all of us, not just the alcoholics or heroin addicts, are repeatedly indulging in behaviours that promise but do not deliver peace and wholeness. We use Instagram or exercise or work as a way to break up the dutiful trudge of achievement and consumption and an underlying fear of meaninglessness. Henry David Thoreau went to live alone in the woods to escape the 'lives of quiet desperation' he saw around him.[2] I think that is probably an overstatement, but a society that tells us our whole purpose is to be successful, sexually attractive and rich is one in which seeking small pleasures to fill the meaning gap makes complete sense.

Because it can also be the longing for more depth, more intensity that drives us to the fridge, bottle or needle. In their beautiful book *Faith, Hope and Carnage*, Nick Cave and Sean O'Hagan reflect on how Cave's heroin addiction came from the same place that is now drawing him towards Christianity: 'they were attempts to remedy . . . a kind of emptiness, I guess, and a hunger'. Sean asks 'a *hunger for what?*'; and Cave answers 'More.'[3] 'More' is also the phrase William James, the early psychologist of religious experiences, uses to speak about what spiritual impulses are orientated to. A slew of recovering addicts including Matthew Perry and Martin Sheen have spoken about their addictions as misdirected quests for transcendence.[4]

While most of us would acknowledge that addictive behaviours don't, ultimately, help us live fully and freely, it's complex. Amy Liptrott, in her memoir of recovery from alcoholism, echoes Cave, saying how drinking *did* made her feel more 'alive', chasing a 'vision for how people could relate more openly, wanting to reach the edges and taste the extremes'.[5] Booze helped confirm her suspicion that there was more to life, but could not get her to that depth in any lasting way.

Because of the ability of dopamine-hacking substances to

expand our horizons, Lewis Hyde in his essay 'Alcohol and Poetry' calls drugs and booze 'spirit guides', in that they can open up new horizons of experience; show, in a crude way 'the possibility of a different life'. They are not actually 'agents of maturation' but make a demand: 'find the path where you can have this experience without the help'.[6] This was certainly how psychedelic drugs were used historically, as sources of insight and connection to the 'more' that needed to be accompanied by wise guides and a rigorous spiritual path. The current renewed interest among many, including many of my friends, in psychedelics as a route to psychological healing and a deeper experience of life reflects this, I think, though I worry that the rigour and long-term aftercare is often missing.

This deeply felt need for 'more' is maybe why addicts in long-term recovery are almost always the most interesting people to meet. I am drawn to them like a magnet, childishly jealous of their community, their entry into the anonymous, no-nonsense twelve-step fraternity. What I see in recovering addicts is people who have felt the same pull I do – to experience life as deeply and fully as possible – who have now committed themselves to surrender, self-scepticism, humility and growth in a way that can't help but make you wiser. The combination is compelling.

The prescription the recovery movement gives for gluttony, drunkenness and all the addictive behaviours we use to take the edges off our day is sobriety. I know the word is beloved in the movement, has expansive and life-giving definitions, but I was for a long time mildly repelled by it. A life of sobriety can't help but be associated in my mind with grey suits and spreadsheets and an utter lack of adventure.

Granted, in the moment of craving, when the pain of being

alive is acute, when I'm anxious or depressed or angry, I probably do need sobriety. I do need to screw up my courage and remain present to the feeling, to acknowledge these hard emotions as part of life rather than stuffing them down. I need to notice what is going on, accept it and thereby let it pass. I find the Psalms immensely helpful for this. They are a book of the Bible, an ancient collection of Hebrew poetry and songs that display the whole complex range of human emotion – rage, desolation, envy, grief, fear, horror, existential angst, hope and joy. The Church has always turned to them as emotion-processing technology, a way of externalising and therefore taming what we experience. Laura Fabrycky says that the Psalms help us 'practice our feelings; through them, we find our humanity acknowledged, alongside the humanity of others.'[7] I find the reflection of my own emotional storm reflected in writing from three millennia ago curiously soothing – I'm reminded that humans have always struggled and wept and raged. The Psalmist didn't have the option of back-to-back Netflix romcoms as anaesthesia, they created art instead. It helps me. I reconciled myself to the concept of sobriety because when I allow myself to feel my feelings, rather than running from them, there *is* more fullness, a sense of life having a wider waveform of highs and lows. I should have known the recovery people would be right. When I manage to resist my gluttonous instincts, it is better, though wilder and scarier, than numbed-out escape. I feel connected to myself, and more able to connect to others.

However, sobriety alone isn't enough to keep my gluttony in check. I find when my life has enough awe, enough wonder and ecstasy in it, the itch to binge on something strikes less often and less acutely.

This is why AA itself is so spiritually grounded. Some

addicts resist it for just this reason and there have been attempts to create atheist alternatives. However, many credit the 'God (however you understand them)' bit with its effectiveness, because the depth addicts chase in their abusing needs replacing. Carl Jung, who along with the Christian organisation the Oxford Group was a major influence on the early recovery movement, wrote in a letter to a friend that a

> craving for alcohol was the equivalent, on a low level, of the spiritual thirst of our being for wholeness, expressed in medieval language: the union with God . . . You see, "alcohol" in Latin is "spiritus" and you use the same word for the highest religious experience as well as for the most depraving poison. The helpful formula therefore is: spiritus contra spiritum.[8]

Spiritus contra spiritum. Jia Tolentino, who is an essayist and staff writer at the *New Yorker*, wrote 'I have always found religion and drugs appealing for similar reasons.'[9] When I am tempted to self-medicate, what I really need is self-transcendence. My guess is we all need more of this. Aldous Huxley, who went on to become a sort of multi-religious mystic, had a breakdown in the 1930s caused by a sense of the meaninglessness of a materialist universe. He argued decades before Abraham Maslow codified it at the top of his pyramid that humans have a 'basic need for self-transcendence'.[10] My self too often feels claustrophobic, petty, without perspective. I spent nearly an hour yesterday researching retinol serums because I was finding the thought of writing terrifying, which is fine, but not a route to existential satisfaction.

Ecstatic experiences

We use all kinds of phrases for what I'm getting at, these experiences of escaping our own internal, self-reflective chatter and feeling connected with something beyond us. Iris Murdoch speaks of the moment that the 'anxious . . . self-preoccupied, often falsifying veil which partially conceals our world' drops away and we can really see.[11] Susan Sontag uses the phrase 'exalted self-transcending moments' and Cole Arthur Riley uses 'wonder', which 'requires a person not to forget themselves but to feel themselves so acutely that their connectedness to every created thing comes into focus. . .'[12] Others call it flow or ego-loss.

Philosopher Jules Evans in *The Art of Losing Control* argues that Western societies are both the historical and geographic exception in having so few 'baked in' moments of shared ritual.[13] These opportunities for 'collective effervescence", as sociologist Émile Durkheim called them, are normal in 90 per cent of cultures but largely missing in mine. In our disenchanted age, we are not taught what to do with our urge for awe, so we either bury it or attempt to sate it in unhealthy ways. We work, then we collapse and passively consume leisure content, then we work again. Evans' thesis is that the lack of opportunities for ecstasy and awe is driving dissatisfaction and even mental health crises, because without these moments humans get 'bored, exhausted and depressed.'[14] Durkheim warned that societies with no collective effervescence, no unselfing, would see a spike in suicide.

There is a stigma around ecstasy though. Fourth generation atheist and political activist Barbara Ehrenreich in her late-life book *Living with a Wild God* confesses what clearly feels to her like a deep and shameful secret: she has had ecstatic metaphysical experiences, a sense of encounter with something beyond.[15] She doesn't know how to explain them logically and materially and couldn't admit them to anyone for most of her life. Jules Evans put some of this shame down to the post-Enlightenment rationalist turn, and a lot down to the lingering stigma of the 1960s, when a search for self-transcendence often ended in narcissism, dysfunctional utopianism and worse.

Evans ultimately argues that we need to shed both these negative associations with ecstasy, because these experiences can be 'healing, inspiring and socially connecting'.[16] He concludes that awe and ecstasy help us find a sense of meaning that is central for our wellbeing, and can even bring comfort in the face of death.

This makes sense to me. When I'm deep in the disconnection of gluttony, what I need is to reconnect with myself and my feelings in sobriety, but also to audit how much transcendence there is in my life. The main place I get this is church.

One of my favourite verses in the Bible, beloved of youth group hedonists everywhere, is 'Do not get drunk on wine, but instead get drunk on the Holy Spirit.' Sadly, when I went back and looked at the verse, it seems I had paraphrased it to myself my whole life, because most translations read instead 'Do not get drunk on wine, instead *be filled* with the Holy Spirit.' I don't think my remembered interpretation is too heretical, however, given that the followers of Jesus in the New Testament are mistaken for being drunk, and elsewhere St Paul warns against worship getting too wild in case visitors got the wrong idea. Snore-inducing hymns in dusty pews this was not.

I am what is sometimes called a 'charismatic Christian'. It doesn't just mean I'm charming (though I am), but instead is a subset of the Church. It's very close to Pentecostalism, which you are more likely to have heard of. Both charismatics and Pentecostals trace our origins to the Pentecost story in the Bible, when the disciples gathered after Jesus had been killed, rose from the dead and ascended into heaven. This was already quite a lot of weird happenings to process, but the text tells us that they then 'received the Holy Spirit'[17]. In practice this meant they experienced an indoor hurricane and tiny fires breaking out on their heads. Pretty ecstatic-sounding, right? There are more mystical and trippy bits of scripture than you might expect if you've never read it. Lots of denominations and churches don't know what to do with them, but charismatics like me believe that the things Jesus' first disciples experienced (healing, prophecy, speaking in tongues, even the wind) can still happen now. Charismatic comes from the Greek 'charisma', meaning gift, because these things are thought of as gifts of the Holy Spirit. Some non-charismatic Christians believe in them in theory but they are not really part of their practice, and some actively oppose them, arguing that this sort of hippie nonsense died out long ago. They think those who do these things are just play-acting. A non-theological definition of charismatic, then, would be that I am even more of a weirdo than you may have already thought. I go to church, not just for the chance to be part of a community, pray, sing with others or hear an uplifting talk, but to speak in tongues, dance around and still sometimes fall on the floor.

The unusualness of this was brought home to me once at the hospital. My dodgy joints were taking me on a dreary carousel of doctors and inconclusive diagnoses. While my third specialist was ruling out MS I was sent for a nerve conduction test. I sat in a black vinyl chair on the fifth floor of King's College Hospital while a technician placed electrodes on the ends of my fingers. He explained that small electrical impulses would help measure the speed and strength of the nerve signal and help diagnose neurological damage. 'Just a tiny shock,' he said. 'If all is well you will give a small twitch.'

Instead, my hand jumped high into the air, followed by my forearm, then upper arm and both shoulders in turn in an overly dramatic Mexican wave. I narrowly avoided cuffing him in the face. 'Interesting,' he said, looking startled. 'Perhaps you're nervous. Try and breathe deeply and relax.' I hadn't felt nervous, but did a bit now. Clearly this wasn't normal. We repeated the test several times, with exactly the same results. He transferred the electrodes to the other hand and the wave of flailing limbs ran in the opposite direction. 'Interesting,' he said again, making notes. 'Has this happened before?'

I had to admit that it had. Regularly. Many, though not all Sundays, while standing in church with my hands upturned. Since I became a Christian in that concrete-floored cowshed, prayer has often been accompanied by these kinds of physical jerks. Sometimes my hands shake, sometimes I need to lie on the floor and bask, I often feel like I'm flying or have an uncontrollable fit of the giggles, but the most common response is this exaggerated, whole-upper-body dance move. It also sometimes happens when I'm listening to someone say something that feels deeply true or significant. I have had people assume I am displaying the physical tics associated with Tourette's Syndrome.

I'm not alone. A group of friends I know who used to pray

together like this a lot got to know each person's usual response so accurately they could do instantly recognisable and very funny impressions of each other. Ask any charismatic Christian who would say they 'experience the Holy Spirit' (the language here is imperfect, but that's the colloquialism) and they will tell you that it often manifests in the same way. For me, it feels like my body is predisposed to dance around in response to [God]'s presence (again, this is theologically complex but I won't bore you with it). It was surprising to discover it reacted the exact same way to electric shocks.

As I explained this, the startled impression intensified. King's is close to Peckham, full of Pentecostal African diaspora churches called things like 'Mountain of Fire and Miracles!' and 'Throne of Healing!' I surely can't have been the first charismatic Christian he'd treated, but physical manifestations of the Holy Spirit possibly hadn't come up in diagnostic conversations before.

'Should I be worried?' I asked, wondering what this all meant for my nerve pain and useless wrists. 'No, I don't think so,' he said, 'the thing we're checking for is too little response. Yours are. . . not that.'

I'm not making an argument that the Holy Spirit is some kind of cosmic electricity, though sometimes it feels like that. I'm not really making an argument at all. I know it sounds aesthetically jarring and deeply unBritish, that you'd likely take me more seriously if I was a cathedral lurker whose religiosity was highbrow and restrained. Jules Evans recounts how sceptics (including other Christians) have tended to sneer at outbreaks of charismatic 'enthusiasm' (from the Greek *en theos*, filled with God) as 'a regression to primitive irrationalism', 'common among women, the working class, ethnic minorities [because] these groups were naturally more unstable, emotional and credulous'.[18] I might get those last three words on a T-shirt. Cultural status in our Western intellectual milieu accrues to the critic, the distanced analyst, the detached and ironic academic. It doesn't accrue to me and my Afro-Caribbean friends in their sixties, waving flags at the back of church in Peckham and sobbing out our sorrows on the feet of Jesus.

I increasingly don't care about their cultural status, but I do still doubt my charismatic experiences, argue with myself over them. I'm sure there is a big dollop of habit and conditioning in there – stirring music and crowd dynamics etc – and maybe something unconsciously performative, but it also happens when I'm alone in our converted garage-chapel or, it seems, when you run a current through me. I don't know how to make sense of it, but it's been happening for long enough that I've learned to just trust and enjoy it. And I really, really do.

The connection between ecstatic experiences and religions themselves is a much debated one. Some people see them as polar opposites – if their experience of religious practice has been very intellectual, driven by having right beliefs, or morality led, focused on right behaviour, the idea that religion might be connected to intense experiences makes little sense.

There is a counter argument though. Abraham Maslow placed mystic experiences and what he called 'religious questions' at the crown of healthy human development. He believed 'the nineteenth-century atheist had burnt down the house instead of remodelling it' by attempting to explain away or repress metaphysical yearnings. He traces the origin of religions themselves to these intense experiences:

> Most people lose or forget the subjectively religious experience, and redefine Religion as a set of habits, behaviours, dogmas, forms, which at the extreme becomes entirely legalistic and bureaucratic, conventional, empty, and in the truest meaning of the word, anti-religious. The mystic experience, the illumination, the great awakening . . . are forgotten, lost, or transformed into their opposites.[19]

Philosopher and psychotherapist Mark Vernon also traces the origins of religion to ecstatic experiences. He argues against the dominant evolutionary explanations for the development of religion, that we invented 'Big Gods' to encourage prosocial behaviour, or that we ascribed 'False Agency' to spirits in the natural world. Both of these theories have come under serious criticism, and the emerging replacement theory places ecstatic experiences and trance states squarely in the foreground of religions' development. The 'Trance hypothesis' argues that developing humans have always experienced awe and wonder, but at some point they figured out they could induce ecstatic experiences through collective singing, chanting, drumming, dancing and in some cases ingesting particular plants. 'It stuck partly because it also helped to ease tensions and bond groups, via the endorphin surges produced in trance states . . . altered states proved evolutionarily advantageous: the awoken human desire for ecstasy simultaneously prompted a social revolution because it meant that social groups could grow to much larger sizes via the shared intensity of heightened experiences.'[20] If you've ever been to a good music festival you'll recognise the feeling of togetherness induced by a collective, music-induced peak experience.

I find the evolutionary theories of religion fascinating, but for me of course they only tell half the story. Most presuppose no gods or spirits exist who might reveal themselves, no truth that human minds are aligning with. The trance hypothesis is at least 'theologically agnostic' in that it doesn't preclude the possibility of connection beyond other humans. What I like about it is it reminds me that my intuition – that my Christianity is not primarily about right beliefs or moral behaviour – is a very old one. The beginning of my story, the driving force for this search, this itch, was a moment of unselfing, a mystical moment of encounter. It's those moments which, even now, keep me here.

That doesn't mean I want to strip out all the rest. I disagree with Maslow that 'the illumination, the awakening' are what 'real religion' are, and that the practices and stories and ideas that cluster around them are somehow in conflict. For a hedonist like me it is so tempting to put a match to the less sexy stuff – the institutions and doctrines, the drudgery of feeding the poor and overcoming my worst self and sitting down to read a complex and enervating book every day. I get bored by multi-verse hymns and long droning sermons and Bible readings done with the same soporific inflections. If I'm honest, it's mainly the ecstatic stuff I love, the sitting in the light of love, those moments when it's like a wild, wise lion rubs their race against mine in exquisite tenderness. (I know the fact that my visual image of [God] is a lion is peak Narnia cliché, but I'm trying to wean myself off caring about originality. None of the truest and most important things are original. Lewis got it from the Bible, after all.) A freewheeling spirituality, severed from its Christian frame, in which my own experiences are the only plumb line, sounds easier than dealing with other people and their ideas. I know though that I need the trellis of rhythms and disciplines, the challenge and accountability of community if I am really going to become fully alive.

Because awe alone can't save us, not least because it isn't easy for everyone to access. My philosopher husband, for example, finds it difficult, though he is very much charismatic in commitment. It doesn't make him less of a Christian, less fully alive. These experiences aren't enough on their own even for those of us who do have them. Though he was resistant to the structures of organised religion, Maslow acknowledged that peak experiences disembedded from a rigorous spiritual path and commitment to change could be next to useless 'without any growth or benefit of any kind beyond the effects of pleasure. The rapture may be very profound but contentless'.[21]

They are also risky. In moments of wonder, ecstasy or ego-loss our rational faculties are dialled down. It's why they are so scary for the left-brained intellectual whose identity rests primarily on that part of themselves. It requires a level of guard-dropping or even surrender to access them. You have to ask in order to receive, seek to find, knock before the door will open. And this requires some courage and some vulnerability.

I feel lucky to have made the leap young, when my self-narration was mouldable and I had high tolerance of risk. I think I'd find it harder to let go for the first time now. I would argue that this seeking and surrender, when done in a safe context, towards a love beyond us, is the only way to know the whole range of human experience, that it's a risk worth taking. However, it does make us uniquely vulnerable. There is a reason cults and coercive gurus use ecstasy. I've seen too many charismatic leaders fail morally to think it's the whole solution, or a guarantee of spiritual health.

My psychedelics-loving friends introduced me to the idea of 'set and setting', which comes from Timothy Leary, a Harvard psychologist and proponent of psychedelics. He argued in the 1960s that healthy ecstatic experiences via psychedelic drugs were reliant on two things: 1) the mindset (intention and expectations) of the user and 2) the environment in which the experience happened (setting).[22] Bad trips, which are not uncommon, are blamed on poor set and setting, while therapeutic use relies on a lot of attention to this area, making sure those taking psychedelics therapeutically are accompanied rigorously by a therapist and helped to make meaning of their experiences.

This concept helped me understand why I want to hold together my ecstatic experiences with the rhythms and practices, scriptures and community of church. I find it helpful to have a Christian frame for my unselfing, because it gives it limits. It is my set and setting. My most extreme, overwhelmed-on-the-floor encounters happen in church, surrounded by people I love and trust, usually with music playing. I can take as much time as I need. Afterwards, I have wise people to process them with, a text to bring them into conversation with. If the presence I encounter in ecstatic worship is not fundamentally loving, it's a red flag.

I also value this idea of set and setting because it stops my search for awe descending into solipsism. The emphasis on spiritual gifts is, like the vast majority of my tradition, doggedly communal. Individual experience that distances us from others is worse than useless. We receive 'words of knowledge' or other spiritual gifts in order to *bless others*. The early church, dabbling in prophecy, is instructed to 'speak to people for their upbuilding and encouragement and consolation', not just to puff themselves up with obscure mystical knowledge.[23] My tradition tells me that if my charismatic experiences are not helping me and/or others become more loving, joyful, peaceful or patient, more faithful, gentle or self-controlled, they are probably not gifts at all but distractions or delusions. Given the dangers of ecstatic experience, this frame feels like safety.

I've traced a circuitous path here, from the numbing and distracting habits many of us are tempted by, to mystic experiences. I am more and more convinced they are linked, and no longer content to settle for the former.

I think the stereotype of the Church is that it would make me ashamed of my appetite for pleasure, for intense experiences, but I've found the opposite. Theology teaches me not to be too easily satisfied. C. S. Lewis said, 'It would seem that Our Lord finds our desires not too strong, but too weak. We are half-hearted creatures, fooling about with drink and sex and ambition when infinite joy is offered us, like an ignorant child who wants to go on making mud pies in a slum because he cannot imagine what is meant by the offer of a holiday at the sea.'[24]

Sometimes, when I am on the verge of numbing out with some substance or activity, this image of mud pies helps me. It's not that mud is always bad, it's just not what I really need. The craving for mud pies is a hunger for something else, and a sign I probably need some shared ritual, some collective effervescence or just to get (safely, healthily) out of my head.

LUST: FROM OBJECTIFICATION TO SEXUAL HUMANISM

I am tempted to start this chapter with a trigger warning. There is a high likelihood it will tempt you to write me off, maybe as a prudish moraliser, maybe as a permissive heretic, depending on where you are coming from. The high creed of our culture is non-judgement, which in practice means pretending we have no opinion about other people's choices. You do you. The trouble is that, in making our own, different choices, and seeking to explain them, judgement is implied. We all do, really, think our way is better, because we wouldn't have chosen it otherwise. And we are quick to read difference or disagreement as threat, rather than expected or even beautiful diversity. Radically different opinions and choices around sex (and parenting, and politics, and vaccines, and and and) can feel as if they make any kind of connection, any kind of friendship, impossible.

I don't believe that's true. I hope we can stay connected. Jesus is entirely clear on quite a small number of things, and one of them is that we shouldn't judge others. As I try to explain some of my intuitions around what makes me feel fully alive in relation to sex, I do not feel judgemental of those who come to different conclusions. If we were in a room together I'd just be curious about your reasoning, keen to hear your experiences (possibly in awkward detail). In this medium, only I get to make my case, and I will try to do so as gently and honestly as possible.

More than in any other area, pointing to Christian approaches to sex as a route to fully aliveness is likely to cause eye rolls, even anger. My experience of these ideas as freeing, as guardrails against the disconnecting, dehumanising tides of our culture do not chime with most people's associations. The damage done by some interpreters of Christian teaching on sex – not least to centuries of 'fallen' women, to those harmed by conversion therapy or hateful rhetoric about LGBT+ people – is real. If you carry scars, religious trauma or a history riven with imposed shame, thank you for getting this far.

We are all formed by our experiences. In my depolarisation and anti-tribalism work I have seen again and again how starting with someone's story, understanding how their experiences shaped their thinking, helps us hear their views with a softer heart. This is why I am going to tell you my story before I tell you the conclusions I've come to. As I tell it, I know yours will be different. Mine does not delegitimise yours. They can both be true.

My medical parents gifted me a very frank approach to bodies. I feel as normal talking about sex as I do about haircuts. I always knew where babies came from, and was taught the anatomical words for body parts first. It was always an anus, a penis, a vulva. I didn't have a tummy, I had an abdomen. This meant I could cast myself as primary school sex fact checker, fount of all knowledge. In year four, on the field amidst forts of sweet-smelling cut grass, I explained the mechanics of a blow job and that you should really call it fellatio. Mr Fisher, our slick-haired, turtle-necked headmaster, had to call my mother into the office to ask why I had been overheard acting like a proto Otis from *Sex Education*.

Later, when I discovered the effect of a power shower

pointed between my legs, it didn't occur to me not to ask Mum about the delicious but slightly scary sensation. That's just an orgasm, she said, wiping down the kitchen sides. It's called masturbation when you give yourself one (tipping crumbs from her palm into the pedal bin). Very good for insomnia.

Because I'd discovered the joys of self-pleasure before my conversion, I had no shame around it. Afterwards, it took me a year or so of youth group to work out this was not the norm. The leaders eventually instigated the sex chat, which included some gentle dissuasion about masturbation. They were lovely, and earnest, and embarrassed, but the whole thing had the ring of something 'on the curriculum' they were obliged to tell us rather than something they really believed. The arguments from the book they wheeled out made no sense to me: 1) Masturbation cuts our imaginations off from [God]. It didn't for me, I felt as close to worship in an orgasm as on the dance floor of a club as in a church. 2) Our fantasies could be damaging, was another. I had dog-eared copies of Jilly Cooper novels so my fantasies were sometimes cinematic (and the word 'jodhpurs' will always have a faint erotic charge) but I didn't really need them. I got their point about how our imagination could be formed in unhealthy directions, so I just decided to manage without the supporting cast. 3) If we got good at pleasuring ourselves it would make our future spouse feel redundant, was offered as the trump card. Wank now, less good sex later. I took that one seriously as I was keen on the idea of good future sex, but it seemed obvious to me that if I knew my body I could teach someone else much better, and hoped they'd do the same for me. It was just efficient. It seemed bizarre to me to think that [God] could have created something as magical as a clitoris and expect us to leave it entirely alone, and also, what did they expect me to do when I couldn't get to sleep? After a few half-hearted weeks of abstinence I fell gratefully, guiltlessly off the wagon.

The other thing on the youth group curriculum was sex outside of marriage, and this was taught with more conviction. I know others who received this message with a side order of hellfire and a persistent sense that sex is dirty and shameful. I didn't. Our leaders gently suggested that sex is a deeply intimate, powerful act, a good gift, and that we needed to wield its power responsibly. Sex without commitment, they argued, was one of the easiest ways to hurt people, or get hurt ourselves. Later, with different leaders, there was some regrettable teaching using a jigsaw puzzle piece (representing us) and superglue (representing sex), implying if we stuck ourselves to lots of ill-fitting jigsaw pieces we'd be broken and covered in glue by the time we found our real fit. They didn't say, but I already knew that being gluey would be worse for girls. Memorably annoying, but not convincing. Those early conversations, though, made sense to me. I liked orgasms, but I couldn't imagine any of the boys I knew being able to give me one. The one girl at school who was vocally having a lot of sex was very cool, and very lovely, but also so clearly mining a deep seam of unhappiness that it wasn't appealing.

On a post-GCSEs girls' camping trip to Newquay my best friend and I started a competition about how many surfers we could snog. We taped up a tally board in our pre-pitched tent among the empty Lambrini bottles and gas-powered hair straighteners. I emerged victorious, lower face red raw with stubble burn, until the last night when she gave a man a blow job on a dark corner of the dance floor. Her laughing description layered triumph over what sounded suspiciously like revulsion. I remembered worrying about how willing she'd been, and felt no regret over losing the contest.

Around that time I was spending a lot of time on dance floors, my other tall friends and I having no trouble getting into clubs from age fourteen. My parents, though not keen, knew banning headstrong teenagers is useless and were rightly confident that I was sensible. As a consequence, they at least always knew where I was, and our home became the default place to pile back to. At school, boys showed no interest, most of them still fitting under my chin, but older men in clubs often approached me. It was helpful for my ego, but I could sense the creepiness.

Unlike many young women, I largely escaped the lurking threat, though not completely. One night out – I must have been fifteen or sixteen – a group of men followed me to the toilet, and in the dark corridor pinned me to the wall and groped me, pulling up my skirt and squeezing my breasts. I bit one of their arms through a navy nylon shirt that stank of Lynx, and they let me go. Shortly afterwards I signed up for kickboxing classes and developed a pull and twist manoeuvre on testicles that I used several times to see off men hitting on me or my friends on dance floors. I just wanted to be left alone with the music.

I don't tell this story because the incident in the club corridor is some deep trauma. I was shaken, but I simply knocked back another Malibu and lemonade and moved on. It is just a depressingly pedestrian example of the way sexual awakenings for women in particular are often uncomfortably adjacent to a sensed malign power. As I became more desirable, that desire didn't always feel as if it had my best interests in mind.

I know now that my height made me lucky. I am five foot eleven and solid. Kickboxing and a certain stubborn swagger gave me an aura of protection that was probably unearned. My brush with sexual violence is neither unusual nor extreme. The reality of the bell curve of average biological strength differences is that almost all men can hurt or even kill almost all women, but not the other way round. This is not a sexy statistic, but a relevant one. My definition of lust is sex without connection, and at the extreme end of sex without connection is violence.

Maybe if I'd not had these early, minor, tragically ordinary experiences I'd have questioned the youth group's teaching. I knew in my bones sex was a good thing, not least because my self-administered orgasms were so clearly a gift, but I saw how often it was on men's terms. It was something my friends began to do because their boyfriends wanted it, because being on the pill conferred status, because everyone else was. There was little suggestion of desire.

After one serious boyfriend in my teens who was extremely patient with what Gen Z would now call my 'celibacy phase' I spent most of my twenties single. I don't think I chose to avoid sex solely because a church told me to. I felt well able to sift and pray and think through other teachings, to hold them up to the light of the divine love I knew and see if they refracted right. I also don't think I was unconsciously protecting myself from sexual violence (though how would I know that?). I wasn't in a hurry to be having the kind of sex many of my friends were having, with entitled men who'd watched too much porn, wanted full pubic depilation and had to be coaxed or wheedled into giving, not just receiving oral sex. It was more a sense of hoarding my sexual power, guarding this glowing orb in my loins like a horny celibate wizard. I knew I had a high appetite for pleasure and a strong need for connection, but I just didn't seem to meet any men I felt were a match for it. Writing this, I now wonder if my weird celibate-sex vibes were just terrifying. It was only years later, reading Audre Lorde's description of erotic power, that I found language for it: 'It is an internal sense of satisfaction to which, once we have experienced it, we know we can aspire. For having experienced the fullness of this depth of feeling and recognizing its power, in honour and self-respect we can require no less of ourselves.'[1] That season of celibacy didn't feel like 'The severe abstinence of the ascetic', which she also condemns, but profoundly and erotically empowering.[2]

I also didn't feel impatient. I was having sensual, even erotic experiences. They just showed up in other places, like prayer.

The sensations of praying can be more or less intense. Whole years can pass when it feels like a very long-distance relationship, borderline theoretical. I pray because I don't know what else to do, where else to root myself, and because I hope to get back to the times when prayer feels like a delicious treat. These barren periods have become less regular as I've aged, however, as my dogged, quasi-mystical search for more meaning has begun to show fruit. In my celibate twenties, and again now in my late thirties, whenever I pray I feel like I'm flying. As soon as I centre down, turn my attention like a glance flicked across a crowded room that connects in eye contact, I feel lift. My skin fizzes and the sensation is of upward and forward motion, even as I sit or kneel. Sometimes it's more like ice skating, or hang gliding. It's delightful.

There have also been times when the flood of sensations – heat, tingling, a pleasant heaviness – are difficult to differentiate from being aroused. I'm suddenly aware of my body, present in my skin. It's undeniably sensual. For years I experienced this and felt faintly disgusted, my mind skidding away from acknowledging the association. Even when you come from a low-shame family and a low-shame faith like mine, an association between the holiness of the divine and human sexuality feels at best counter-intuitive, at worst, pure ick. But a strict separation between the topics of sex and [God] isn't the only, or even the best way of reading my tradition.

The Song of Songs is one of the odder books of the generally quite odd collection that makes up the Bible. It's a frankly erotic dialogue between two lovers who are panting to get their hands on each other.

He says: 'Your stature is like a palm tree; your breasts are clusters of fruit. I said, I will climb the palm tree and take hold of its fruit.' She responds: 'Your mouth is like fine wine flowing smoothly for my love, gliding past my lips and teeth!' And propositions him: 'Come, my love, let's go to the field; let's spend the night among the henna blossoms. There I will give you my love.'[3]

It's been read for centuries as an allegory for the love between [God] and human beings and between Christ and the Church, as well as an unabashed celebration of sexual desire. So prayer feeling pretty sensual has some precedent.

The medieval mystics, who wrote about ecstatic encounters with [God], also didn't shy away from the sensual in describing their connection with the divine.

The ecstasy of St Teresa, a sixteenth-century Italian mystic, has been repeatedly depicted in art and sculpture, partly because it's a Freudian field day: 'I saw in his hand a long spear of gold, and at the point there seemed to be a little fire. He appeared to me to be thrusting it at times into my heart, and to pierce my very entrails; when he drew it out, he seemed to draw them out also, and to leave me all on fire with a great love of God.'[4]

Margery Kempe, a few centuries earlier, was less veiled, reporting that [God] spoke to her: 'Therefore I must be intimate with you, and lie in your bed with you . . . you greatly desire to see me, and you may boldly, when you are in bed, take me to you as your wedded husband.'[5]

Most of the more openly erotic mystics were women, presumably because in a heteronormative world that popularly depicted [God] as male it was mildly less awkward for them. However, it wasn't unknown to men – John Donne didn't edit out this element of his spiritual life:

> Except you enthrall me, never shall be free,
> Nor ever chaste, except you ravish me.[6]

Reading about these mystics, I have to ask: Is this the shadowy psycho-sexual drive behind all this church stuff? Do I just want to have sex with [God]? The female mystics now get written off in psychoanalytic and feminist terms as repressed virgins, expressing their sexuality in the only legitimate way open to them. Maybe that was the story of my pre-marriage years.

The honest answer is I have no idea. You'd have to ask a therapist. I do like sex, and I do hunger for these intense encounters with [God]'s love more and more. I am increasingly comfortable with holding some confusion around this, with the untidiness of an adventure in being fully alive. If I am horny for [God] I don't really mind. The things of the body and the things of the soul are hard to separate, and it's only since Descartes that we think we should.

To return to Audre Lorde, she expands the definition of

erotic beyond sexual intimacy. She sees it as 'a form of creative, life-giving energy that is generated out of sharing deeply and joyfully any pursuit with another person . . . this kind of connection . . . is a way of overcoming numbness and self-negation'.[7] In my case, it seems the other person doesn't have to be a human.

Margery Kempe doesn't fit the stereotype of a frustrated virgin either. She was married, and gave up sex with her husband in search of deeper mystical union with [God]. Maybe he was just terrible in bed, or maybe she was after something else. I want both. Like many parts of my faith, I can feel people trying to explain this away, tidy it into a neat rational box, and the subversive in me wants to keep blowing up the boxes. I feel a very similar rush of bodily pleasure, a deep pulse of life on a sweaty dance floor, moving my body rhythmically with others. I felt it when I was breastfeeding, and it scared me then too, because the deep sensual pleasure of mothering, the joy of touching and being touched felt taboo because the only category we have for it is sex. But if it's connection itself that is sensual and pleasurable, as it is for me, then it can show up all over the place.

I just couldn't see it happening in casual sex. I didn't see the draw, even in my atheist period, though I thought I should. This means I am in many senses startlingly innocent, fundamentally unqualified, at least in experience terms, to write a chapter on sex. I was a virgin till I was twenty-eight. I did eventually meet a man who I could sense would match me, mind and body, and he did. We got engaged, spent months dry humping, drunk on hormones, and when we finally had sex on our wedding night it was clumsy but glorious. It's been my sex story ever since (less clumsy now). I even find his marginalia sexy. I still have erotic experiences while praying but have no desire to leave him and become a nun. Maybe we're the exception that proves the rule.

It's hard to talk about being happy without it sounding smug. I fear exposing my 'couple privilege', causing a pang of envy or lack. I think it's worth the risk, because almost all writing about sex is by people who are less vanilla than me, and it can make us feel that the only route to sexual satisfaction requires wild experimentation with multiple partners. I want to balance out the narratives available to us. I was sensually satisfied when I was single and celibate. Now, my marriage makes me feel free enough to go on erotic adventures, to feel sexy with my saggy post-pregnancies belly and the silver threads in my hair. Neither of us need to perform and primp, but can ask for what we want, give and receive pleasure joyfully. I'm extremely satisfied, is what I'm saying, the former twenty-eight-year-old virgin who's only had sex with one man. If connection is not your kink, maybe it sounds like unhealthy repression. But it doesn't feel that way to me.

The other life, the one where I'd never gone to the festival in the cowshed, seems likely to have led to a woman who had sex earlier and with more partners. My need for intense experiences, for depth, means I imagine her taking psychedelics, maybe even being polyamorous, attending sex parties. Various beloved friends do all these things. Probably I am drawn to these people (as well as my Christian friends who will probably be horrified at the line above) because they still feel PLM in some deep sense – though I have expressed fully aliveness differently, we are looking for adjacent things. I see that other me sometimes, out of the corner of my eye, and wave. She's much more sophisticated, less earnest, way more sexually experienced. Not necessarily less happy, just different.

Hook-up culture

She would, however, have had to navigate the dominant sexual culture I chose to secede from.

In 2015, a viral essay was published in *Vanity Fair* entitled 'Tinder and the dawn of the dating "apocalypse"'.[8] It analysed what was then a relatively recent phenomenon – the ability to swipe for sex.

'It's like ordering [Deliveroo],' says Dan, the investment banker, 'but you're ordering a person.' The comparison to online shopping seems an apt one. Dating apps are the free-market economy come to sex . . . ' online, the act of choosing consumer brands and sex partners has become interchangeable.'

Two male regular users of Tinder were asked about what connection, if any, they felt with the women they sleep with:

'We don't know what the girls are like,' Marty says.

'And they don't know us,' says Alex.[9]

We've come a long way since the King James version of the Bible used 'know' as a coy euphemism for sex, as in 'Adam knew Eve and she conceived a son.' Sex as a form of intimate knowledge, in the context of the Tinder apocalypse, sounds as archaic as the translation that uses it.

It's impossible to think about sex now without reference to changes in the way we date. Researchers have described the sharp increase in 'hookup culture' in recent decades as a 'sexual paradigm shift'.[10]As in other areas of life, advances in information technology have completely upended generations of social norms.

In 2022, another dating app essay was published, this time in the *New Yorker*.[11] The female journalist is ostensibly singing the praises of Feeld, a newer 'hookup app for the emotionally mature' defined by 'openness and respect' in contrast to the 'cold and unfeeling' wilderness of app dating elsewhere. She implies that the concerns of the 2015 piece about Tinder and other apps have been addressed on Feeld by discouraging unsolicited dick pics and general male entitlement, and encouraging sexual expression in all its forms.

The writer was driven to Feeld by the breakdown in a relationship: 'I was thirty-nine and scared by the idea that I would not be reproducing the kind of heteronormative nuclear family I had grown up in.' She describes herself as having a 'preference for monogamy' but finding on Feeld 'an alternative to the fantasy of family I was letting go of.' The piece implies that the writer is letting go of it, not for political or principled reasons, but because the dating culture around her has made it impossible. Her thinly veiled shame at still desiring monogamy and family is painful to read. I wanted to hug her.

It would be easy for the war-on-woke brigade to mock Feeld, with its endless options for gender identity, obscure sexual acronyms and high tolerance of sweetly nerdy fetishes. It reads to me as a more transparent and possibly kinder alternative to older apps for the gender-fluid generation, with less body shaming. What is not clear to me, even in this article supposedly in praise of it, is that more options to access casual sex, no matter how polite or inclusive the platform, is what most people – and especially women – really want. One line struck me as almost unbearably sad: 'For single people, casual sex is not a glib lifestyle choice but a serious attempt to be happy within a specific reality . . . This was one way to make my unwanted future tolerable, to at least make it interesting for myself.'

My instinctive linking of sex and connection is drawn, I

think, as much from my feminism as from my Christianity, though those two things are so entangled I'd struggle to differentiate them. My sense is that these seismic changes, which I'll summarise as a culture of casual sex, widespread pornography use and a decrease in marriage, are not, in the main, an especially good thing for women.

Some elements of the longer-term changes are, of course, good ones. Not having my sexuality policed by men, choosing who and when to marry, and how and if to have children. I am grateful for these things. I am no trad wife, keen to return to 1950s gender roles.

It is also important to note that hook-up culture seems, at least in the short term, to be working fine for some people. Studies tend to show that between a quarter and a third of people engaging in it do so without ambivalence, with little to no regret and high levels of enjoyment.[12] That is a proportion of the population, including, perhaps, you, for whom sexual variety severed from deep connection seems to work fine. You presumably are very certain that your partners feel the same way, because I don't think you would have got this far without being an ethically alert person. Statistically, while a handful are women, you are overwhelmingly more likely to be male.[13] Whatever gender, you can skip the rest of this section, because it's not really for you.

My definition of lust is not just desire, or sexual pleasure. Those things are not sin, either in my sense of it or in church tradition. Lust, for me, is sex absent from an acknowledgement and awareness of our partner/s as fully, complexly human, and vulnerable. Sex without due care to avoid treating people as objects or abusing our power. And I have a sad intuition that lust in that sense runs right through our culture, and that it is making too many people, the chunk of the population that do share my intuitive linking of sex with connection, feel less than fully alive.

Alongside the proportion doing fine with it, one study of hook-up culture on college campuses found that a different third of students say that their intimate relationships have been 'traumatic' or 'very difficult to handle'. Many of them experience a persistent malaise, a deep, indefinable disappointment. And one in ten says that they have been sexually coerced or assaulted in the past year. Even those commentators who want to paint a broadly positive picture quote young people as saying 'if anything . . . sex is too available' and 'The one thing that's wrong with this generation is they always put sex before connection.'[14] For those who do not feel comfortable with hook-up culture, it is not working at all, and most of them are women.

Louise Perry, feminist and former *New Statesman* columnist, in her book *The Case Against the Sexual Revolution* makes this point from a non-religious perspective. She cites data that shows that women in anonymous surveys have an overwhelming preference for committed relationships over casual sex, have fewer orgasms during hook-ups than with a committed partner and experience troublingly high levels of bad, coercive, uncomfortable, painful or even downright dangerous sex in casual encounters.[15]

In America Christine Emba, in her book *Rethinking Sex: A Provocation,* makes a similar case.[16] She thinks there is no such thing as casual sex, especially for women, because of the inherent vulnerability of the act. Both authors argue that consent as the sole ethical lens through which we view sex is insufficient. It's the bare minimum we should require. They are nervous of what Emba calls 'uncritical sex-positivity', which fails to grapple with power imbalances and the complex, culturally conditioned nature of consent. Which, for fear of 'kink-shaming', refuses to question even practices like the rise in choking and 'rough sex', which are self-evidently more likely to harm women. Even some who, unlike Perry and Emba, would call themselves 'sex positive' are making similar noises. One session at a 2022 sex positive conference was titled 'Towards an ethic of consent *and care*' in order to 'articulate why some sexual interactions leave the participants and the surrounding community with the moral intuition that something wrong has gone on, *despite being formally consensual*' (my italics).[17]

Perry's argument is that the current sexual settlement is designed around the preferences of the highly 'sociosexual' – those with a high appetite for a variety of sexual partners. At population level, though there are of course many individual exceptions, the highly sociosexual are overwhelmingly male.[18] These (mainly) men are at least outwardly thriving in a dating culture that has normalised casual sex and removed social encouragement for faithful commitment, but a lot of people, especially women, are not.

I'm still pondering both Perry and Emba's argument (and honestly, as someone who never experienced this evolution of dating culture, I feel ill-equipped to judge if it is as terrible for women as it appears) but it's that 'consent and care' line that has stayed with me. Sex that cares for the other, which takes their personhood seriously, is close to the theological principles I'll unpack below. It saddens me that so few people are finding it. I can't help wondering if celibacy, as the second-wavers argued, is as legitimate an expression of feminism as the current social default of sex positivity. What if masturbation and a massage instead of a casual hook-up is, for most women, closer to actual liberation than conforming their desires to what a particular generation of men have been taught to want? Interestingly, some members of Gen Z, the group most raised in hook-up culture as a default, are coming to the same conclusion. I spent an hour in *#celibacytiktok* so you don't have to, where a vocal minority are simply opting out. Not because a church told them to, but because it seems to them to be what taking care of themselves looks like.

Porn

The link between hook-up culture and pornography is both intuitive and evidenced. One study concluded 'that more permissive sexual scripts mediated the association between more frequent pornography viewing and hooking up'.[19]

Humans have looked at arousing images for as long as culture has existed, but when I was younger porn was available only from newsagents and seedy video stores. Now I can find a Jilly Cooper-inspired fantasy or a violent gang bang on my phone in the time it takes for me to walk to the toilet from this desk. In fact I could just open another tab right here.

I won't though. Full disclosure, I have watched porn. Once, with my husband in those exhausting early parenting years when finding the time to get aroused felt impossible. We were delirious with sleep deprivation and hadn't had sex for months, were scratchy and distracted with each other. I thought it might speed things up, help us reconnect. Even the softest, 'ethical' female-friendly stuff I could find left me conflicted. My overdeveloped pastoral instinct always kicks in. It's the same reason I can't watch reality TV. I start googling 'qualified psychologist on set?' and 'aftercare plan for contestants?' and going on to the stars' social media to check how badly they have been trolled. As you can imagine, in the context of porn this is not super sexy. Next time we need a marital sex boost I'll seek out literary erotica instead, because I'm happier treating imaginary people as props in my fantasies. Maybe that's problematic too, but there you go.

My pastoral instincts around porn are not entirely unfounded. In a sex-positive society, consent is our one remaining sexual principle. And it's a good one. A vital baseline. Porn, whatever the content, if made and consumed by consenting adults is morally neutral within that framework.

The trouble is, consent is contextual. It depends on the choices offered to you, your economic independence, how assertive you are, your formative experiences. Some people are more likely to consent to things that might harm them than others, especially if they are in need of money. According to one study, actors in adult films are much more likely to have experienced the care system and domestic violence and to be living in poverty than the wider population.[20] Tellingly, if you look at just male porn performers, experiences of the industry are nothing like as negative.[21] There are creators working hard to change the industry, to be as responsible and transparent as possible, to centre women's desire and show a range of bodies and take the wellbeing of performers seriously. Even they have been dealing with their own *#metoo* moments, working out if it's possible to constrain power on a porn set.[22] They are trying, and sometimes failing, to make performers feel safe. Given that this industry is here to stay the attempt feels important. But it's a tiny, tiny proportion. Aside from these pockets where the questions are at least being asked, far too much porn is not consensual by even the thinnest definition. Pornhub, the largest pornsite on the internet, has been found to carry footage of victims of child rape, kidnapping and sex trafficking.[23]

I nearly wrote, 'I'm sorry if that last line is a turn off,' before I realised, with deep sadness, it won't be for everyone. Because the other thing the proliferation of increasingly hard-core forms of pornography has done is normalise violent fantasies. The sexual imagination of more than a generation of young people, and especially males, has been taken through a giant, unregulated experiment.[24] What happens when you can get a rape or choking or BDSM fantasy on your phone in an instant, and do so repeatedly? Does this make it easier or harder to have sex defined not just by consent but by care, which connects you with another vulnerable human person? The correlative link between porn use and desire for 'rough sex' is well established, and violent sexual offenders tend to be heavy violent-porn users, though causation remains unclear.[25]

I wonder if the only way to really enjoy porn, even the soft stuff, is to just surrender to the dehumanisation, to let the actors be objects. That's the social contract, and at least some performers will have properly consented to it, not just be pursuing this career because they have no other choice. Some porn performers speak of finding it empowering, and I have no right to question their experiences. I'm not a stranger to the paradox that being objectified can be arousing, feel counter-intuitively powerful. But because connection is what I think life is really about, it raises a red flag. Objectification, of myself or others, seems spiritually dangerous. I can't help but feel for the humans involved, and what I feel is not (only) arousal but worry.

Audre Lorde argues that 'pornography is a direct denial of the power of the erotic, for it represents the suppression of true feeling. Pornography emphasises sensation without feeling.' [26] Lorde's use of the word 'suppression' helped me name something. We speak of restrictive sexual cultures as 'repressive', and they of course can be. But I've come to see sex without connection, for many, as a different form of repression. If one of the things we are looking for in sex is real human connection but we're taught that is not a sexy or legitimate thing to be looking for, we are made to repress a part of our selves. And that can be just as damaging.

The death of commitment

The final element of our current sexual culture is a reduction in marriage rates. This has been declining since the 1970s and stands at a historic low. Eighty-three per cent of men born in 1940 were married by the age of thirty, but for the millennials born in 1980 the figure was only 25 per cent.[27] Again, for some people this change will be a positive one – I would not have wanted to have been pregnant and hastily married at twenty-two like my nanny – but it has huge knock-on effects for how we connect with each other at an intimate level.

In Sally Rooney's novel *Beautiful World, Where Are You?* Alice, the protagonist, muses on the loss of marriage as a social norm:

> People our age used to get married and have children and now everyone is still single at thirty and lives with housemates they never see. Traditional marriage was obviously not fit for

> purpose . . . but at least it was an effort at something and not just a sad sterile foreclosure on the possibility of life . . . when we tore down what confined us, what did we have in mind to replace it?[28]

I have a group of friends who are mainly activists and socially radical, and they echo Rooney's question. Hook-up culture and non-monogamy are norms for them, certain sections of Gen Z and younger millennials. This year I had three conversations with women in their thirties who were increasingly dissatisfied with their situations, but didn't know how to ask for more and still sound 'chill'. Women agonising over how to be 'chill' around men has a specific ability to pique my feminist rage. Not at them, but at a culture that has told them what they want is shameful, that their desire to love and be loved by one person, to raise children, is uncool. These deepest, most tender human longings are wise and rational, because they orientate us towards things that are objectively good for us, but they are derided for them, labelled needy or emotional or desperate. Several are freezing their eggs, because the men they know seem a million miles from being ready for the responsibility of kids, and they seem embarrassed about that too. I hate it.

Rooney's line 'a sad sterile foreclosure on the possibility of life' haunts me when I speak to these friends. Casual sex and continually delayed couple formation has been sold as life-giving, but at least for a large chunk of my single female friends it no longer feels that way. Rooney indicates an understanding that life sometimes requires a curtailment of instant individual freedoms, being able to follow our every sexual whim, in the service of something more lasting. Like Rooney, these friends assume 'traditional marriage' is no longer a legitimate choice because it sounds patriarchal, authoritarian and constraining, but have nothing solid to replace it with. I'll return to why I think they are wrong.

Given that the current sexual settlement is not, to put it mildly, working for everyone, I think the Christian sexual ethic has something to offer. This is yet another way in which the public story of my faith departs wildly from my actual experience. Christianity is not (or shouldn't be) primarily about morality but about connection, about the relationship between us and other people, and us and [God]. Love [God] and love your neighbour is how Jesus summed up the law. If I'm attempting to follow him, that principle should shape the moral and sexual choices I make.

I think it is entirely possible to read the Christian sexual ethic as a kind of sexual humanism. My summary of it rests on the same foundation as the rest of the Christian ethic – the dignity and value of each human person, and the call to learn to love each other better.

I am not a pastor or a theologian, so please don't make major life decisions based on what I'm about to say. This is just a normal woman's summary of where I find life in my tradition. It teaches me that sex is an amazing, powerful gift for connection, and to take it seriously. Practically, this means firstly avoiding using another person as an object or a means to an end. Don't treat people like a sex toy. Even if they have consented to it. It's bad for us. People get hurt, and people are sacred. Secondly, it teaches me to be wary of sex across big imbalances of power, because the potential for harm is high. Again, people get hurt.

People are not objects

The idea that we should avoid treating people as objects underlies my uneasiness with hook-up culture and with porn. If you need a non-religious place to ground this principle, Kant said basically the same thing in the second formulation of his categorical imperative (not that Kant was in any real sense non-religious but he's read that way). His foundational principle for ethics was to avoid treating humans 'merely as a means but always as an end'.[29] And I feel it especially strongly as a woman because, in the words of Simone de Beauvoir, a woman – 'a free and autonomous being like all human creatures – nevertheless finds herself in a world where men propose to stabilise her as an object'.[30] It is of course possible for women to do the same to others, to treat romantic partners as less than fully human, to seek sex or relationships for instrumental reasons, not real connection. Either way it doesn't sound very erotic to me.

Take power seriously

The biblical condemnation of 'fornication' is stark, and, read now, extremely uncomfortable. It was only when I started reading some of these difficult passages through the lens of the protection of the vulnerable that it began to make sense to me. The primacy of the vulnerable is the leitmotif of the Hebrew Bible. The infamous and misleading 'angry God of the Old Testament' is angry, when he is, for the most part at the oppression of the poor, the migrant, the widow and the orphan, a group of people who theologian Nicholas Wolterstorff refers to as 'the quartet of the vulnerable'.[31]

Misusing power and failing to protect the vulnerable is uncomplicatedly a sin in scripture.

Condemnations of sexual activity in the New Testament are inseparable from this principle. The Greek word *porneia*, for centuries translated as 'fornication', now most often translated as 'sexual immorality', is etymologically inseparable from its origins in prostitution. As theologian Luke Bretherton points out, prostitution in New Testament times 'was bound up with a political economy of slavery (most prostitutes were male or female slaves) and systems that rendered moral the sexual exploitation of women and men who lacked status'.[32] Whether you think modern prostitution is always oppressive or not, in the ancient world it certainly was. While *porneia* came to be used more broadly, Bretherton thinks it is legitimate to read fornication – which is basically how I am defining lust – as similar to 'the insatiable and destructive desire for money that renders everything for sale . . . fornication names an extractive desire to possess. It knows no limit and instrumentalizes others.'[33] Basically, lust can't help trending towards dynamics of oppression. You can therefore read the biblical condemnation of fornication as not a prudish distaste of people's fun, but a deeply political opposition to extractive and oppressive forms of sex in which the most vulnerable bear the cost.

Adultery and fornication are condemned in scripture in a culture where most women had almost no agency, where sex outside marriage often resulted in pregnancy, which led to ostracism. A stark imbalance existed – which has not completely disappeared – between the risks borne by men and women in the sexual act. A blanket ban on adultery and sex outside marriage has been too often used to shame only women and let men sleep around with impunity, but it can also be read as extremely pro-women, seeking to restrain male power to ruin their lives, requiring men to take responsibility for their sexual actions.

More controversial are the passages about same-sex sexual activity. This part of what has been culturally transmitted as the 'Christian Sexual Ethic' has too often resulted in horrific individual and social scarring. A guest on my podcast and dear friend, Casper ter Kuile, who is married to a man, said in his interview that for most of his life the word [God] just sounded like 'I hate gays',[34] and that, of course, sounds like 'I hate you'. Fascinated by spirituality and searching for meaning and belonging, for decades he looked everywhere but church, convinced, not without cause, that he would not be welcome there. It breaks my heart.

The passages that have been read as condemning same-sex sexual activity are few, outnumbered hundreds of times over by themes like money and justice, but they exist. It is not intellectually honest for anyone wanting to take this book seriously to just wish them away. I'd love to cherry pick the sections I like. Thomas Jefferson approached the whole Bible this way, excising vast swathes in the process. It's ballsy. It makes me uneasy though, this instinct. I have reasons to be sceptical of myself. Part of what feels weirdly refreshing about this whole path is the ability of something outside of myself, outside of this precise cultural moment to call me, and it, into question.

Some of the pain caused to gay people has been from deliberate and hateful bigotry, but much of it is unintentional, the collateral damage of Christians desperately wrestling with this ancient, multi-vocal, multi-language, multi-context, multi-genre text, and seeking to stay faithful to the spirit of it. Not least because it's the same text that commands them to love their neighbour.

I'm neither a queer Christian nor a church leader laden with the weight of responsibility for souls that office entails. I've spoken to several decent men and women for whom this tension is tortuous, watched them trying to work out how to reconcile their reading of scripture with their commitment to the people in their care, or their own desires. In many ways this is not my fight. My instructions are clear: love your neighbour as yourself, and don't judge. I put too little faith in my own interpretative ability to have any level of certainty, but the vulnerability and power lens helps me read these sections with less wincing. My understanding is that committed, equal relationships between two people of the same sex did not really exist in the ancient world. Where sex did take place between (usually) two men, it was within the context of large power imbalances – masters and slaves, older male patrons and adolescents or with prostitutes. One reading of these confronting, painful sections is that what is being condemned is the same thing being condemned basically everywhere the Bible condemns sex – extractive fornication and disconnecting lust that always harms the least powerful; indeed, the Bible implies, harms everyone involved.[35]

The theological instinct to hold together sexual desire and connection or emotional intimacy has traditionally been simplified to, as it was for me, saving sex for marriage. It clearly isn't the case that deeply intimate, mutually honouring sex is only possible inside marriage. This was brought home as I discussed this chapter with friends who have come to different conclusions from me. One is polyamorous, and one of the most morally serious people I know. She sees her choices as also in opposition to hook-up culture, because ethical non-monogamy, done well, requires a level of clarity and honesty and, yes, commitment. She has experienced it as honouring and connecting as well as liberating, the opposite of treating people like objects. Another, who has moved away from a fundamentalist evangelical childhood that left her with a troubled relationship with her sexuality, now goes to sex parties with her husband and describes a sense of deep, albeit temporary, connection, with others there. I wouldn't make their choices, and they wouldn't make mine, but in talking about them in the context of friendship, surfacing these rarely discussed issues of power and instrumentalisation, we've all got clearer about how we want our sex lives to align with our values, not just the dominant culture.

Despite all this, and the ghost of Mary Whitehouse hovering close, I want to argue for the place of committed, faithful relationships as the most obvious container for connected sex. I'd even go so far as to cheerlead 'traditional marriage', by which I mean two equal people committing to care and support each other, to share and struggle together over time. A set of serious, socially witnessed, legally binding and economically impactful promises are the strongest protection we have come up with against extractive sex. It's harder for me to treat you like an object if you own half my stuff. I think marriage is still *a* good container for this kind of sexual humanism because like every virtue, every habit that makes me feel fully alive, it takes structure and repetition. Connected sex, in which the other person's particular pleasures and their emotional state are as front of mind as our own, takes practice. It doesn't come naturally to me, or, I'd guess, to any of us. Luke Bretherton puts it more eloquently: 'covenantal faithfulness [like marriage] is the context for cultivating intimacy over time with others . . . Rather than a territory to be defended or a narrowly prescribed set of actions to be performed, such covenantal relations are a way of talking about a set of virtues and practices through which we learn to relate fruitfully and truthfully.' He describes marriage beautifully as 'an expansive social practice and vocation . . . [not] marriage understood as a bounded territory.'[36] When being married or not becomes a cosh to beat people with, a form of social currency, it is a disgrace. But when we can see it as 'an expansive social practice and vocation' that trains us to connect in a disconnection culture, it is a jewel. In the same way that the rituals and rhythms of church provide 'exercises in attention' to help overcome my acedia, marriage has helped me channel my sexual appetites in the direction of connection and intimacy, in ways that I experience as life-giving and deeply erotic.

In cheerleading marriage, I don't want to sound like the 'family values' politicians who turn out to be shagging the staff and seek to shame single parents rather than support them. Shaming and social censure are disconnecting, dehumanising, the opposite of what I see Jesus doing (except with those who use their power to oppress the vulnerable). Also, Christianity is not such a natural ally of 'family values' as many proponents of that nebulous and now faintly sinister phrase seem to think. Jesus was unmarried, as were many of the disciples. Whole swathes of the New Testament are deeply ambivalent about marriage, noticing, rightly, how it tends to narrow our field of care and distract us from our callings to the rest of community.

My case for marriage is much closer to Bretherton's above. It's one way we can learn to attend to the full humanity of another person, over time, even when it's hard. And I believe that this pursuit, whether in marriage or committed friendship or close community, is what helps us be fully human ourselves.

As I write, I fear the arrow of my words lodging in your heart. It's what makes this whole subject (maybe all the important subjects) so fraught. My dear single friends don't need to be reminded of the benefits; most of them are stuck navigating the Tinder/Hinge/Bumble apocalypse, or the Feeld plan B, feeling locked out of couple world. It is salt in the wound. My dear divorced friends would really rather not hear that I wish more marriages would survive. Knowing these things bring pain, I want to say quickly in the very next sentence, *of course* lots of married people are miserable, lots of single people are happy, which is easy because it is true. We have all seen it. I simply want to argue that marriage is still a good thing to aim for, a good thing to protect, something revolutionary despite its normcore clothes. It can teach us to care. Like Thoreau going to the woods to pursue a deep life in one place, committing to one person need be no less of an adventure.

If you are intrigued by what I've said, and how it might apply to your own life, you could start by thinking about power. The sexual humanism I am talking about requires an awareness of differing levels of vulnerability and agency, and embraces care and commitment as a bulwark against objectifying people. It knows sex can be a source of blessing, one of the deepest and most beautiful forms of human connection, but can also cause harm, can disconnect us from ourselves and others at an equally deep level.

It may be that my obsession with connection is what makes the Christian sexual ethic feel like it goes with, rather than against, the grain of my soul, the grain of my feminism. I am convinced that it's possible to keep that central, golden thread of sexual humanism and strip away the shame and judgement that have accumulated around it, but I guess it depends where you are starting from. If your thesis of being 'fully alive' is different from mine, if connection is not so central to it, then sex can presumably just be sex and this all seems like unnecessary ethical hand wringing. Either way, I hope I haven't lost you. Because we're about to tackle the Big One.

PRIDE: FROM INDIVIDUALISM TO COMMUNITY

Pride is the shapeshifter of the sins. The word is, as sociologist and ethicist Michael Eric Dyson puts it, 'rhetorically pliable'.[1] As a culture we have an ambiguous relationship to it, using it more commonly as a positive than a negative. Take pride in yourself, you should be proud, I'm so proud of you. We might say 'too proud to ask for help', but it's hardly a stinging insult. When we really don't like someone's overinflated ego we'd call them arrogant, not proud.

It is also a contextual concept. Dyson argues that Black pride in particular is a courageous and vital response to an inheritance of humiliation. Pride in an oppressed person can be more like medicine than poison. Dyson's use of pride here is similar to how I would use belovedness, a stubborn connection with one's own deep sense of dignity. Pride in his sense can be another act of resistance to injustice, a way of keeping alive the logic of a different world. It can be beautiful.

Some have even argued that it can be virtuous. If a genuinely good person is surrounded by vicious and grasping souls, wouldn't acknowledging the difference be the truer, better thing? Denying it be false humility? This reveals one of the most common usages of pride, a sense not just of individual worth, but comparative value. Ultimately, a sense of superiority.

I don't believe that when we are genuinely superior, as

almost all of us will be in some context, being honestly aware of that is a problem. I am a world-class blower of delicious, percussive raspberries and denying my prowess would be dishonest. Give me a belly or a non-Michelle Obama upper arm and I will make a noise that will make you smile. I don't care how old or cynical you are. I try to value my raspberry-based superiority for its own sake as little as possible, and acknowledge my self-assessment might be faulty, but cringing and contrived inferiority never looks very alive to me. I am happy to claim my crown.

Neither do I fear the 'pride' related to mastery. My son passed a test in his swimming lessons recently. He's not up until now demonstrated a lot of aptitude in the water, so has been splashing expensively about in the shallows for years. Taking kids to swimming lessons to try to insure against future drowning is one of my least favourite aspects of parenting. But it paid off when he passed the test to finally move up a group, and almost exploded with delight. He danced, shivering, on the side of the pool, and sang for joy in his out-of-tune little voice. He felt proud, is one way of putting it, and I shared in his joy. Few things are as satisfying as learning to do something we couldn't do before. It's one of the key predictors of people's satisfaction with their jobs. Celebrating our achievements is a great thing, though we almost never reach them alone. My son is too little as yet to thank me for the hours I've spent enduring humid and cacophonous changing rooms rammed with hangry, verruca-ridden children. If he is still overlooking other people's help as an adult, I will have failed. Celebrating achievement without acknowledging what we've received is a clue to the kind of pride that *is* a problem.

The concept is also conflated with vanity or vainglory. I

see them as quite different, and indeed in most early lists of sins or bad thoughts they were separate. Vanity is still, I think, weakly relational, in that we care how others perceive us. I am vain, in that I sometimes care what I look like and spend a lot of time reading skincare reviews, but I'm not worried about it, soul-wise. Maybe I should be. I deliberately didn't choose one of the lists of sins that include it because it seems at worst like a baby sin. Some days, yes, I worry about my weight and my outfit because I'm somehow performing femininity, seeking to conform to the packet instructions of what a woman should look like. There is no aliveness in anxiously smoothing out my wrinkles in the mirror and sucking in my belly. I do this less often now though. More regularly when I'm thinking about what I look like I'm enjoying being creative with my second-hand clothes and putting on one of my twelve bright lipsticks because it cheers me up. Of course there are more important things, but when kept in proportion an awareness of appearance feels like a benign hobby, like cooking. It connects me with myself, what I like, my own body, and that is an important part of connection too. I dearly hope a wise, grounded, spiritually alive woman can still have style, if it brings her joy. Why wouldn't she?

If it's not belovedness, the joy of mastery or vanity, does pride even exist, then, as a source of disconnection? It's tempting to just skip this chapter altogether. And yet the great hearts and minds of my tradition have all agreed that something about pride *is* a problem, is the opposite of aliveness, and I'm learning that this tradition usually has something to teach me.

In fact, many of these teachers have spoken of pride as the fundamental temptation. St Augustine called it 'the beginning of sin'.[2] Maybe it's hard to define because it's so foundational, the drive to disconnect itself, and all these other chapters have been about the ways we do it. For Augustine, pride is a problem because humans are made for and orientated towards relationship – primarily with God, but also with others. It's our proper 'end', *telos* or goal. It's why we exist. Pride though resists that orientation, making our own soul 'an end to itself'.

Pride in this sense sells us a superhuman vision of ourselves. My pride disbelieves that connection is worth striving for, because hell is other people, and who needs them anyway. It's the part of me that thinks surrender is shameful, and that those around me are bit parts in my drama. I wish with all my heart I did not believe this, but part of me does.

This kind of pride disconnects me from myself, because what I ambitiously conceive of as my true self does need others, deeply, and is less human without them. It builds a wall between me and them, me and [God]. And it goes all the way back to the beginning.

In Christian thought, the Fall is the first crack in the world, and the deepest. The moment of fracture at the very start of the Bible is the relational equivalent of the Big Bang. The universe and humans are still feeling the effects of both.

I don't know if you've ever read those first dense, layered chapters of Genesis. The inciting incident happens so fast it's hard to get your bearings. The world is made in a series of joyful creative flourishes, people emerge, tenderly and carefully from [God's] hands. For a beat it's all harmonious and beautiful and then it's broken. [God] warns the people he's made about the dangers of one particular tree, a serpent tells them to ignore [God] because who needs him anyway, and it's done. Dislocation and alienation enter a world of ease and intimacy. It's entirely possible to read these stories as Nietzsche would – a paternalistic god punishing people for daring to question his authority. I don't. I see a world designed *for* relationship, created by a God defined *by* relationship, in which humans almost instantly pull back into themselves. The temptation that the serpent presented to the first man and woman was a chance to not need God, and it was done by questioning God's character. A relationship of trust and companionship, in which God and people walked together through the trees in the cool half-light of evening, was soured.

Augustine and later Luther used the phrase *Homo incurvatus in se* as a synonym for sin – humanity turned in on itself.[3] Something designed to reach outwards instead burrowing in like a septic toenail. John Donne summed up this self-harming tendency: 'Nothing but man, of all envenomed things,/Does work upon itself with inborn sting'.[4] As anyone who has ever dealt with ingrown hairs knows, things designed to grow outward cause trouble when they don't. The decision to ignore God's warning shatters the loving, uncomplicated friendship between humans and God, and between the man and woman. The text is painfully psychologically astute. The humans blame and finger point like toddlers: 'She did it! He did it!' They feel shame, suddenly, to be naked, and so they hide from each other and from God. And God responds by making them clothes. The creator of the universe sews them an outfit each. It always makes me think of the worn-down parents of an adult addict finally needing to ask them to move out, making themselves draw the healthy boundary, but tucking a wad of cash in their child's bag all the same. Even as God is trying to let humans experience the consequences of their disconnecting choice, the parent-creator can't help but soften it.

Despite the clothes, a great distance driven by distrust opens up between the man and woman. The consequences they face are different, making them incomprehensible to each other. In the narrative logic of the Bible, the Fall is the break and God's desire for reconciliation drives the rest of the story.

There are many other ways to read these passages – as a Jungian fable of adolescence, for example, or just a confused mishmash of timelines from multiple ancient texts being crunched together. They are all illuminating, because I find this book endlessly generative, never seeming to wear out from over reading. But what I primarily take from it is a story of disconnection. What was it about intimacy with the divine and each other that was so scary? How was the serpent persuasive enough to convince two people *in paradise* to curve away from it? And how do I avoid becoming ingrown?

So far, my working definition of pride is this sense of a sequestered, solipsistic self, determined to never compromise, never surrender. We often think humility is the opposite of pride, but I'm now wondering if the true opposite is love. Iris Murdoch famously said that 'love is the extremely difficult realisation that something other than oneself is real'.[5] And when I'm proud, love is what I am missing. For me, believing I'm the centre of the universe looks like a shameful mix of entitlement, subtle disdain for others and a desire to insulate myself from their suffering, their needs. And when I let it rule me, I also insulate myself from my own full humanity. It's death dressed up like self-esteem.

This chapter will explore the best container for my quest to become less proud and more loving: in two expressions of community. It's the most effective way I've found to dig out the toenail, and curve towards life instead. After that, finally, you can read about [God] directly if you want to, though the distinction is somewhat artificial. I believe humans are blinking icons of the divine, after all. As my patron saint Martin Buber says, disagreeing with someone who gave up his fiancée because he thought her a barrier to God, '[people] are not the hurdles on the road to God. They are the road'.[6]

Community: intentional community

In times of prosperity and peace, it is possible for an individual, couple or nuclear family to get on fine largely by themselves, brushing up against others only in casual social contact or financial transactions. A few friends just like us who we occasionally text, party or brunch with will do. When systems are working fine and there are enough resources to go around, the payoff from individualism in freedom and convenience seems attractive. It is easy to default to this way of living, and our social structures make it more and more likely. The trouble is, committed reciprocal relationships over time (yes, the kind that inconvenience us) help us flourish, and without them life begins to feel meaningless. But unless we hit a crisis we can go a long time before that becomes apparent to us.

For almost all of us, our times do not feel like settled peace and prosperity, and I can't imagine they will again soon. Compared to most of the world, and most of history, we still have it incredibly easy in the West, but turbulence appears to be the new normal, and ramping up. Coupling that with a steady decrease in social cohesion is a terrible plan. Jonathan Sacks in his book *Morality* echoed many commentators by bemoaning an 'overemphasis on the I and a loss of the we'.[7]

I don't need to quote you loneliness figures and hand-wringing policy reports to convince you we no longer really know how to be together. We are fracturing, exactly when we are most going to need each other.

Because in unstable times, people who are members of diverse and committed groups are at a huge advantage. This is part of my drive to live more closely with others. It's as selfish as that, on one level. I do feel genuine fear about my children's future. Continuing to raise them as if the world they inherit will be the same one we did feels irresponsible. I don't know what their world will look like, what monsters under their bed they will have to fight. But I know that being knitted into a small group of people who love them, who they have seen up close learning to love each other, resisting their disconnecting pride, sharing their skills and capacity and energy for the good of all, is one way I can prepare them.

I want to show them that, although it requires sacrifice of individual autonomy and preferences and is not compatible with unfettered self-actualisation, being part of real community is worth that cost. I think true self-actualisation, becoming more fully ourselves, does actually happen best in healthy community, in places we are fully known, but it looks different. I honestly think, other than an unshakeable knowledge of their parents' love, and an openness to the possibility of God's love, this is the best gift we can give them.

It's climate anxiety then, alongside my own fear of disconnection, that has driven our unusually drastic action. My family and I 'live in community'. This is one of those vague and grandiose phrases that can signify a lot of different things. I mean, almost all of us live in community in some sense, unless we have moved into a cell in the desert, and even then someone brings the food. For us, it means we have pooled our resources and bought a home with another family, entwining our lives to make a tiny urban monastery.

This isn't something you just fall into, especially in your thirties with two kids. I'd long had a hunch that the nuclear family was a weird building material for a society – not sufficiently load bearing for the weight placed on it, and leaving lots of other options lying around, unloved. Anyone who has been single while everyone else is settling down, or trying to raise kids far from support, may have had the same intuition. We know, in theory, that the 2.4 children suburban-semi blueprint is unusual, historically, and we can feel the ominous cracking, but there are very few viable-seeming alternatives. All the incentives and narratives act as tram tracks, funnelling people in one increasingly isolated direction, and it takes some stubbornness to change course.

I think this is why it took me so long to realise it might be possible. I had one friend who had pursued her climate-activist calling into an intentional eco-community in woodland in the south-west. We visited once, seeking out alternative paths, and she was boiling nappies for her newborn over an open fire while rain poured into their partially tarpaulin-covered roof. I knew then that I was not cut out for the kind of full-blown, off-grid community they had found. People like me who 'need' a good mattress and nice sheets just didn't seem the type.

It took the realisation that we definitely could not afford to stay in London in the traditional way to move us from wistful idea into action. We were part of a church that we loved, in a city we felt called to, but the housing market was bearing down on us. Friends kept getting swept away, uprooted from necessity rather than choice. I was also continually drawn back to the narratives of the early church, that economically radical model in the biblical book of Acts. They depicted a diverse, underdog community who lived in and out of each other's houses, met each other's needs. They shone off the page at me, these plucky pockets of egalitarianism in the midst of empire. Love one another, this book whispered, surrender to each other, seek each other's good. That way everyone will be cared for. The formative power of my own culture, in comparison, the because-I'm-worth-it, follow-your-bliss, how-dare-you-ask-me-to-care-or-compromise messaging felt irresistible without a much stronger counterweight. I wanted to listen to the radical invitation of my own tradition and wondered if it was even possible to be a disciple of Jesus locked in our own little hutches.

Without having any real plan, we started asking friends at church if they'd like to explore living together. They did not. We began propositioning people we knew less well. Tumbleweed. At every stage of trying to work out how to live differently there have been barriers. It's hard work, deciding you want to set up your home life in more relational ways. There are challenges in the soft stuff – who to do it with, how to discuss money, how much conflict is too much. There are hurdles with the hard stuff, the legal model, the Houses of Multiple Occupation legislation that means that people who aren't related or employing each other are more expensive for landlords to let to, the fact most banks won't give mortgages to more than two people.

It's not that there isn't an appetite for living differently. We can all do the maths with a housing crisis and a loneliness crisis and a climate crisis and see how urgently we need to rethink, but none of us were trained for it. A good life still means our own space, set up just how we like it, and not having to engage with people we're not related to before coffee. Ideally not even them. And all the systems are set up for that vision of a good life, not for the one we were increasingly drawn to.

I was nervous, in particular, about the kids. Lots of people experiment with more communal ways of living when their lives are relatively unencumbered. Communalists cluster in their twenties and their fifties and sixties. The middle years of grind, for those of us lucky or foolhardy enough to have procreated, easily feels like a time of hunkering down and withdrawing, rather than seeking to connect outwardly more deeply. As well as there being reduced capacity for the demands of community, living in an unconventional way felt like we were taking a huge risk with our children's childhoods. What could turn into a short experimental chapter for us would form their whole life, for better or worse, because what we experience in our early years is so foundational. I was hyper aware that our utopian dreams could harm them, crowding out the parent–child bond, failing to give them sustained attention or sufficient space, or even make them vulnerable to abuse. So many communities built on high ideals end in flames, and the children involved are too often collateral damage.

And yet. The hard-headed pragmatist in me couldn't quite squash the sense that fully aliveness lay in this direction. I was beginning to think the whole thing was a pipe dream when our heads were turned by a new couple in church. They were younger, recently married, but had both lived in community houses before. They seemed wise beyond their years, and their experiences had been positive enough that they were keen to live in community again. We pounced.

It took three years to get to where we are now. After establishing we were both serious we spent one night a week together, basically dating each other. I needed to trust the bones of anyone who would be living so close to my children, and we really didn't know each other at all. Things got intense fast. We talked about our values, our expectations of home, our childhood wounds. We did personality tests and discussed them, examined conflict styles. We talked about money, that most British of taboos, how much we each had, how much we wanted to share, how far off we still were from being able to afford to stay in the area we'd made a life in. We prayed together and for each other. We went on field trips to other communities. We wrote a vision and sketched a rule of life together. And finally, towards the end of 2020, as the dangers of isolation got ever clearer, we jumped.

We've now been living together, first renting and now jointly owning, with the help of a band of visionary souls who have invested in the project, for over three years. We have a joint mortgage, a joint account, a joint fridge and a joint table. All the chores are divided up, so I cook twice a week and never do the shopping. One housemate is the quartermaster, in charge of stores, one the CFO, who keeps us on budget, one the Head of Estates, who leads on DIY, and I'm. . . I'm now worrying that I'm not contributing, but I think in fact I'm Head of Planning and Hospitality, always asking, 'What's next?', 'Who shall we invite for dinner?' and 'When is the next party?' Parties are high on our list of house values.

I love living as an extended household, almost always supplemented by anything from one to four guests who need somewhere to stay. We have our own bedrooms but share all the common space. We shop and eat together, cooking on a rota, chalking up a blackboard to indicate how many people are in, how many extras we are bringing. We order bulk from a whole-food cooperative, because you're not a proper commune if you don't always have 5kg of lentils on-site. Once a week we have house nights, a mix of connecting with each other and admin, and it's sacrosanct, requiring permission from everyone to skip. This small constraint on my freedom chafes on my proud independence sometimes but I know I need it. The distracting tides of life will pull us away from each other unless we create, and commit to, the structures to stop them.

I think we're here for the long haul. I want to be. I know it's partly because I am getting old, but fully aliveness feels like it means sticking, not twisting, at least for the foreseeable. Early monastic vows included a promise of stability and many orders still ask members to commit to staying in one place. It sounds easier than poverty, chastity and obedience, but for my generation at least it might be harder.

Commitment sounds constraining but has felt liberating. Meaningful relationships take time, and my desire to keep my options open in case a better offer comes along was continually undermining that. I am so grateful for the technologies that mean it is possible to maintain friendships and family relationships over distance, but my experience is that community requires proximity.

I know not everyone is going to move into a commune, even a micro one, but I think a move in this direction is possible for those less weird than us. If there are people in your life that you want to commit to, long term, what would it look like to give them a stake in moving decisions? To take into account not just convenience and lifestyle and economics when deciding where to live, but the web of relationships you would either strengthen or weaken? I know groups of friends – and this gets harder as people have kids – who have done exactly that: committed to making decisions about moving collectively, to give others a say. It is a small but surprisingly radical step, and a tiny act of resistance to the proud individualism that tells us completely unfettered choice will make us happy.

An even smaller step in this direction might be relinquishing full control of your time. A set appointment with the people you want to be growing alongside, just a regular lunch or a walk, can be enough of a structure to keep you connected. It can sound intense, being the one to suggest it, and it's even harder to express a hope you will all try to protect it, to flake only if it's really important. Asking commitment of each other, offering it ourselves, goes against the grain of our current social scripts. It is hard enough in romantic relationships. But it can be transformative. Conversations can stretch out and continue rather than just being the usual download of news. You can come to know each other more deeply, to be more deeply known, and the sacrifice of turning down other options to protect that time gets easier.

Some people, motivated by duty, who know they thrive on structure, will find this easier than I do. I'm naturally spontaneous and distractible, always on the lookout for my next adventure, but in locking myself into a community against my flibbertigibbet tendencies I feel only relief. The constant horizon scanning of where we might move and how we might live is over. It's done. We're here. This green grass is our grass and other people's grass is not my business. Now how can we love these neighbours?

I love living in community. And I hate it some days too. But mostly I feel grateful to have manoeuvred into a situation that provides scaffolding against my own disconnecting tendencies. And also some distress at how visible these proud tendencies now are.

I know living in community, even a micro one like ours, sounds idealistic. And it is, in so far as we have certain ideals about what community can and should be like. We think it's possible to structure life together so that there is more care and more capacity to go around. We think the inevitable conflict, when managed with commitment and compassion, can be a source of deepening intimacy. We believe that a bunch of imperfect, selfish, proud and fragile humans can become a little less selfish, a bit braver and a lot more use in our hurting world by living in close proximity.

We don't, however, expect perfection. Far from it. Living in community rapidly strips you of any rose-tinted expectations. Idealism that doesn't reckon with the reality of human nonsense is useless. We believe the things above to be possible, but far from guaranteed, and we think without divine help the chance *we* will embody it becomes vanishingly small. We are not doing this because we have some kind of relational superpower. Believe me.

This week we had an emotional two-hour conversation about the dishwasher. I've felt grumpy about it three times since. We need a new one and can't decide which type. I want my way and so does everyone else. Trying to decide things via consensus is time consuming, often boring and the opposite of efficient. I'm always in a hurry and have had to learn to tolerate my housemates still talking about a question I thought we'd solved an hour ago. They've had to tolerate my low attention to detail and tendency to bodge my way through things. I think done is better than perfect, another housemate thinks if something is worth doing it's worth doing properly. We've had tense house nights where all the ways we are different were laid bare.

Walking our way through our differences, as slowly and

honestly as we can, is a ritualised embodiment of our value that relationships are more important than tasks, that we want to move from pride to love. If that sounds romantic, it is not. My experience is that community kills the romantic idea. Illusions die here, especially my illusions about myself. I really am petty enough to mind about an ugly mug being on show and who mopped the floor last. I am snippy and critical when I am overwhelmed, or before 10 a.m. I forget that other people are really real, too often relegate them to an audience for my main character energy. And the only way through is to bring all that out into the light. Anything unsaid festers like a dead mouse in a trap.

We have a slot in our weekly house night for what has become known as 'gear grind love wells'. This started because one housemate likes to talk in terms of 'how we can love each other well', for example, by putting the lid on the butter or not leaving the back door unlocked. Another thinks this is sentimental dressing up of what should actually be called 'what grinds my gears'. So we use both, a weekly slot to raise the things that bug us rather than swallow them. It comes halfway through a straightforward agenda of practicalities (who is in the guest room this week, who is cooking when) and when we get to it there is often a beat, a breath in as we lightly brace ourselves. Raising annoyances can't help but give us a tiny dose of fight-or-flight. If I'm the one sharing something, I fear looking petty or intolerant, so feel exposed. If I've annoyed someone else, I too easily get defensive. There is always a choice about how to respond, whether to meet the feedback with a soft heart or shut down. Recently when I was tired and fragile I got defensive and snappy in response to a housemate's totally reasonable request not to leave toothbrushes by the sink in the kitchen. Learning to breathe through these feelings has been vital. It underlines, week by week, that annoying each other can coexist with loving each other, being completely for each other. It's a tiny practice of tolerating the tension of difference.

This sometimes-excoriating culture of honesty corrodes my pride. I have to admit when I'm hurt and be vulnerable, ask for what I need. I would rather not know that I hurt or irritate others, and say sorry, but it's essential to prevent distance from creeping into our home. There is no hiding. And there is, it seems, no need to hide. Thus far, when I've brought the worst of myself into the light, it's been met with grace and humour and understanding. My household doesn't love me because I'm perfect. I'm not. Neither are they. We love each other and affirm the best of each other because we've chosen to. We are covenanted together, which is more like a vow than a contract. We are all wanting to grow up in the same direction.

If you've ever wondered about living more relationally, beyond the small steps above, I'd encourage you to follow that curiosity. Centuries of monks and nuns have left a rich body of wisdom to help us. You'll have to push quite hard against the stories and structures that block the path, but it is possible. Despite the challenges, I can't imagine, now, living another way. I have grown more steadiness of soul in the last three years than in the previous twenty combined. I think that the world that is coming, the societies that emerge as the world as we have known it passes away, will force many of us into more forms of communal living in any case. Choosing to learn how to do it well now feels like work worth doing.

I have come to think of living in community, along with many of the practices in this book, in terms of hormesis.

Hormesis is the biological term for a beneficial or stimulatory effect caused by exposure to low doses of something that is harmful in large doses.[8] For instance, cold-water swimming will kill you if you stay in too long, but a few minutes of immersion shocks your body in a way that strengthens multiple systems. Pushing our muscles too hard can injure them, but going to just before that point, creating micro tears, is what strengthens them. The body overcompensates, essentially. And this is true for our mental health too. Psychologists use the phrase 'eustress' for types of short-term, boundaried stress that lead to neurological growth.[9] Plants have a similar response, reacting to stress by releasing bio-active compounds that can confer stress resistance. This is part of why eating plants is so good for us, because we get those compounds second hand. Any gardener knows that stressing plants on purpose is part of tending them. Unpruned plants will not flourish.

None of this is to say that everything that does not kill you makes you stronger. Some things traumatise or crush us. Long-term stress can be as horrific for health as eustress is good. Like most truths, it's complex.

But eustress or hormesis (or indeed pruning, the biblical metaphor) give me a language for why the less pleasant bits of community still feel like they are making me more fully alive. As iron sharpens iron, the biblical book of Proverbs says, so one person sharpens another. Friction can graze, or it can polish. If we were having violent arguments every day, it would be harming me. Regular, contained conflict, which we are all committed to navigating well, feels instead like it is helping me learn. My pride is being slowly, imperfectly, suffocated to death. And it feels like the kind of death that is necessary to really live.

Even as I write this I am aware I am not selling it, even to myself. Yay, death! Why on earth would I choose a life that is harder? Taking a less comfortable path on purpose is counter cultural. The economy relies on our insatiable appetite for smoothing out the highway. The entrepreneur's mantra is find a 'need' (code for an inconvenience) and create a product to solve it. It's that pesky hedonic adaptation again. Ordering over the phone and walking to pick up a takeaway used to just be how you got a takeaway. Now that delivery apps exist it feels like a massive ball-ache. If I had enough money I could optimise effort right out of my life, as I imagine the super rich do.

If the eustress/hormesis theory has any legitimacy though, this might be another reason money doesn't make us happy. I think we want, deep down, something to be asked of us. We want to rise to the challenge of life. I'm haunted by the children's film *Wall-E*, in which humans circle the earth on a giant spaceship after they've made the planet uninhabitable with their rubbish. Aboard, life is a cruise ship, requiring nothing. People become too overweight and unfit to walk so use mobility buggies and are constantly hypnotised by their hyper-personalised devices. By designing out discomfort and challenge, the whole race has become overgrown babies, passively consuming what is fed to them, like a mass regression. It's a piercing parody that reveals the eventual endpoint of all this optimisation. Getting our own way all the time does not make us happy, it makes us lonely and lost in purposeless leisure – usually on the backs of a class of people who pay for it. In *Wall-E* it's robots. In our world, it is not.

Living beyond the nuclear family is one of the ways I have tried to break the spell of the *Wall-E* cruise ship of comfort. Only semi-successfully, obviously. I still love comfort. I just spent too many hours researching and too much money buying a second-hand Loaf bed with a squishy velvet-covered headboard. It's not exactly a monk's cell. But the minor discomforts of community are a gesture, a doable-feeling contribution towards creating a tiny pocket of alternative logic. I can't be the only one who wants to resist the prevailing values of wider society, to 'give [it] the slip', as Christian anarchist Jacques Ellul wrote in the 1930s. I don't have grandiose dreams of triggering a new civilisational order, but I do want to more clearly become a citizen of a different kingdom, one where I'm growing outwards, not inwards. And it turns out having to talk to people before I have had my coffee helps.

Community: church

The other community that I am allowing to chip away at my pride may be more familiar. I love church. People don't say this much. The stories of institutional failure, hypocrisy and disappointment are real and well known. At a national and institutional level, most church bodies are almost laughably disappointing, despite some good people's best efforts. Throughout history they too often have been far worse than that, complicit in deep injustices, from slavery to child abuse. The leader of the festival where I became a Christian the first time was found by the Church of England's National Safeguarding Team to have used 'coercive and controlling behaviour' with people under his care.[10] The leader of the organisation running the theology weekends that were so formative in my return to faith was later exposed as a sexual abuser.[11] If it wasn't so tragic it would be funny. Church can hurt us.

I've been hurt by church in more direct ways too. We chose to leave a church, that much-loved church which first made us want to commit to the city, because of a catastrophic relational breakdown between leaders. Their falling out became bitter and was apparently unresolvable, exacerbated perhaps by being unable to meet in person during the pandemic. I joked, darkly, at the time that at least there was no abuse and no affair. Still, it was painful watching people we respected fail to resolve their differences, get angrier and more wounded. Not least because Jesus was pretty clear that Christians should be known by their love for each other. Their conflict was a relational bomb going off in the heart of our community, and many of us scattered like shrapnel.

Psychologists talk of the wounds of belonging. It harms us to be lonely and disconnected, but with any community comes risk. We've experienced the grief of committing to a group of people that imploded. It would be easy to let that experience colour our whole posture towards church, but it doesn't. The way things end does not define what they are. The story I want to tell about that church community has a sad ending, but that is just one page in the book. Prior to the implosion, we benefitted from a decade of solidarity and growth and tender care. We met every week with people different from us who we supported and felt fully supported by. The church was small enough that we all knew each other. If I'd had an emergency, a sick child or just been locked out, I could have picked up the phone in the middle of the night to any one of them, and known they'd come.

A fixed point in the week when you see the same people without having to schedule it acts as a trellis for relationships. Ideals need structure. They need a critical mass of committed people, who can be broadly relied on, who are all willingly being formed by the same things, repeatedly turning their attention in the same direction. When the terms of engagement are clear, it self-sorts. People come who are longing to belong to something meaningful, who share the vision, and those people stay. It's increasingly hard to find as we lose the habits of being committed and reliable, though I've seen it happen, for seasons at least, in community choirs, in unions, in experiments with non-religious spiritual community like The Sunday Assembly or The Nearness.

Philosopher Byung-Chul Han describes how many of us, especially younger generations, do not have that kind of scaffolding. He uses the memorable phrase 'where all that is solid melts into information' to give a sense of how destabilising a hyper-personalised, low-commitment, largely digital existence is.[12] Zygmunt Bauman called it 'Liquid Modernity', the sense of sloshing beneath our feet as all the structures and stories we've inherited begin to dissolve.[13] Han's prescription for this bewildering and unsettling condition sounds a lot like church to me: 'What we need most are temporal structures that stabilize life . . . Stability comes over long stretches of time: faithfulness, bonds, integrity, commitment, promises, trust. These are the social practices that hold a community together. They all have a ritual character.'[14]

Those structures can provide some very concrete benefits. A functioning church is a living experiment in the gift economy. Stuff is shared, resources flow where they are needed. Let there be no one poor among you, one of the New Testament letters to an embryonic church commands. Not 'Don't let the poor in', far from it. Rather, don't let them stay poor when you are rich. The early church in the biblical book of Acts sounds full-blown communist:

> All the believers were one in heart and mind. No one claimed that any of their possessions was their own, but they shared everything they had . . . And God's grace was so powerfully at work in them all, that there were no needy persons among them. For from time to time those who owned land or houses sold them, brought the money from the sales and put it at the apostles' feet, and it was distributed to anyone who had need.[15]

In our last church, when we were pregnant with a toddler and were dragging bags and buggies and childcare detritus around the country on public transport, all while my pelvis was coming apart, we were gifted a car anonymously. It's common practice in many churches that old cars aren't sold, but donated, so the owners asked the pastor who needed it. He said that we might be glad of it. In that pastor's excruciatingly sad leaving service, he said that this had been his favourite part of the job, being able to act as a sort of Father Christmas for all the gifts that passed among us anonymously. A couple of years later an envelope appeared after church in my handbag labelled 'for therapy', containing a thousand pounds in cash. My husband was in the middle of a breakdown. I have no idea who it was, to this day. It could have been any of them. They all knew what was going on. We knew these things about each other. My pride always wants to present a neat and tidy narrative of my life, to be someone with her shit together. That instinct gets rapidly worn away in real community. When someone asked, 'How are you doing?' I would actually tell them, and they me. The sense of being seen and held was so intense I'd often cry just walking through the doors from relief. I still miss it.

I regret no part of our time at that church, despite the bewilderment as it all fell apart. As the Jack Gilbert poem

'Icarus' says, just because something ended it doesn't mean it failed. Maybe we, like Icarus, were just coming to the end of our triumph. Being part of a functional, loving, committed community for ten years sometimes did feel like flying. I don't want the grief of what seemed a bitterly unnecessary ending to erase my memories of, my gratitude for, what came before it.

The church we are in now is life-giving in different ways. It's a local Anglican, doing what parish churches do best, pulling in a real cross-section of the neighbourhood. It is a refreshingly functional local civic institution. It is racially and socio-economically more diverse than any gathering I have ever been part of. The worship band includes a wealthy Dulwich-based classical composer and a young mum in insecure, mouldy social housing. There are many people with disabilities and additional needs, over-educated graduates like us, more than a hundred children. Members of the congregation have been in parliament and in prison. It runs a prison ministry, a food bank, a debt advice centre and multiple toddler groups. Recently I went to help make tea and coffee for the debt advice training course. That evening, huddled in a corner of the cavernous space with just one radiator on because of the bills, I met a Syrian refugee, a local art student covered in piercings, a female taxi driver resplendent in corn rows and multiple gold chains, a straight-talking Scottish nurse and a weary-eyed social worker. Church is social cohesion in action. It's messy, and sometimes embarrassing, theologically confused and absolutely beautiful. I feel enormously privileged to be a part of it, to have it at the bottom of our road. I suspect churches like this are not to be found everywhere, but I also think there are more of them than we realise.

I am team church. It's common now for thoughtful

Christians to check out, to practise their faith privately. The gap between what church should be and what it often is can ache and chafe. The racial diversity in our current church has required painful conversations, prayer and wise navigation over recent years. People have been hurt and said unwise things. Given the seismic shifts in the Church of England, I'm sure discussions around sexuality are going to get equally painful. I'd bet a lot of money that we don't all agree. It's very far from a perfect community.

But we already hear the stories of church gone wrong. I have my own. I am not trying to discount them – I want to hear them with a soft heart. I am though trying to balance them, for the sake of accuracy. We don't hear the stories of happy churches, like we don't hear the stories of happy marriages and happy families. Maybe they are boring, as Tolstoy implied. Bits of church *are* boring – the bad sermons, the rotas, the people you don't really like telling you a long story over coffee. Sometimes I sit there and critique it, wincing at the clanger in the prayers or the tone-deaf comments in the sermon, but that just disconnects me. I can't be part of it when I'm feeling superior, when I let my pride be the lens through which I see it.

I have concluded all these irritating things are part of the deal. When I take my eyes off Church with a capital C, the big institutions and bishops and televangelists, and just look at this imperfectly glorious huddle of ragtag local people, my heart softens into love. All this mess is the compost on which community grows, and it's not made in my image, to my design, thank God.

Being part of a local congregation is my weekly dose of pride-prevention medicine. It reminds me that I am interconnected, interdependent, and that the prize of overcoming my judgey nature is feeling part of this joyful, semi-competent, unlikely group of people. It's rare and strange and fragile and difficult. It's a different kingdom, a different economy, in a normcore disguise, hidden under a steeple.

I wonder where you find the scaffolding for community. Church may not be for everyone, but we all need somewhere to belong. It requires vulnerability, to name this need, to go looking for it, and will inevitably involve disappointment. We are formed into good little consumers and the mental and emotional shift required to commit to something that does not adapt to our preferences is a big one. Oliver Burkeman, a writer on productivity and self help, concluded, however, that 'Freedom . . . is to be found not in achieving greater sovereignty over your own schedule but in allowing yourself to be constrained by the rhythms of community – participating in forms of social life where you don't get to decide exactly what you do or when you do it.'[16]

Community will always require something of us, and that is annoying. I still find it annoying. I want the benefits without the cost. I want to know connection – love, even – without surrendering my sovereignty, my pride. But I've seen enough to know that this kind of healthy community is a pearl of great price, and what it asks of me is more than worth paying.

THE G BOMB

And so here we are, the place the steeple above my church claims to point to. I hope I have not just been dodging, but circling, circling the summit rather than attempting a direct ascent. It feels important to creep up on the idea of [God], not because [God] is skittish, but because we are. We're easily spooked by the psychological depth charge of the possibility of unconditional love. Under the hustle and cynicism and responsibility, how many of us also know that raw and bitter-sweet longing? Abi Morgan in *This is Not a Pity Memoir* says, 'I cry for a God who I neither trust nor even think exists.'[1] She expresses the ambiguity so many people feel, the ambiguity I knew when praying all those years ago in Manchester, 'I don't believe in you.'

Maybe it comes from our buried child selves. Who wouldn't want to be known and loved, exactly as they are, by something wiser and kinder and stronger than we can conceive? Rowan Williams explains what this means for him: 'I do not have to be my own origin. I do not have to try and be a self-creator. There is a level of affirmation bringing me into and holding me in existence which I do not have to work for.'[2]

I feel relief even writing that, a desire to lean back into it, but also a heavy duty of care. I'm not in the room with you. The possibility of something akin to a cosmic parent can't help but be bound up in our experiences of our own parents and, as Larkin said, they fuck us up.[3] I don't know your wounds and resentments, the colour of your bruises, whether this sets off an emotional firestorm of contempt or just leaves you cold and completely baffled. Ultimately, what if I'm wrong? How dare I risk raising that most flammable of hopes, in *this* world, its beauty shot through with blood? Trying to write about [God] is terrifying.

As well as my fear of causing harm, the tools all seem unfit for purpose. Striving to convey something about [God] in words is like trying to net a storm cloud. It's been done so badly that the endeavour itself now smells faintly dishonourable. Any attempt to capture the divine in a 'cage of concepts' is like trying to fit a dragon into a kennel: it can only end in injury.[4] There is a school of theology called apophatism, which responds to this problem by refusing to talk of [God] positively at all. It's sometimes called negative theology, and rests on the conviction that the essence of [God] is unknowable and therefore attempts at description should be avoided. It is sounding very attractive right now. Orthodox Jews refuse to speak or write the divine name out of a similar sense: it is dangerous presumption.

I often feel like the army general quoted by C. S. Lewis who rejects theology because the ideas and systems don't seem to relate to his actual experience: 'I know there's a God. I've felt Him: out alone in the desert at night: the tremendous mystery. And that's just why I don't believe all your neat little dogmas and formulas about Him. To anyone who's met the real thing they all seem so petty and pedantic and unreal!' Lewis admits that when the general 'turned from that experience to the Christian creeds . . . he was really turning from something quite real to something less real. In the same way, if a man has once looked at the Atlantic from the beach, and then goes and looks at a map of the Atlantic, he also will be turning from something more real to something less real: turning from real waves to a bit of coloured paper.'[5]

I can't show you the waves. When I'm swimming in the sea I am not thinking about how to communicate the experience, I am just in it. You can only swim in the sea for yourself. You can only decide one day to strip off your protective layers and dive right in. The best I can hope to create is a crayon drawing, a bit of coloured paper that might tempt you to go for a seaside walk one day, sniffing the air. Which might make those of us who do regularly go for a dip seem 5 per cent less mad. I followed someone else's crayon drawing down to the shore, after all.

I am not saying anything the mystics have not been saying for centuries. Those who have meditated faithfully for decades tell of a form of consciousness not accessible to the rest of us, like a secret level in *Mario Kart*. You don't even have to put [God] into the equation directly if it's too scary. Jeffrey Kripal, who holds a Chair in Philosophy, writes in his book *The Flip* about the emerging school of panpsychism, which claims that consciousness is present in all material things. The intuition is that there is a mind at work, indeed a mind *in*, all matter, and it is gaining some highly qualified adherents. Kripal admits that 'abstract third person knowledge . . . of that mind is seldom, if ever sufficient . . . it usually takes a deeply personal and direct encounter with the minded cosmos to convince an intellectual or a scientist'. He also acknowledges that this means we are trying to talk about these encounters across a great chasm, because it is 'so convincing to those who have known it, and so unconvincing to those who have not'.[6]

If you have not experienced what Kripal calls 'the flip' I can't help but be unconvincing. This process is hurting my writerly ego, because I don't know how to write about my best thing. My best thing is not enclosable in words. The words themselves are beginning to fall apart in my hands. [God]. That sign of a million signifiers. The brackets are failing to hold all the meanings in now. It's a noun, not a proper name. Sitting like a stone on my tongue threatening to go down the wrong way.

Maybe it would help to go back to pride. Pride is the big cheese of sins in theology not just because it keeps us from the intimacy and community we are designed for but because it makes an encounter with God impossible. Pride disconnects us because it regards need as the enemy. Relationships of broad equality or sycophancy are all that are acceptable to pride, and any connection with the divine is not likely to deliver that. Almost all religions conceive of God as above and beyond us, and approaching with a swagger as liable to end badly.

I find the fact that Frank Sinatra's 'My Way' is the most popular funeral song genuinely horrifying. I feel angry even thinking about it. Not only because it's a bad song (don't @ me) but because generations have been infected, at their most vulnerable moments of deep reflection, with the idea that a proud individualism is something to celebrate.

The last verse of 'My Way' contains the line that best explains my hatred. It argues that a man has nothing but himself, and warns against being 'one who kneels', that last phrase sung with a stylish sneer.

This song summarises pride for me. It is no surprise that Donald Trump danced to it at his inauguration ball. It's a con. What we have, at the end of our lives, if we have lived them well, is not ourselves, but a team, a family (whether biological or chosen), a weighty legacy of encounter and relationship that rings a note in eternity. The desire to be invulnerable, so scared of coercion or the demands of mutual care that we consistently cut the threads between us and other people is poison. It is sin. And its high priest is Ol' Blue Eyes.

I know that kneeling, like gratitude, can sound weak or abject. It's a posture of respect and submission and we don't want to submit. Again, this is often for good reasons. Women spent too many centuries submitting. So did people of colour. They had no choice. To stand, eye to eye with each other, with dignity and honour, does feel like life. When we always metaphorically kneel when other people are standing, there is something wrong.

But I believe there are some doors we can only pass through on our knees.

In Christian thought, doing it 'my way' is the wide and foolish road, leading to a bleak and shrunken island. An acknowledgement of our need is the necessary condition for fullness of life. We kneel in prayer, in reverence, in respect. I kneel, regularly, in church, despite it not being a normal part of our services, because I want to put my body in a position that will help my stubborn heart line up. I don't find it abject, or humiliating. My pride is the tyrant in this situation and I want her tamed. I find it freeing.

I can spend so much of my time clenched against my circumstances, strategising and catastrophising my future, defending my patchy scrap of self. Kneeling is a way of embodying surrender, of saying, 'I am not God, I have not got this, but it might be ok anyway'. I find it the quickest way to a sense of abundance and rest and compassion. Kneeling almost always feel like relief.

I guess it depends who you think you are kneeling to. Irish

philosopher John Moriarty wrote a book called *Nostos*, meaning homecoming, in which he recorded his 'genuine search for the truth . . . a truth I would surrender to'.[7] Maybe it's weakness, to want that, but Christianity has again taught me to be less scared of weakness. In its inverted status system, that is where the treasure is. Even so, I am proud, so find surrender of all kinds difficult. Get behind me, Nietzsche. Spiritual surrender is only possible (or wise) to someone who feels trustworthy enough. Rowan Williams again – one of the few writers I can actually read on this subject – calls what he is willing to surrender to 'The Other who does not compete, with whom I don't have to and can't bargain; the Other beyond violence, the regard that will not be evaded or deflected, yet has and seeks no advantage.'[8]

The other who holds me in a loving regard. The other I believe I am kneeling before is not a distant deity demanding obsequiousness from cowering servants. It feels instead like this Other is meeting me, and the mental image that rises unprompted when I pray is of us forehead to forehead, in a posture that therefore implies (and perhaps this is skirting heresy) that God is kneeling too.

This posture is a clue for me. Maybe I was struggling to write about God because the concept tends to abstraction. And Christianity is shot through, not with theses and propositions but with the 'scandal of particularity'. Scripture indicates that we can learn about the divine better in a story than on a spreadsheet. Seventeenth-century scientific prodigy Blaise Pascal wrote about a profound religious experience, sometimes known as his 'night of fire', which sounds a lot like my experience in the cowshed:

The year of grace 1654
Monday, 23 November.
From about half past ten in the evening until half past midnight.

Fire
'God of Abraham, God of Isaac, God of Jacob,' not of philosophers and scholars.

Certainty, certainty, heartfelt, joy, peace.
God of Jesus Christ.
God of Jesus Christ.
My God and your God.

. . .

Joy, joy, joy, tears of joy.[9]

Pascal met God, and found there 'not the God of the philosophers or scholars.' Not a God he could capture in a pithy formulation, or a hypothesis to be tested. The God of specific people, in a specific story. The God of the incarnation, in which the divine lives in and through a helpless immigrant outcast baby, son of a shamed woman and later of a widow. The echoes with the 'quartet of the vulnerable' ring loudly. The God of the crucifixion, in which the power of the universe knows betrayal, suffers in a way reserved for the scum of the earth. My God is not a parody of power, but instead one who makes themselves woundable. This is no superhero story. My experience of the divine is not through theory or argument. My God is personal, and the only way to encounter a person is to seek them out.

In a novel I was reading recently, a delightful, Pulitzer Prize-winning romcom about a middle-aged man called Arthur Less, I was struck by this paragraph:

> Arthur says nothing, and Robert says nothing. He knows the absurdity of asking someone to explain love or sorrow. You can't point to it. It would be as futile, as unconveyable as pointing to the sky and saying 'that one, that star, there.'[10]

One of my favourite hymns also pairs love and sorrow, which is maybe why these lines stood out to me. 'When I Survey the Wondrous Cross' describes the crucifixion of Jesus with a focus on these two tender terms:

> See from His head, His hands, His feet,
> Sorrow and love flow mingled down!
> Did e'er such love and sorrow meet,
> Or thorns compose so rich a crown?[11]

You may have noticed I haven't talked a lot about the crucifixion in this book. I don't trust my own sense of my motivations, but at least a conscious reason is that I don't think I can make it 'useful'. This is a book designed for those in search of spiritual core strength and curious about what the practices, postures and principles of Christianity might have to teach them. It's not primarily for those actively seeking faith. That wasn't the book I felt called or able to write. And the crucifixion, for me, is Holy Ground, a place to approach only if you fall into the latter category.

The crucifixion of Jesus is where we derive the word 'excruciating' from, and also 'crucial'. It is, literally, the crux of the matter. In Christian thought, and in my life, it is a place of love and sorrow, two things more truly expressed in poetry than in propositions.

People do make propositions out of the cross, of course. Those with minds formed differently from mine might tell you it's simple. The symbol becomes quasi-mathematical, a plus on top of a twisted minus. Our sin plus Jesus' death equals freedom.

I was never very good at maths. I can't get hold of this sum.

Thankfully, I don't find a sum in the text I've chosen to treat as sacred. The New Testament speaks of the crucifixion using complex, kaleidoscopic imagery, a rich and textured tapestry of metaphor. After the Gospels, which narrate it from slightly different perspectives, every biblical writer who touches on it offers a subtly different account of its meaning. It's a scandal, an offence, a shameful death in solidarity with the enslaved, a substitutionary act, a ransom payment, a prophetic proclamation of the path of self-emptying. It's a ritual re-enactment of the Exodus, a recapitulation, a stitch across an open wound, the liberation of a besieged city.

In her magisterial book on the cross, Fleming Rutledge helped me relax about the fact I don't seem able to make it work like maths: 'None of the symbols, motifs and themes "work" in any logical way, either as analogies or as theories to explain what God in Christ is doing on the cross. They are figures of speech, and as such require imagination and participation. As people of faith, we do not interpret them so much as we inhabit them – and indeed . . . they inhabit us.'[12]

The cross is ground zero of connection for me. It is the narrative climax, the repair of what was broken at the beginning, in Eden. I just keep turning and turning the kaleidoscope, inhabiting the story as the cycle of the year unfolds.

I've shifted emphases over time, had different favourite,

worn-smooth sections of the tapestry. The most vivid thread, which I find woven through every patch, is grace. Whatever happened on the cross, it somehow sweeps away the economic story of debt and credit, earning and striving, and instead pours out unearned compassion. When I can accept it, it reconnects me without me having to try, and so makes me relax my shoulders. This place of love and sorrow feels to me like a still point in the swirling story of the world. It's a place for me to stand. Somewhere I can shelter. I don't know why exactly, how this relates to all the other stories we tell about the world or ourselves, why this one story, this one symbol liberates me so fundamentally. I just receive it.

I am aware that this chapter will be driving some of you bonkers. I am doing the precise opposite of what books on faith are supposed to do. My argument, and it is more like an invitation, is that the only way to understand what Christians mean by God is to train your attention in a different way. Or: if you want to understand it you have to inhabit it.

If this all still sounds unbearably insubstantial, maybe some neuroscience would help make what I mean clearer. That is how we make things convincing nowadays, after all. I've spoken to many people on my podcast, *The Sacred*, about what they believe. One of the most memorable was Matthew Taylor, the former head of the RSA and Tony Blair's policy unit, now chair of the NHS Federation.[13] His father Laurie Taylor is a life-long atheist, and Matthew was raised to atheism. He is, however, taking his daughter to church, because, as he admits, he'd like her to be able to believe. He would like to believe himself, though he currently doesn't. We spoke about this seeming inconsistency. Why, many would ask, would you want your child to believe something you cannot prove is true? Together, we grasped at this sense that there are many forms of knowledge, and those of us formed in a world that privileges a narrow range can nevertheless sense that there might be more. The work of psychiatrist and neuroscientist Iain McGilchrist has been immensely helpful for me on this. He argues that our different brain hemispheres have different modes of attention – the left is concrete, linear, mathematical, theoretical. It sees the world as inanimate and breaks things down into component parts. The right sees the whole, how things connect together, is the seat of intuition, creativity and what we might call spirituality. Importantly, McGilchrist thinks, it is the better hemisphere at grounding us in reality.

Because our brains are plastic, formed by our habits and what we repeatedly pay attention to, when we live in a world that heavily emphasises one way of knowing, we can lose touch with the other function. We lose fluency in the other, innate language until it sounds like gobbledygook. It isn't that the language of the other hemisphere no longer makes sense, but *we* can no longer make sense of *it*. McGilchrist argues that contemporary Western societies have dangerously and repeatedly prioritised left-hemisphere forms of attention over right. We measure and dissect and pin the butterfly to the wall. And this has consequences in our neurobiology. Because we can only really see what we pay attention to, not fleetingly, but over time.

McGilchrist argues that understanding these different modes of attention is foundational, because they control 'nothing less than the way we relate to the world. And it doesn't just dictate the kind of relationship we have with whatever it is: it dictates what it is that we come to have a relationship with.'[14] Matthew Taylor and I concluded we both take our kids to church out of the same instinct that makes us sign them up for music lessons, to literally form their minds through habits of attention. To widen the range of what they can see and hear. A child who has played an instrument will encounter an orchestra differently than one who hasn't. They will experience more. The instinct is not to constrain their choices, but to keep their options open. I don't want them trapped in a solely left hemispheric world, for the possibility of divine love to slip out of their field of vision like the gorilla at the back of the basketball game. If my kids have been exposed to religious ways of knowing it will be easier for them to conceive of the possibility of God, even if they later choose to reject it.

Another guest, Professor Tom Shakespeare, recounted to me how he moved from being agnostic to Christian after taking up a friend's invitation to read the Gospels every day. If you do it, something will change, she said, and it did. Jesus went from being an interesting ethical teacher to someone profoundly present in his own life.[15] I wonder if immersing himself in a right-hemispheric world for long enough cleaned his glasses, cleansed his palate enough to see and taste something else. Something that – he would say – had always been there, just out of the range of his perception.

In trying to broaden our set of epistemologies, I'm not going to convince you that God exists. I honestly think only encounter can do that, though removing some intellectual barriers can help. My goal here is more modest, to show that an instinct that there isn't a God might not be as neutral or obvious as it appears, but the outcome of a set of social conditions, cultural stories and formative practices. It is possible that it is a result of what you have chosen to pay attention to, the way your culture has formed what you can and can't perceive.

Blaise Pascal, who had an ecstatic experience in his 'night of fire', is more famous for a piece of writing that has become known as Pascal's Wager. It has been distorted and diluted in cultural transmission, as so many things about my tradition are. I thought it claimed that people should believe in God because the consequences for not believing and being wrong were worse than the opposite. It's much subtler than that, and reads as freshly honest four centuries later. He was too smart to say that you could make yourself believe in God on the basis of odds. He recognised the tension of people who aren't sure, saying: 'If I saw nothing . . . which revealed a Divinity, I would come to a negative conclusion; if I saw everywhere the signs of a Creator, I would remain peacefully in faith. But, seeing too much to deny and too little to be sure, I am in a state to be pitied . . . I envy those whom I see living in the faith with such carelessness.'[16]

Pascal vacillated between doubt and faith himself, and didn't think you could make yourself believe in anything. The piece is a dialogue, with someone (himself?) who says, 'I am so made that I cannot believe. What, then, would you have me do?' The conclusion is very similar to mine, and comfortingly prosaic: 'Learn of those . . . people who know the way which you would follow, and who are cured of an ill of which you would be cured. Follow the way by which they began; by acting as if they believed, taking the holy water, having masses said, etc.' Basically, if you would like to believe, but don't, you might as well go to church. It goes on, 'Even this will naturally make you believe, "But this is what I am afraid of."– And why? What have you to lose?'[17]

This final astute awareness – 'this is what I'm afraid of' – puts a finger right in the middle of the painful mental knot I worried at during my attempted atheism. I didn't want to be fooled, to let wishful thinking dictate my life. I didn't, deep down, want to be aligned with the irrational, the children, the poor and the needy who flocked to Jesus. Who still flock now, around the globe. I wanted to be better than that. I wanted to be a grown-up. I was scared of losing myself, losing, in fact, my pride, and also desperate for it.

The *Pensées* in which the wager features were written two or three years after Pascal's 'night of fire', his ecstatic encounter with the divine. I had assumed the chronology was the other way round. Faith is rarely as linear as that. A powerful experiential encounter with God didn't settle the question forever. It is possible to feel you have met God, and still not know if you believe in God. It happens to me still. But on those days, I land again pragmatically where Pascal did. I turn my attention to rituals and practices that seem most likely to form me into the person I want to become. I go to church. And I have never once regretted it.

I had a long argument with myself about leaving God till last. I have feared being complicit in the instrumentalising of religion, taming and tidying my faith for secular tastes. Much of what came before this chapter could be understood in a purely materialist universe, requiring no transcendent actor in the play. The strange and category-shattering presence of the divine has long been tucked away, hidden like a Victorian table leg under starched rationalist cloths. Since the Enlightenment and the Reformation before it, Christianity in the West has slowly morphed into a polite and civilised order with a focus on private devotion and ethical reform. Its wild and disruptive elements were tidied up, stewarded by the poor and marginalised, and the public face became instead about right action and right belief. Eventually it could be embraced even by philosophers like Voltaire and Hume who rejected its providential theological claims. And I've wanted to keep those of you with Voltaire tendencies on side, to not scare you with my Wild God. Partly because my pride still wants to impress you, resists surrendering my right to be seen as part of an imaginary intellectual elite. Less shamefully, because I do believe that what I've offered here (forms of attention, paths to peacemaking, an invitation to belovedness, awe, gratitude, sexual humanism and community), the themes I find in my tradition and which also show up elsewhere – are treasures that can be of use beyond their frame. Yes, some of these practices and insights shorn of their theological moorings, lifted out of the (broadly) coherent ecosystem of thought do sometimes remind me of that bottle of booze brought back from a sunny holiday – not so delicious out of original context – but that doesn't mean they are useless. Far from it.

But in suggesting you can start with them, and leave the God question open, I don't believe I've betrayed my tradition or asset stripped it for the secular market. I don't think it's possible to live in this different mode of attention, this alternative imaginative universe, and not be changed. I'm with Pascal. I think you can belong without believing, pray without believing, sabbath without believing, and gain a lot from those things, but that, *if you want them to*, they can form your mind and soul in ways that open a door to a different kind of perception. And you may thereby find that there was something worth surrendering to, all along.

AFTERWORD

When I was twenty I was baptised. Again.

I had come home from university for the summer after breaking up with my first serious boyfriend. I was getting more serious about my faith, had found Christian friends who I could both pray and party with for the first time in my life, and the fact that he didn't understand any of it had become increasingly painful for us both. He had tried to go on an Alpha course, I'd tried not to mind when it didn't 'take'. We had the same tearful arguments on repeat. In the end, I could see I was torturing him, wanting him to be something he wasn't. I had, without meaning to, made my love conditional, and conditional love is worse than no love at all. I knew I had to end it. I was indecisive though, and in my dithering further mashed his heart. The end of term was the firebreak we needed. I felt relief to have a boundary to help me follow through on the decision I was sure was right, but also guilty for the harm I'd caused, and heartbroken.

I had been christened as a baby, in that routine way people still did in the eighties, but had, of course, no memory of it. That summer I felt the need of a fresh start. When I went to the vicar of the local Anglican church to ask to be baptised as an adult, he refused. I now understand the theological reasoning much more – it's supposed to be a one-time thing – but then I felt rejected and angry. I wanted to choose this path for myself, to mark the day in the cowshed, belatedly, with a public declaration.

There was a small evangelical church in the next village along that mainly met in people's houses but had access to a tiny Nissen hut with a baptismal pool. They somehow heard of my desire, and offered to baptise me there.

And so, one Saturday afternoon, we gathered. I'd brought just my family and my schoolfriend James, an atheist performance artist always trying to convince me to take ketamine, who was curious. The entire church had shown up, about thirty of them, with enough home-baked cake to feed a hundred. I'd only met the pastor before, and was essentially using them for their baptismal theology and their building, but they greeted me with hand-written cards containing carefully chosen Bible verses and personalised words of encouragement. They had, it seemed, been praying for me for weeks. I started crying before the service even began, overwhelmed by this display of unearned love from strangers.

There was nothing aesthetically pleasing about that day. Another lot of plastic chairs clustered carelessly under another corrugated tin roof. I tried not to think about the asbestos probably lurking beneath the ancient peeling posters on the walls. The band got halfway through a slow and discordant rendition of the modern worship song I'd requested and ground to a halt. It was beyond them. They only knew five songs and the only one I recognised from the list the guitarist hurriedly whispered to me was 'Shine Jesus Shine' so they played that instead. Then I descended down the tiled steps into the pool, about the size of a large rectangular hot tub, or a very big grave. I was fully dressed, and worried that my top would go see-through and James would remember that rather than anything else, my breasts foiling my outreach attempt. Two people I'd never met waded in on either side and asked me if I accepted Jesus Christ as my Lord and Saviour. Then they held my elbows and leant me backwards into the water.

It is so brief, baptism. Even the 'full immersion' approach that I experienced, though it's more dramatic than a polite sprinkling at a font. It can sound scary, like being held under by school bullies. I am claustrophobic, and as the water washed up over my eyes I felt a spike of panic. The strangers holding my arms were not really trying to drown me, and my head was under and then out again before I knew it. But that split second of fear is maybe part of the point, because it is, really, about drowning. Baptism represents dying.

In his book on what might be beyond climate collapse, environmental writer Dougald Hine underlined the importance of ritualised encounters with our own death. He argues that industrial societies, only possible because of the millennia of dead things that fossil fuels represent, have tried to hide death from us. We think talk of it morbid, and tidy the dying away, outsourcing their care mainly to the underpaid and undervalued. And this death-phobia hampers our ability to become 'grown up'. Adulthood, in healthier societies than ours, is not something that happens by default through sheer survival or duration of education. It's something your community must bring you into. 'It takes a work of initiation on which much of the life of your community is focused,' Hine says. And across cultures, many of these moments of initiation into adulthood contain a form of ritual death. Christianity and myriad other wisdom traditions offer this counter-cultural thing, a very serious staged confrontation with our mortality.

Hine's point is that the loss of these rituals, the community participation in bringing children across the threshold of adulthood, is just one of many things we have lost in our culture of disconnection. Because when we deny death, we deny limits, think we are above cause and effect. 'To be a grown-up,' he argues, 'is to live alert to consequences, to know the cost of your living. It is hard to be a grown-up in the world we have made.'[1]

It is hard to be a grown-up.

Today I am having one of my regular spikes of climate anxiety. My husband says I have prepper tendencies, and I do deal with the overwhelm by planning to bulk-buy seeds and dig a well. I am more prone to fear than I am to anger, or sadness, which is just a temperamental quirk. It's awkward though, because the Bible seems pretty comfortable with those other two emotions. God, and God's people, regularly weep and mourn, or rage against injustice. There is an expectation that these emotions can coexist with being fully alive. Fear is a different thing. The text apparently says 'Do not be afraid' 365 times, which is clearly one of those made-up stats like the 'fact' we lose 80 per cent of heat from our heads. But both tell us something broadly true – if you're cold, try a hat, and the polyphonic voices of my scriptures don't want their readers to be full of fear, even while being very direct about how hairy things might get.

These voices invite me to be part of a story in which I was always going to play only a tiny role, and which was always going to end. I am going to die. So are my children and my friends; eventually, ultimately, so is this planet. It all might happen sooner than I'd have chosen, much of it might be our fault, but it was always going to end.

When I let it, my faith helps me sit with this. It helps me to accept rather than resist those cold hard facts. It helps me do that most adult of things and look death in the face. And I find, when I let the fear drain out of me, that she looks like neither an enemy nor a friend, but a sister.

I started this book wanting to be fully alive. I thought it might make me into the kind of grown-up Tim Minchin's song envisages. Have I grown strong enough to carry heavy things, wise enough to answer hard questions, brave enough to fight the battles ahead of me, ahead of us? Probably not. And I'm more sure now that those things are not the main aim.

My aim is growing up and outwards into Love – the greatest thing, the Bible says, the one that remains. It is not a three-month or even a five-year goal. It's not a project, not something I can ever tick off my list. Which is quite liberating, actually. All my other projects, my work stuff and health stuff and house stuff, need to be secondary to this, and it helps keep them in their place. I can't pass or fail, in this growing, which is part growing up and part growing down, becoming more like a real child and a real adult. I can just move, on any given day, towards Love or away from it. I can choose to grasp out beyond the boundaries of my self into connection, or I can refuse. And the days I refuse are not irrevocable. I believe that because of another death, the death I sought to participate in through baptism, the path is always open for me to turn round. Re-pent just means think again. Sometimes it does feel like a little death, this changing, but it turns out some deaths are good.

When I came up from enacting my own death, as the water streamed from my nose and face and eyes, I felt a serious joy. Joy is not a shallow shiny thing. It always seems to stay threaded, like an umbilical cord, to something sorrowful, but it is good. I saw that deep joy, Pascal's joy, reflected back at me from thirty smiling, crying strangers.

Baptism was not a once-and-for-all solution to the pain of being a person, clearly. Enacting one's death one day does not make the prospect of our end, the end of the world, suddenly a comfortable thought. I think a part of me did begin to grow up that day, though. I'd go on to lose my faith and find it again, and who knows where I'll be by the time this book comes out. I know I will suffer, because life does that, and so will the people I love. The world outside of Eden will break all of our hearts.

We had a reading from the Song of Solomon at our wedding, that includes these verses:

> Set me as a seal upon thine heart,
> As a seal upon thine arm:
> For love is strong as death. . .
> Many waters cannot quench love,
> Neither can the floods drown it[2]

Whatever is ahead of me, ahead of us, it will include many deaths, but Love remains. I hope I can remember to surrender, again, to the tide that is always trying to pull me home.

NOTES

Introduction

1. Thomas Merton, *The Man in the Sycamore Tree: The Good Times and Hard Life of Thomas Merton Edward Rice* (Harcourt, 1985), p. 48.
2. This term was coined by Edwin H. Friedman, a rabbi and family systems therapist. See Edwin H. Friedman, *A Failure of Nerve* (Seabury Books, 2007).
3. Julian Barnes, *Nothing to be Frightened of* (Jonathan Cape, 2008), p. 3.
4. Francis Thompson, 'The hound of heaven', *Merry England*, v. 15, no. 87 (July 1890), pp. 163–8.
5. 'Staying Power', Jeanne Murray Walker, *Poetry* (Chicago, May 2004).
6. Paul Ricoeur, *The Symbolism of Evil*, translated by Emerson Buchanan (Boston, 1969), p. 349.
7. Alain de Botton, *Religion for Atheists* (Penguin, 2012), p. 17.

The Human Propensity to Fuck Things Up

1. Francis Spufford, *Unapologetic* (Faber and Faber, 2013).
2. Martin Buber, *I and Thou* (First Scribner Classics, 2010), p. 26.
3. Martin Buber, *Between Man and Man*, translated by Ronald Gregor-Smith (Routledge, Taylor and Francis e-library, 2004).
4. Rom. 7:15–25.
5. Richard G. Newhauser and Susan Ridyard (eds), *Sin in Medieval and Early Modern Culture: The Tradition of the Seven Deadly Sins* (York Medieval Press, 2012).
6. David Brooks, 'The Moral Bucket List', *New York Times* (11 April 2015).

Wrath . . . *From Polarisation to Peacemaking*

1 Jeanne Marie Laskas, 'Dear Mr President', *Guardian* (18 August 2018), https://www.theguardian.com/books/ng-interactive/2018/aug/18/barack-obama-reveals-how-letters-from-the-american-people-shaped-his-presidency-interview
2 Ephesians 4:26.
3 *The Sacred* with Willie Jennings (11 August 2020), https://podcasts.apple.com/gb/podcast/the-sacred the-sacredid1326888108?i=1000487851698
4 Noel Annan, *Our Age* (Weidenfeld and Nicholson, 1990), p. 182.
5 Jon Yates, *Fractured: Why our societies are coming apart and how we can put them back together again* (Harper North, 2021).
6 Amy Chua, *Political Tribes: Group Instinct and the Fate of Nations* (Bloomsbury, 2018), p.1.
7 See Bill Bishop, *The Big Sort: Why the Clustering of Like-Minded America Is Tearing Us Apart* (Houghton Mifflin Harcourt, 2008).
8 M. Levine *et al.*, 'Identity and emergency intervention: how social group membership and inclusiveness of group boundaries shape helping behavior', *Personality and Social Psychology Bulletin*, 31(4) (April 2005), 443–53, https://pubmed.ncbi.nlm.nih.gov/15743980
9 Gaba, Sherry, 'Understanding fight, flight, freeze, and the fawn response', *Psychology Today*, https://www.psychologytoday.com/us/blog/addiction-and-recovery/202008/understanding-fight-flight-freeze-and-the-fawn-response (2020).
10 Rich Bartlett and Elizabeth Oldfield on friendship, lineage and a demonology of the culture wars, YouTube November 2022, https://m.youtube.com/watch?v=a5_mMz_VHjo
11 Fathali M. Moghaddam, *Mutual Radicalization: How Groups and Nations Drive Each Other to Extremes* (American Psychological Association, 2018).
12 Joanne Sheehan, 'Decades of Nonviolence Training: Practicing Nonviolence', *The Nonviolent Activist* (July–August 1998).

13 Elizabeth Alexander, 'Ars Poetica #100: I Believe', from *American Sublime* (Graywolf Press, 2005).
14 Evagrius Ponticus, 'Praktikos 11', *The Praktikos & Chapters on Prayer*, translated by John Eudes Bamberger, quoted at https://thepocketscroll.wordpress.com/2013/03/07/anger-with-a-little-help-from-the-desert-fathers-and-evagrius
15 Quoted in Ed Pavlić, 'On James Baldwin's Dispatches from the Heart of the Civil Rights Movement, The Making of an Iconic Essayist', *Lit Hub* (10 December 2018), https://lithub.com/on-james-baldwins-dispatches-from-the-heart-of-the-civil-rights-movement
16 James Baldwin, 'A Letter to My Nephew', *The Progressive* (1 December 1962), https://progressive.org/magazine/letter-nephew

Avarice . . . *From Stuffocation to Gratitude and Generosity*

1 Oliver James, *Affluenza* (Vermillion, 2007) p. xiii.
2 *Ibid.*, p. xx.
3 P. Brickman & D. T. Campbell, 'Hedonic relativism and planning the good society', in M. H. Appley (ed.), *Adaptation-level Theory: a Symposium* (Academic Press, 1971), pp. 287–305.
4 John Maynard Keynes, 'Economic Possibilities for our Grandchildren', *in Essays in Persuasion,* first published in *The Nation and Athenæum* (11 and 18 October 1930).
5 https://ourworldindata.org/historical-poverty-reductions-more-than-a-story-about-free-market-capitalism
6 James Wallman, *Stuffocation: Living More with Less* (Penguin, 2015).
7 Sarah O'Connor, 'The mysterious decline of our leisure time', *Financial Times* (5 October 2021).
8 Prov. 23:4.
9 Alexis de Tocqueville, *Democracy in America*, edited and translated by Harvey C. Mansfield and Delba Winthrop (University of Chicago Press, 2000), pp. 511–14.
10 Quoted by Dougald Hine at https://dougald.nu/the-capacity-for-second-thoughts-ivan-illich

11 Karl Polanyi, Conrad M. Arensberg and Harry W. Pearson, *Trade and Markets in the Early Empires* (The Free Press, 1957).
12 René Girard, 'Generative Scapegoating', in Robert G. Hammerton-Kelly (ed.), *Violent Origins: Walter Burkert, René Girard, and Jonathan Z. Smith on Ritual Killing and Cultural Formation* (Stanford University Press, 1987), p. 122.
13 Donella Meadows, *Beyond the Limits* (Earthscan Ltd, 1992), p. 216.
14 Eve Poole, *Buying God* (SCM, 2019), p. 83.
15 Ernest Becker, *The Denial of Death* (Free Press, 1973).
16 John Maynard Keynes, 'Economic Possibilities for our Grandchildren', in *Essays in Persuasion*, first published in *The Nation and Athenæum* (11 and 18 October 1930).
17 Dougald Hine, *At Work in the Ruins* (Chelsea Green, 2023).
18 *The Sacred* podcast with Vanessa Zoltan, 25 January 2022, https://m.youtube.com/watch?v=Dte5Db1a97g
19 Andy Crouch, *The Life We're Looking For* (Hodder and Stoughton, 2022), p. 72.
20 *Ibid.*, p. 73.
21 Oliver James, Affluenza (Vermillion, 2007) p. 20.
22 Luke 18:18-30.
23 Phyllis Tickle, *Greed* (Oxford University Press USA, illustrated edition 2004), p. 22.
24 St Basil the Great, *On Social Justice*, translated by Paul Shroeder, Popular Patristics Series (St Vladimir's Seminary Press, 2009), pp. 69–71.
25 https://www.themarginalian.org/2014/02/18/martin-seligman-gratitude-visit-three-blessings
26 Martin Seligman, *Flourish: A new understanding of happiness and well-being and how to achieve them* (Nicholas Brealey Publishing, 2011).
27 John Maynard Keynes, 'Economic Possibilities for our Grandchildren', in *Essays in Persuasion*, first published in *The Nation and Athenæum* (11 and 18 October 1930).
28 Elizabeth W. Dunn, Lara B. Akin and Michael I. Norton, 'Spending Money on Others Promotes Happiness', *Science*, 21, vol. 319, Issue 5870 (March 2008), pp. 1687–8.

29 Charles Eisenstein, *Sacred Economics: Money, Gift, and Society in the Age of Transition* (North Atlantic Books, 2011).
30 I have not been able to fully substantiate this story, but it is quoted in Matt Friedman, 'The Accountability Connection', *New Man*, July–August 1994, p. 12.
31 Thomas Traherne, 'Desire', in *The Poetical Works of Thomas Traherne 1636?–1674*, edited by Bertram Dobell (Dobell, 1903).
32 Schweiker, William, 'A Preface to Ethics: Global Dynamics and the Integrity of Life', *Journal of Religious Ethics*, 32 (1):13–38 (2004), p. 269.

Acedia . . . *From Distraction to Attention*

1 Patricia Lockwood, *No One Is Talking About This* (Riverhead Books, 2021).
2 J.K. Rowling, *Harry Potter and the Philosopher's Stone* (Bloomsbury, 1997), p. 157.
3 Quoted by Jonathan L. Zecher in 'Acedia: the lost name for the emotion we're all feeling right now', *The Conversation*, 27 August 2020.
4 Geoffrey Chaucer, 'The Parson's Tale', accessed at https://chaucer.fas.harvard.edu/pages/parsons-prologue-and-tale
5 John of the Cross, 'The Dark Night', *The Collected Works of Saint John of the Cross*, translated by Kieran Kavanaugh and Otilio Rodriguez, third edition (Institute of Carmelite Studies, 2017.), pp. 1.7–2.3.
6 Aldous Huxley, 'Accedie', *On the Margin: Notes and Essays by Aldous Huxley* (George H. Doran Company, 1923), pp. 25–32.
7 Thomas More, 'The Four Last Things', edited by W. E. Campbell in *EW* 1931. 1: pp. 457–99, accessed online at https://thomasmorestudies.org/wp-content/uploads/2020/08/Four-Last-Things-Part-1.pdf
8 Dorothy L.Sayers, *Murder Must Advertise* (Hodder and Stoughton, 1983), p. 99.

9 Psalm 90:12.
10 St Augustine of Hippo, *Confessions*, 1,1.5.
11 There have been many studies about the effects of prayer and meditation (and about the difference between the two). Defining prayer is clearly difficult, as it means different things to different people, and so the field is a tricky one to navigate. Some studies find explicitly 'spiritual' forms of prayer and meditation have stronger calming effects than secular, some find the opposite or that they are the same. As with most studies using fMRA imaging, they should be handled with some care (see one paper on complexities here: https://www.researchgate.net/publication/276501619_Neuroimaging_of_Prayer_Questions_of_Validity) but my reading is that the beneficial effects of prayer have been reliably observed.

This article provides a balanced and helpful overview of the state of the field and some of the controversies for laypeople: https://www.vice.com/en/article/nzpk9w/how-prayer-and-meditation-changes-your-brain

For a deeper dive this academic book provides a more rigorous overview: Andrew Newberg, *Neurotheology: How Science Can Enlighten Us About Spirituality* (Columbia University Press, 2018).
12 E. A. Maguire, K. Woollett and H. J. Spiers, 'London taxi drivers and bus drivers: a structural MRI and neuropsychological analysis', *Hippocampus*, 16(12) (2006), 1091–101, https://pubmed.ncbi.nlm.nih.gov/17024677
13 Jenny Odell, *How to do Nothing* (Melville House Publishing, 2019), chapter 4.
14 See Jon Kabat-Zinn, *Wherever You Go, There You Are: Mindfulness Meditation in Everyday Life* (Hyperion, 1994).
15 Morning Prayer from The Book of Common Prayer, http://justus.anglican.org/~ss/commonworship/word/morningbcp.html
16 *Common Worship: Holy Week and Easter* (Church House Publishing, 2010).
17 Casper ter Kuile, *The Power of Ritual* (Harper One, 2020), p. 165.
18 Pico Iyer and Elizabeth Gilbert, *On Being*, 18 November 2021,

https://onbeing.org/programs/pico-iyer-and-elizabeth-gilbert-the-future-of-hope-3

19 Vanessa Zoltan, *Praying with Jane Eyre* (TarcherPerigee, 2022).

20 Walter Breuggeman, *Sabbath as Resistance* (Westminster John Knox Press, 2017).

21 Abraham Joshua Heschel, *The Sabbath: Its Meaning for the Modern Man* (Farrar, Straus and Giroux, 2005), p. 14.

22 James K. A. Smith, *Desiring the Kingdom: Worship, Worldview, and Cultural Formation* (Baker Publishing, 2009).

23 James K. A. Smith, *Who's Afraid of Postmodernism?: Taking Derrida, Lyotard, and Foucault to Church* (Baker Academic, 2006), p. 57.

24 Rowan Williams, *Being Human: Bodies, Minds, Persons* (SPCK, 2018), all quotes in this section from chapter 4.

Envy . . . *From Status Anxiety to Belovedness*

1 Exod. 20:17.

2 Andy Crouch, *The Life We're Looking For* (Hodder and Stoughton, 2022), p. 3.

3 Virginia Woolf, *A Room of One's Own* (Hogarth Press, 1929), chapter 3.

4 William James, *The Principles of Psychology* (Henry Holt and Company, 1890), pp. 292–3.

5 Charles Taylor, *Sources of the Self: The Making of Modern Identity* (Cambridge University Press, 2006), p. 14.

6 Abraham Tesser, 'Toward a Self-Evaluation Maintenance Model of Social Behavior', Paper presented at the 93rd Annual Convention of the American Psychological Association (Los Angeles, CA, 23–27 August 1985), https://files.eric.ed.gov/fulltext/ED267303.pdf, accessed 27/2/23.

7 Thomas Hobbes, *Leviathan* (Andrew Crooke, 1651).

8 S. K. Kierkegaard, *The Sickness unto Death*, edited and translated by E. Hong & H. Hong (Princeton University Press, 1980), p. 86.

9 James Baldwin, 'The Black Boy Looks at the White Boy',

Esquire (May 1961), https://classic.esquire.com/article/1961/5/1/the-black-boy-looks-at-the-white-boy-norman-mailer
10 Larry Seidentop, *Inventing the Individual* (Allen Lane, 2014), pp. 347–53.
11 Larry Seidentop, *Democracy in Europe* (Penguin, 2001), chapter 10.
12 Victor Hugo, *Les Misérables*, translated by Christine Donougher (BBC Books, 2018), p. 99.
13 Terry Eagleton, *Culture and the Death of God* (Yale University Press, 2015), p. 68.
14 James 2:5.
15 Karl Marx, 'A Contribution to the Critique of Hegel's Philosophy of Right', first published in *Deutsch-Französische Jahrbücher* (7 & 10 February 1844), accessed at https://www.marxists.org/archive/marx/works/1843/critique-hpr/intro.htm
16 M. Shawn Copeland, *Enfleshing Freedom: Body, Race, and Being* (Fortress Press, 2010).
17 Tom Holland, *Dominion: The Making of the Western Mind* (Little, Brown, 2019).
18 David Foster Wallace, *This is Water: Some Thoughts, Delivered on a Significant Occasion, about Living a Compassionate Life* (Little, Brown, 2009).
19 Isa. 44:20.
20 Kathryn Chetkovitch, *Envy* (Granta, 2003), https://granta.com/envy
21 Ada Limón, *The Hurting Kind* (Milkweed Editions, 2022).
22 Rowan Williams, 'On Being Creatures', 4th Esa Lecture 1989, https://www.scribd.com/document/466064196/Rowan-Williams-On-being-creatures-4th-esa-lecture-1989
23 Simone Weil, 'Reflections on the right use of school studies with a view to the love of God', in *Waiting for God* (G. P. Putnam's Sons, 1951).
24 Sebastian Moore, *The Inner Loneliness* (Crossroad, 1982).
25 See Glynn Harrison, *The Big Ego Trip* (IVP, 2013).

Gluttony . . . *From Numbing to Ecstasy*

1 Meredith Melnick, 'The Growing Link Between Alcoholism and Obesity', *Time* (6 January 2011), https://healthland.time.com/2011/01/06/study-the-growing-link-between-alcoholism-and-obesity

2 Henry D. Thoreau, *Walden*, edited by J. Lyndon Shanley (Princeton University Press, 1971), p. 8.

3 Nick Cave and Sean O'Hagan, *Faith, Hope and Carnage* (Canongate, 2002), p. 85.

4 See for example https://www.christianitytoday.com/ct/2011/octoberweb-only/fatherbecomesson.html; Matthew Perry, *Friends, Lovers and the Big Terrible Thing* (Headline, 2022).

5 Amy Liptrott, *The Outrun* (Canongate, 2018), p. 214.

6 Lewis Hyde, 'Alcohol and Poetry', https://lewishyde.com/wp-content/uploads/2021/11/18AlcoholandPoetry.pdf accessed 11/7/23

7 Laura M. Fabrycky, 'Acedia, Liberalism, and the Demonic', unpublished paper delivered at Breaking Ground Retreat, 17–20 November 2022, Laity Lodge.

8 https://www.saltlakeaa.org/2015/01/spiritus-contra-spiritum-carl-jungs-letter-to-bill-wilson-january-30-1961. Original viewable at https://fifthavenuesteppress.com/carl-jung-letter

9 Jia Tolentino, 'Ecstasy', in *Trick Mirror: Reflections on Self-Delusion* (4th Estate, 2019), p. 143.

10 Quoted in Jules Evans, 'Perennial Philosophy', *Aeon* (19 February 2020), https://aeon.co/essays/what-can-we-learn-from-the-perennial-philosophy-of-aldous-huxley

11 Iris Murdoch, *The Sovereignty of Good* (Routledge, 2001).

12 Susan Sontag, 'The Pornographic Imagination', in *The Susan Sontag Reader* (Farrar, Straus and Giroux, 1982); Cole Arthur Riley, *This Here Flesh* (Hodder & Stoughton, 2022), p. 37.

13 Jules Evans, *The Art of Losing Control: A Philosopher's search for Ecstatic Experience* (Canongate, 2017), p. xiv.

14 *Ibid*, p. xiii.

15 Barbara Ehrenreich, *Living with a Wild God: A Nonbeliever's Search for the Truth about Everything* (Twelve, 2014).

16 Jules Evans, *The Art of Losing Control: A Philosopher's search for Ecstatic Experience* (Canongate, 2017).
17 Acts 2:4.
18 Jules Evans, *The Art of Losing Control: A Philosopher's search for Ecstatic Experience* (Canongate, 2017), p. 31.
19 Abraham Maslow, 'Religions, Values, and Peak Experiences', quoted at https://academyofideas.com/2016/09/maslow-peak-experiences-solitary-individual
20 Mark Vernon, 'Divine Transports', *Aeon* (7 November 2019), https://aeon.co/essays/how-trance-states-forged-human-society-through-transcendence
21 Quoted in Timothy Pytell, 'Transcending the Angel Beast: Viktor Frankl and humanistic psychology', *Psychoanalytic Psychology*, vol. 23, no. 3 (2006).
22 Ido Hartogsohn, 'Constructing drug effects: A history of set and setting', *Drug Science, Policy and Law*, 2017:3, https://journals.sagepub.com/doi/10.1177/2050324516683325
23 1 Cor. 14:3.
24 C. S. Lewis, *The Weight of Glory* (SPCK 1942).

Lust . . . *From Objectification to Sexual Humanism*

1 Audre Lorde, 'The Uses of the Erotic: The Erotic as Power', in *Sister Outsider: Essays and Speeches* (The Cross Press, 1984), pp. 53–9.
2 *Ibid.*
3 S. of S. 7.
4 *The Life of St. Teresa of Jesus*, chapter xxix, paragraph 17, https://www.gutenberg.org/files/8120/8120-h/8120-h.htm
5 *The Book of Margery Kempe*, book 1, section 36, pp. 126–7.
6 John Donne, 'Batter my heart, three-person'd God', Holy Sonnets, *Norton Anthology of Poetry* (Norton and Company, 1996), p. 289.
7 Audre Lorde, 'The Uses of the Erotic: The Erotic as Power', in *Sister Outsider: Essays and Speeches* (The Cross Press, 1984), pp. 53–9.

8 Nancy Jo Sales, 'Tinder and the Dawn of the "Dating Apocalypse"', *Vanity Fair*, September 2015 https://www.vanityfair.com/culture/2015/08/tinder-hook-up-culture-end-of-dating

9 *Ibid.*

10 Caroline Heldman and Lisa Wade, 'Hook-Up Culture: Setting a New Research Agenda', *Sexuality Research and Social Policy*, 7 (2010), 323–33.

11 Emily Witt, 'A Hookup App for the Emotionally Mature', *New Yorker* (11 July 2022), https://www.newyorker.com/culture/annals-of-inquiry/feeld-dating-app-sex

12 For example Lisa Tulane, 'The Rise of Hookup Culture on University Campuses' (25 August 2017), scholars.org: https://scholars.org/brief/rise-hookup-sexual-culture-american-college-campuses

13 See, for example, Andrew P. Clark, 'Are the correlates of sociosexuality different for men and women?', *Personality and Individual Differences*, vol. 41, no. 7 (2006), 1321–7.

14 Eleanor Halls, 'This Is What The Sex Lives Of Gen Z-ers Are Actually Like', *Vogue* (6 August 2022).

15 Louise Perry, *The Case Against the Sexual Revolution* (Polity, 2022).

16 Christine Emba, *Rethinking Sex: A Provocation* (Penguin Random House, 2022).

17 Quoted in Susanna Shrobsdorf, 'Why there is no such thing as casual sex', *Time* (24 March 2022). I accessed this webpage in March 2022 but it has now been removed.

18 Louise Perry, *The Case Against the Sexual Revolution* (Polity, 2022).

19 Scott R. Braithwaite, Scott *et al.*, 'The Influence of Pornography on Sexual Scripts and Hooking Up Among Emerging Adults in College', *Archives of Sexual Behavior*, 44 (2014).

20 Corita R. Grudzen *et al.*, 'Comparison of the Mental Health of Female Adult Film Performers and Other Young Women in California', *Psychiatric Services*, vol. 62, no. 6 (June 2011), 639–45.

21 James D. Griffith *et al.*, 'A Comparison of Sexual Behaviors and Attitudes, Self-Esteem, Quality of Life, and Drug Use Among Pornography Actors and a Matched Sample', *International Journal of Sexual Health*, 24:4 (2012), 254–66, https://www.tandfonline.com/doi/abs/10.1080/19317611.2012.710183
22 Tracy Clark-Flory, 'Is Feminist Porn Having Its Me Too Moment?', *Jezebel* (8 September 2018), https://jezebel.com/is-feminist-porn-getting-its-metoo-moment-1828173419
23 Sheelah Kolhatkar, 'The Fight to Hold Pornhub Accountable', *New Yorker* (13 June 2022), https://www.newyorker.com/magazine/2022/06/20/the-fight-to-hold-pornhub-accountable
24 See for example, Dong-ouk Yang and Gahyun Youn, 'Effects of Exposure to Pornography on Male Aggressive Behavioral Tendencies', *The Open Psychology Journal*, 5 (2012), 1–10.
25 T. Kohut, I. Landripet and A. Stulhofer, 'Testing the confluence model of the association between pornography use and male sexual aggression: A longitudinal assessment in two independent adolescent samples from Croatia', *Archives of Sexual Behavior,* 50 (2021), 647–65; or Emily Vogels and Lucia O'Sullivan, 'The Relationship Among Online Sexually Explicit Material Exposure to, Desire for, and Participation in Rough Sex', *Archives of Sexual Behavior*, 48 (2019).
26 Audre Lorde, 'The Uses of the Erotic: The Erotic as Power', in *Sister Outsider: Essays and Speeches* (The Cross Press, 1984), pp. 53–9.
27 Esteban Ortiz-Ospina and Max Roser, 'Marriages and Divorces' (2020), published online at https://ourworldindata.org/marriages-and-divorces#:~:text=The%20percentage%20of%20couples%20divorcing,marriage%20has%20also%20fallen%20significantly.
28 Sally Rooney, *Beautiful World, Where Are You?* (Faber and Faber, 2021), p. 186.
29 Immanuel Kant, *Groundwork of the Metaphysics of Morals*, translated by James W. Ellington, 3rd edition (Hackett Publishing Co Inc, 1993), p. 36, 4:429.
30 Simone de Beauvoir, *The Second Sex*, translated by H. M. Parsley (Penguin, 1949), p. 20.

31 Nicholas Wolterstorff, *Justice: Rights and Wrongs* (Princeton University Press, 2008).
32 Luke Bretherton, *A Primer in Christian Ethics* (Cambridge University Press, 2023), chapter 12.
33 *Ibid.*
34 *The Sacred* podcast with Casper ter Kuile (17 October 2018), https://thesacredpodcast.podigee.io/26-24-casper-ter-kuile
35 If you're interested in this argument, see Eugene F. Rogers Jr, *Sexuality and the Christian Body: Their Way into the Triune God*, Challenges in Contemporary Theology (Basil Blackwell, 1999).
36 Luke Bretherton, *A Primer in Christian Ethics* (Cambridge University Press, 2023), chapter 12.

Pride . . . *From Individualism to Community*

1 Eric Michel Dyson, *Pride* (Oxford University Press, 2006), p. 5.
2 Philip Schaff (ed.), *A Select Library of the Nicene and Post-Nicene Fathers of the Christian Church: Volume ii St. Augustin's City of God and Christian Doctrine* (T&T Clark, 1886), chapter 13.
3 Matt Jenson, *The Gravity of Sin: Augustine, Luther and Barth on 'Homo Incurvatus in Se'*, (Bloomsbury Academic, 2006).
4 John Donne, 'Elegie for the Lady Markham', *The Poems of John Donne* (George Rutledge, 1896).
5 Iris Murdoch, 'The Sublime and the Good', in *Existentialists and Mystics: Writings on Philosophy and Literature* (Penguin, 1999), p. 215.
6 Martin Buber, *Between Man and Man*, translated by Ronald Gregor-Smith (Routledge, Taylor and Francis e-library, 2004).
7 Jonathan Sacks, *Morality* (Hodder and Stoughton, 2020), p. 37.
8 K. Kouda and M. Iki, 'Beneficial effects of mild stress (hormetic effects): dietary restriction and health', *Journal of Physiological Anthropology*, 29(4) (2010), 127–32, https://pubmed.ncbi.nlm.nih.gov/20686325

9 Juliette Tocino-Smith, 'What Is Eustress? A Look at the Psychology and Benefits', *Positive Psychology* (15 Jan 2019), https://positivepsychology.com/what-is-eustress
10 Madeleine Davies, 'Safeguarding concerns about Mike Pilavachi substantiated, review concludes,' *Church Times* (7 September 2023).
11 'Law firm details sexual misconduct by global ministry leader Ravi Zacharias', Associated Press (21 February 2021).
12 Byung-Chul Han, 'All That Is Solid Melts Into Information', *Noema* (21 April 2022), https://www.noemamag.com/all-that-is-solid-melts-into-information
13 Zygmunt Bauman, *Liquid Modernity* (Polity Press, 2000).
14 Byung-Chul Han, 'All That Is Solid Melts Into Information', *Noema* (21 April 21 2022), https://www.noemamag.com/all-that-is-solid-melts-into-information
15 Acts 4:32–37.
16 Oliver Burkeman, *Four Thousand Weeks: Time Management for Mortals* (Vintage, 2022), p. 33.

The G Bomb

1 Abi Morgan, *This is Not a Pity Memoir* (John Murray, 2022), p. 153.
2 From Rowan Williams, 'Faith and Human Flourishing: Religious Beliefs and Ideals of Maturity, an Oxford University Podcast', uploaded 12 February 2014, https://podcasts.ox.ac.uk/rowan-williams-lecture-faith-and-human-flourishing-religious-belief-and-ideals-maturity
3 Philip Larkin, 'This Be the Verse', *Collected Poems* (Farrar, Straus and Giroux, 2001).
4 Scott Daniel Dunbar, Lecture on Religious Philosophy (St Peter's College, SK. 2007), quoted from https://www.newworldencyclopedia.org/entry/Negative_Theology_(Apophatic_Theology).
5 C. S. Lewis, *Beyond Personality: The Christian Idea of God* (Geoffrey Bless, 1944), p. 9.

6 Jeffrey Kripal, *The Flip: Who you really are and why it matters* (Penguin, 2020), p. 13.
7 John Moriarty, *Nostos: An Autobiography* (The Lilliput Press, 2011).
8 From Rowan Williams, 'Faith and Human Flourishing: Religious Beliefs and Ideals of Maturity, an Oxford University Podcast', uploaded 12 February 2014, https://podcasts.ox.ac.uk/rowan-williams-lecture-faith-and-human-flourishing-religious-belief-and-ideals-maturity
9 Blaise Pascal, *Oeuvres complètes* (Seuil, 1960), p. 618.
10 Andrew Sean Greer, *Less* (Lee Boudreaux Books, 2017).
11 Isaac Watts, 'When I Survey the Wondrous Cross', *Hymns and Spiritual Songs* (1707).
12 Fleming Rutledge, *The Crucifixion: Understanding the Death of Jesus Christ* (Eerdmans, 2015), p. 6 (in 2017 edition).
13 *The Sacred* with Matthew Taylor (10 April 2019), https://thesacredpodcast.podigee.io/39-36-matthew-taylor
14 Iain McGilchrist, *Ways of Attending* (Routledge, 2014), p.13.
15 *The Sacred* with Professor Tom Shakespeare (20 June 2018), https://soundcloud.com/thesacredpodcast/tom-shakespeare-final
16 Blaise Pascal, *Pensées* (E. P. Dutton, 1958), p. 229.
17 *Ibid.*, p. 233.

Afterword

1 Dougald Hine, *At Work in the Ruins* (Chelsea Green Publishing, 2023), pp. 36 and 37.
2 S. of S. 8:6–7.

ACKNOWLEDGEMENTS

This book is a fruit of community. Without the many, many people who have encouraged, challenged, cheerled, inspired, informed and advised me, it would not exist.

I am grateful for my indomitable agent, Sophie Lambert. Despite being pretty sceptical about religion herself, she asked me 'what do you really want to write?' and didn't balk when I said 'theology for everyone else'. Her faith in my voice and willingness to take on a challenging sell of a book made me think that something like this might be possible. Thanks also to Alice Hoskyns, Sophie's right-hand woman whose feedback was invaluable and who will be an amazing agent in her own right any day now, and to Rhik Samadder for believing in me enough to introduce us.

Joanna Davey, my editor at Hodder, fought to bring the book there, and has championed it doggedly ever since. It is such a wonderful thing to have her in my corner and the gentle wisdom of her editing improved the text immeasurably. Huge thanks to the wider Hodder team also, Alice Graham, Rosie Gailer, Rhoda Hardie, Jenny Campbell, Meaghan Lim, Andy Lyon and Lydia Blagden for the beautiful cover.

Thanks to Katelyn Beaty, Jeremy Wells and the team at

Brazos for taking a punt on a sweary Brit who may make all their tender North American readers blush, but you believed would also make them think. I'm so glad you took this on!

Many friends have read and offered feedback at various stages, and I am very grateful for having this many people who I can trust not to destroy my fragile confidence and also offer genuinely helpful input. Thanks go to Nell, Jenn, Sarah, Anne, Luke, Andy and Doris, Millay, Nessa, Jen, Leanne, Rhik and Andy. Alicia and Lizzie helped hugely with the wider project of finding my voice in public.

In our community house, we say 'community makes you brave,' so I want to thank my housemates for their dogged commitment to my creativity, for their company when things were hard and for celebrating every win. My mum and dad, Chris and Janet, who gave me love steady enough to build a life on, and fed my ravenous hunger for books without complaint. You made me brave too. Sue and Bernard, your care and practical support has been part of what made this possible.

Finally, to my kids who make me want to grow up my soul in order to contribute to the world they need, I love you. I hope you know it in your bones. And Chris, heart of my heart. You have never made me feel too much, too honest, too questioning. Instead, you affirmed my intuitions and helped me ground them, and cheered me on all the way along. Sometimes I don't know where your mind ends and mine begins and I'm so grateful to be attempting to grow up into faith, hope and love by your side. (And thanks for letting me talk about our sex life.)